The Roman goddess Diana on Pegasus

Adolescent, unmarried girls in ancient Greece competed every four years in the Games of Hera, named for the goddess of women and earth. Wearing chitons (loose-fitting garments that left their right shoulder and breast exposed), the girls ran barefoot or in sandals. The winners received part of a cow sacrificed to Hera.

The beginnings of ancient Olympic competitions can be traced back to approximately 776 B.C. It should come as no surprise that women were banned from participation in any of the events. Eventually virgins were admitted as spectators, but married women were threatened with death if caught in attendance. This rule remained in place throughout the 1,600 years the ancient games existed. It would be 1,503 years before Olympic competition returned.

In Greek mythology, there is a tale of one woman's athletic skills. Her name was Atalanta, the goddess of the hunt, and it is said that she thrived on the challenge of competition and could outperform any of the men of her era. The mythological tale begins with Atalanta being abandoned in the woods by her father because he had wanted a son. Raised in the wild by a she-bear and hunters, Atalanta grew up to be beautiful, swift of feet, and as strong as a man.

Brave and adventurous, Atalanta sailed with Jason on his quest to find the legendary Golden Fleece. When she at last returned home to her family, they pressed her to marry. She reluctantly agreed, but only on condition that the successful suitor could beat her in a footrace. Many tried and failed.

Atalanta, Greek goddess of the hunt

Finally, young Hippomenes came along and with the help of Aphrodite, Hippomenes succeeded. Armed with three golden apples from the Garden of the Hesperides, Hippomenes strategically threw them in Atalanta's path during their race. After he won the race, Hippomenes and Atalanta were married, and she later gave birth to a son.

101

Peggy Fleming
1948–
Figure Skating

120

Olga Korbut
1955–
Gymnastics

139

**Nancy
Lieberman-Cline**
1958–
Basketball

106

Sheila Young
1950–
Speed Skating, Cycling

125

**Martina
Navratilova**
1956–
Tennis

144

**Florence
Griffith Joyner**
1959–1998
Track and Field

110

Anita DeFrantz
1952–
*Rowing, Sports
Administration*

130

**Nancy
Lopez Knight**
1957–
Golf

149

Nadia Comaneci
1961–
Gymnastics

115

Chris Evert
1954–
Tennis

134

Joan Benoit Samuelson
1957–
Marathon

154

Jackie Joyner-Kersee
1962–
Track and Field

161

Paula Newby-Fraser
1962–
Triathlon

181

Bonnie Blair
1964–
Speed Skating

201

Steffi Graf
1969–
Tennis

166

Tracy Caulkins
1963–
Swimming

186

Katarina Witt
1965–
Figure Skating

206

Myriam Bédard
1969–
Biathlon

170

Cynthia Cooper
1963–
Basketball

192

Silken Laumann
1965–
Rowing

210

Janet Evans
1971–
Swimming

174

**Shooting Stars:
Women in
Basketball Today**

196

Gail Devers
1966–
Track and Field

215

Kristi Yamaguchi
1971–
Figure Skating

Women Athletes From Ancient Times to 1896

"I don't think being an athlete is unfeminine, I think of it as a kind of grace."
—Jackie Joyner-Kersee

Despite the restrictions and bans imposed upon them by society, women have been participating in competitive sports for centuries. By examining the artifacts of the ancient civilizations in Greece and Rome, a pictorial history emerges. A close look at the individual pieces of pottery and sculpture begins the story—an Etruscan vase adorned with women runners going all the way around its base; a bronze sculpture of a young Spartan girl frozen in a runner's pose.

The early Greeks believed that the mind and body were one. Physical exercise was required of both boys and girls, but for different reasons. For young males, a fit body was an indication of health and strength, the ability to excel in competition, and readiness for combat. For young women, it was less about athletic success, and more about believing that by making their own bodies healthy and strong, women would be better prepared to endure the exhausting and painful process of labor and childbirth, and produce strong, healthy sons. Once women reached adulthood, however, athletic competition was forbidden. Their place in society was confined to the roles of wife and mother.

EXTRAORDINARY Women★ ATHLETES

BY JUDY L. HASDAY

Children's Press
A Division of Grolier Publishing
New York • London • Hong Kong • Sydney
Danbury, Connecticut

This book is dedicated to the extraordinary women in my life, past and present, who have inspired me by their courage, strength, and wisdom. The pioneers: great-grandmothers Ida Fairbanks, Maizul Goodman, Elizabeth Isaacson; grandmothers Gussie Jean Fairbanks, Molly Hasday; my mom, Shirley Hasday; aunt Eleanor H. Klein; teacher and mentor, Florence Keiff; and my life friend, Cheryl Hendler Cohen.

Special thanks to my very first editor, my colleague, my friend, Therese De Angelis, for encouraging me to take the plunge into the world of writing.

Visit Children's Press on the Internet at:
http://publishing.grolier.com

Library of Congress Cataloguing-in-Publication Data

Hasday, Judy L., 1957-

    Extraordinary women athletes / by Judy L Hasday.
      p. cm. — (Extraordinary people)
    Includes bibliographical references and index.
    Summary: Presents brief biographies of more than fifty women athletes from the twentieth century, including Ora Washington, Althea Gibson, Tenley Albright, Wilma Rudolph, Chris Evert, Nancy Lopez Knight, Jackie Joyner-Kersee, and Janet Evans.
    ISBN 0-516-21608-2 (lib. bdg.)   0-516-27039-7 (pbk.)
    Women athletes—Biography v Juvenile literature. [1. Athletes. 2. Women—Biography.] I. Title. II. Series.

GV697.A1 H36 2000
796'.082'0922—dc21
[B]   99-049335

Contents

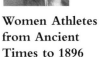

45

Toni Stone
1921–1996
Baseball

62

Tenley Albright
1935–
Figure Skating

80

Margaret Smith Court
1942–
Tennis

49

Althea Gibson
1927–
Tennis

66

Kathy Whitworth
1939–
Golf

85

The Girls of Summer
1943–1954
*All-American Girls
Baseball League (AAGBL)*

54

**Patricia Keller
McCormick**
1930–
Diving

70

Wilma Rudolph
1940–1994
Track and Field

90

Billie Jean King
1943–
Tennis

58

Larissa Latynina
1934–
Gymnastics

75

Jody Conradt
1941–
Basketball coach

96

**The Battle
of the Sexes**

The modern Olympics were resurrected in 1896 by Baron Pierre de Coubertin, a French physical fitness patron. After securing enough support for the idea of resuming Olympic competition, de Coubertin set the opening date of April 6, 1896, 1,503 years after Emperor Theodosis I banned the ancient games. Fittingly, King George I of Greece announced the start of the first modern Olympic Games, held in Athens. Women's participation in the games, however, was not permitted by de Coubertin in any capacity beyond being mere spectators applauding the men's athletic efforts.

One woman, Melpomene, did petition the International Olympic Committee to participate in the grueling 26-mile (41.8-km) marathon race. She was denied official entry, but Melpomene was going to run anyway. On the last day of the these first modern Olympics, several dozen men gathered at the starting point at the bridge in Marathon, Greece. Melpomene ran outside the view of the officials, following a parallel path of the men's course through the countryside, each runner intent on being the first to enter Panathenaic Stadium.

French runner Albin Lermusiaux led the way throughout the first part of the race. Meanwhile Melpomene, having lost sight of the competitors, just tried to pace herself until they appeared in view again. She stopped for some refreshment in the town of Pikermi, passing some of the participants now lying exhausted along the roadside. In the end, a Greek shepherd from the Marousi hills named Spiridon Louis entered the stadium first. The cheers of thousands of spectators greeted the appearance of the first modern Olympic marathon winner. He had completed the race in 2 hours, 58 minutes. When Melpomene finally reached Panathenaic Stadium, she could not enter. Instead she finished the race by running a lap around the outside of the arena. There were no cheers, and no one to greet her and congratulate her on finishing the race. Her time of 4 hours, 30 minutes was not official, but it was the first triumph for all the women who would follow in the games to come.

Women in Sports: the Few, the Determined, the Pioneers

*"In company with the first lady ever to qualify
at Indianapolis, gentlemen, start your engines."*
—Modified starter's call at the Indianapolis 500, May 29, 1977

The 1996 Summer Olympic Games in Atlanta, Georgia, marked more than just the celebration of the 100th anniversary of international athletic competition. At the first modern Olympic Games of 1896 in Athens, Greece, women were limited to the role of spectators—cheering and clapping for the 200 male athletes competing in 9 sports over a two-week period. A century later, more than 3,000 women assembled in Atlanta to compete in 100 of the 271 events held. The 1996 Summer Games also saw the addition of two new sports for women: softball and soccer.

Women athletes today are the beneficiaries of more than a century of struggles by their predecessors to break through the gender barriers placed in their paths. These women pioneers have dared to enter many once "male-only" sports, and have had to work harder to prove that they, too, deserve the opportunity to participate in whatever they choose—baseball, auto racing, horse racing, soccer, ice hockey, officiating, or other sports endeavors. But it has not been without many sacrifices along the way.

In 1922, tired of being excluded from Olympic track and field, women decided it was time to show the International Olympic Committee (IOC) "boys' club" and the International Amateur Athletic Federation (IAAF) how determined they were to compete. The fight against Pierre de Coubertin and his colleagues was led by Frenchwoman Alice Milliat. A translator by profession, Milliat was also an avid sportswoman, active in rowing and sports administration. When the IOC and IAAF refused to add women's track and field events to the Olympic program, Milliat established a women's Olympics program.

The Fédération Sportive Féminine Internationale (FSFI) was founded by Milliat and some of her colleagues in 1921. Comprised of six countries including France, Great Britain, and the United States, the FSFI staged its first Women's Olympics, a one-day competition on August 20, 1922. More than 20,000 spectators filed into Paris's Stade Pershing to watch the 18 athletes compete in 11 events. The day was a smashing success and included some new world records. In keeping with the format of the IOC Olympic Games, the FSFI held its next Women's Games four years later in Göteborg, Sweden. Now showcasing the talents of women from 10 nations, the games had more pomp and pageantry, including an opening-day ceremony that was attended by the Swedish royal family. The 1926 Women's Olympics competition was extended to three days, incorporating 13 events.

The success of the Women's Olympic Games finally forced the IOC to reconsider its position. By a 12-5 margin, the members voted to add five track and field events to the 1928 Olympic Games in Amsterdam, the Netherlands. It was a minimal concession compared to the number of events featured by the FSFI, but it was still a major victory for the women's athletic movement. Through perseverance and working together, women were beginning to change the old-fashioned restrictions that had been placed upon them for

Katherine Switzer, embraced in 1973 by the Boston marathon official who once barred her from running

centuries. Now that women were gaining entry into the once male-controlled world of athletics, opportunities began to open in some of the least expected places.

From childhood, many of today's female athletes have been told that girls are supposed to play with dolls, not baseballs or footballs, or in any sport considered "unfeminine." The Women's Sports Foundation's executive director, Donna Lopiano, dreamed of playing baseball for the New York Yankees. She was told that women didn't play in the major leagues. Tell that to Ila Borders. Women haven't made it yet onto the major league fields of teams like the New York Yankees or the Atlanta Braves, but it is just a matter of time. As for Borders, she made history on February 15, 1994, when she became the first woman to pitch in a men's college baseball game.

And then there is Pam Postema. She was one of the first women to wear the uniform of an umpire, calling balls and strikes behind the plate in men's professional baseball. Despite the insults and the verbal abuse from fans, Postema stood strong and continued to move along in the minors. In 1989, she even umpired the Hall of Fame game in Cooperstown, New York. Then she was passed over for promotion to the major leagues. When she was dismissed from her job for "deterioration of her work" later that same year, Postema filed a sex-discrimination lawsuit against major league baseball (MLB). Though nothing has changed and there are currently no other women umpires working in MLB, the door has been opened. Someday, women will stand on the baseball diamond calling the balls and strikes, not just retrieving balls hit out of play.

Women have often been very creative in finding ways to get around the "no women allowed" exclusion from sports they wanted to be a part of. Take Katherine Switzer, for example. An avid runner, Switzer wanted to compete in the 1967 Boston Marathon. The only problem was that the Boston Athletic Association (BAA), which sponsored the race, did not permit women to enter. This is exactly what faced Melpomene in 1896 in Athens, so she decided to run hidden from view. Switzer registered as K. Switzer, and her boyfriend picked up her official race number. It didn't take long for BAA officials to see that a woman was running as an official entrant. Though they tried to physically

Indy 500 driver Janet Guthrie's determination is a key factor in her success.

remove her from the course, Switzer finished the race in 4 hours and 20 minutes. Often, courage and determination have prevailed, as they did for Switzer. She was at the start line ready to go at the 1972 Boston Marathon, the first time the race was finally and officially open to women. Many great marathoners have followed, including 1984 Olympic Marathon champion Joan Benoit Samuelson.

The gender barrier has been even tougher to break in sports that are considered extreme or dangerous, such as auto racing. The idea that women were not capable of auto racing was so ingrained that the traditional call, "Gentlemen, start your engines," had to be modified in 1977 when Janet Guthrie, the first woman to qualify for the Indianapolis 500, joined the other

Indy drivers at the starting line. It was believed that women were not strong enough to handle the pressure of driving at such high speeds, and to this, Guthrie replied, "I'm going to *drive* the car around the track, not carry it." She credits her parents for having raised her to believe that she could accomplish anything she wanted to do—even when it came to competing in sports.

Libby Riddles and Susan Butcher faced similar objections when they began competing in the annual Iditarod Trail Sled Dog Race, a grueling 1,200-mile (1,930-km) trek from Anchorage to Nome, Alaska, that can last from 10 to 20 days. Riddles became the first woman to win the race in 1985, finishing the last leg in blizzard conditions 18 days after leaving Anchorage. Butcher was forced to withdraw from her first race that same year after she and her dogs were attacked by a moose, but she won the Iditarod four times between 1986 and 1990. After her third consecutive win in 1988, Joe Redington, who had established the race and was a good friend of Butcher's, quipped, "It's getting pretty damn hard for a man to win anything anymore."

Donna Lopiano, who was forbidden to play in Little League, must have been thrilled when, on August 23, 1989, a youngster named Victoria Brucker became the first girl to play in the Little League World Series. Victoria was not only one of the San Pedro team's best hitters, but also one of their finest pitchers. On that historic day in August, Brucker became the first girl to get a hit and score a run in a Little League World Series game. Today, little girls don't have to worry about being turned away from Little League baseball tryouts. Perhaps one day in the near future, Victoria Brucker or a little girl very like her, will pitch the first game of a major baseball league season, making her dream come true.

Annie Smith Peck

1850–1935

Mountain Climbing

Enjoying international travel, Annie Smith Peck climbed mountains throughout the world. In her 40-year career, she climbed the Matterhorn in the Swiss Alps at age 45, and Mount Huascarán in the Andes when she was 58. A progressive woman in an era when most women stayed at home, Annie was always pushing the limits. Having scaled 14,692 feet (4,478 meters) to reach the summit of the Matterhorn, Annie set a record as an American woman climber. Impressive as that feat was, the international headlines reported more about her clothing—she removed her long skirts in favor of a pair of knickerbockers during her climb.

Annie Smith Peck, born on October 19, 1850 in Providence, Rhode Island, was the lone girl among three brothers. Annie was raised in a family of wealth and prominence. Her father, George Peck Sr., was a well-respected lawyer with a very successful practice. His daughter was more progressive than the times, and as a conservative gentleman, he was quite uncomfortable when Annie announced that she wanted to attend the University of Michigan. Mr. Peck even suggested that he might cut his daughter off financially if she went against his wishes. But Annie was a strong-willed, intelligent young woman who understood the power of reason. She reminded her father that he had urged his three sons to get college educations, and supported their academic endeavors at Brown University. Was it fair that she should be denied the same opportunity just because she was a woman? Annie made her case, and her father acquiesced.

In 1874, at the age of 24, Annie Smith Peck entered the University of Michigan at Ann Arbor. She proved to be an excellent student, and earned her Bachelor of Arts degree in Classics four years later. Mr. Peck was very proud of his daughter's accomplishment. After graduation, Annie taught college for a few years, and then returned to Rhode Island to pursue her Master of Arts degree. She wrote her thesis on Thucydides (d. ca 401 B.C.), a Greek historian and soldier, who documented the events of the Peloponnesian War between Athens and Sparta in 431 to 404 B.C.

Completing her degree in less than a year, Annie accepted an appointment as Professor of Latin at Purdue University in Indiana in 1881. While at Purdue, Annie attended a lecture by Stanford University president Dr. David Starr Jordan. In his lecture, Dr. Jordan described his experience of climbing the Matterhorn, the imposing, snowcapped mountain in the Swiss Alps. Though Annie was captivated by his story, something Jordan said toward the end of his talk left an equally important impression—he said that only a few men, and certainly no woman, could endure the physical and mental demands of such a climb. Perhaps one day, Annie thought to herself, she would challenge that statement.

In 1884, Annie decided to give up her teaching post and move to Europe to pursue her studies. Before settling into another program, however, Annie spent some time traveling in Italy, France, Austria, and Switzerland. While she was in Switzerland she made sure her itinerary included a view of the Matterhorn. Seeing the mountain, and remembering what Dr. Jordan had said a few years earlier, Annie promised herself somehow, someday, she would raise the funds and attempt the climb.

Before she made history as a mountain climber, however, Annie achieved an academic first. In 1885 she became the first woman admitted to the School of Classical Archaeology in Athens, Greece. After a year of study there, Annie returned to America and taught Latin at Smith College for a few years. Soon Annie grew restless and decided to try earning a living as a lecturer on Greek literature and archaeology. While on the lecture trail, Annie also wrote articles about her travels in Europe and America.

Finally, in 1888, Annie embarked on her first mountain climb in eastern California. With her brother, George Jr., Annie hiked the 10,000 feet (3,000 m) to reach Cloud's Rest, in Yosemite, which was established as a national park in 1890. The climb was all Annie had hoped it would be, and she was exhilarated by the experience. She continued to make other climbs, including New York's Adirondacks and New Hamphire's White Mountains. Each time she climbed, she wanted to go farther, higher, reaching new peaks and achieving new goals.

In May 1895, Annie felt ready to attempt an ascent of the Matterhorn, and she set sail for Europe. To pay for the trip, Annie agreed to write articles about her expedition for *Century Magazine*. Through the summer, in preparation for the Matterhorn, Annie climbed other mountains in and around the Alps. Finally, on August 20, Annie and her guide, Jean Baptiste Aymonod, began the climb to the summit of the Matterhorn. The following day, Annie successfully completed the journey, becoming the first American woman to do so.

Her success in the Alps made mountain climbing Annie's passion. She went on to climb higher and higher peaks, including Pico de Orizaba, Mexico's highest mountain, rising 18,400 feet (5,600 m) above sea level. Soon, she decided it was time to set her sights on higher mountains that had never been scaled by anyone, man or woman. Annie chose 21,276-foot (6,232-m) Mount Illampu, in Bolivia, South America. Though she failed in two attempts to make it all the way to the top, she did manage to reach 18,000 feet (5,486 m).

Undeterred, Annie then targeted Mount Huascarán in the Andes Mountains of Peru. At the age of 58, on her fourth attempt, Annie made the 21,812-foot (6,768-m) climb, setting a record for the highest ascent in the Western Hemisphere. Annie was honored with a medal from the Peruvian government, and the peak she had reached was named *Cumbre Aña Peck*.

When Annie returned to the United States, she wrote a book about her experiences—*A Search for the Apex of America,* published in 1911. She remained passionate about travel and mountain climbing, and also became involved in the struggle for women's suffrage. When she reached the top of Mount Coropuna, Peru, at age 61, Annie left behind a banner that read "Votes for Women." Ever the innovator, Annie convinced the newly established South American commercial airline to allow her to fly around the continent and write about her experiences. She began this seven-month aviation journey in late 1929 and returned to New York in June 1930.

In 1934, after returning from a short trip to the West Indies, Annie checked into New York's Memorial Hospital. She thought she was suffering from exhaustion, but tests revealed that she had uterine cancer. She rested for a while, and then at age 84, she took off again—on a trip around the world. However, she got only as far as Athens, Greece. While climbing the Acropolis, she became very tired, and had to come back to the United States. Annie Smith Peck died in New York on July 18, 1935.

Ora Washington

ca. 1898–1971
Tennis, Basketball

"Courage and determination were the biggest assets I had."
—Ora Washington

It is unfortunate that America was still so torn by widespread racial prejudice and discrimination when Ora Washington was born. Had she been born just 30 years later, Ora, along with Althea Gibson, may have sent the predominantly white, upper-class sport of tennis on its heels. Ora's position in the all-black American Tennis Association (ATA)

was so dominant that she retired from the sport to encourage other players to compete in tournaments without having to face her.

She never had the opportunity to play against the white tennis champions of her time, such as France's Suzanne Lenglen or America's Helen Wills Moody. Perhaps if she had, then the record books would read a little differently.

Born in Philadelphia, Pennsylvania in 1898, Ora grew up in the Germantown section of the city. There, on October 4, 1777, George Washington failed in his attempt to regain the area from the British during the Revolutionary War. The cobblestoned, tree-lined streets were a reminder of the neighborhood's historic significance. Ora took up the game of tennis at the suggestion of some friends who were trying to help her cope with the death of her sister. They hoped that the athletic activity might help Ora with her grieving, and eventually ease the pain of the loss.

Ora's athletic gifts quickly became apparent. In 1924, she beat Dorothy Radcliffe in an ATA singles championship at Druid Park Hill, Baltimore. Though she had a very unusual grip, holding the racket shaft halfway up the handle, and she rarely followed through on her swing, Ora was such a powerful player that she rarely lost a match. In some years, she didn't suffer a single defeat.

From 1929 to 1935, Ora was the ATA singles champion. She won the title again in 1937, for an unprecedented nine singles championship titles. A good doubles player as well, Ora also won seven straight doubles titles. Though she would have welcomed the opportunity to play Helen Wills, the U.S. Lawn Tennis Association (USLTA) singles champion, her challenge was never accepted.

Ora retired from the game of tennis twice. She was persuaded to return to the courts by Detroit's Flora Lomax, then the reigning ATA singles champion. Flora suggested the two meet head-to-head to see if Ora could win back her title. Ora won without much difficulty, and played again for a while. However, she bowed out of tennis a second time when some officials expressed concern that other tennis hopefuls might be discouraged from playing because she was so dominant.

Ora was not idle during her retirement, though. A multitalented athlete, she was also playing competitive women's basketball. As an 18-year member of the Philadelphia Tribune, Ora was their star center, winning top scoring honors several times. The Tribune was a barnstorming team that traveled around the country in search of other teams to play. They accepted all challenges and rarely lost a game. Ora also played one season for the Germantown Hornets in 1929-30 as the team's captain. But her basketball fame really came from her years with the Tribune. In nine years of play, the Philadelphia Tribune lost only six games.

On the road, Ora also enjoyed running basketball clinics and demonstrations with her teammates. She participated in sports at a time when athletes were not highly paid, but Ora believed that hard work and determination led to success, no matter what sort of work you did. Ora saved enough of the money she earned doing housework to buy an apartment building.

Never far from her Germantown roots, Ora spent many years giving back to the community. She is best remembered there for offering free training sessions as well as volunteering to coach youngsters interested in learning basketball and tennis. The neighborhood lost a good resident and graceful champion when Ora Washington passed away in 1971.

Helen Wills Moody

1906–1998

Tennis

"Tennis is a diversion, not a career."
—Helen Wills, from her autobiography *Fifteen-Thirty*

Throughout her career, reporters referred to Helen as "Little Miss Poker Face" and "Queen Helen," because of her stoic expression on the tennis court. However, Helen's unemotional demeanor may have been one of her greatest assets. As a true pioneer in women's sports, Helen helped dispel the stereotypical views about participation being too strenuous and "unfeminine" by wearing makeup during her matches. She has been decribed by her opponents as the hardest-hitting tennis player they ever faced. Both her forehand and backhand shots could go the length of the court. Curiously, though she achieved tremendous success and is remembered as one of the greatest tennis players in the illustrious history of the sport, Helen never considered herself primarily an athlete. She was a Phi Beta Kappa graduate of the University of California at Berkeley, and traveled in well-to-do social circles with the likes of Lady Astor and George Bernard Shaw.

Born in Centerville, California on October 6, 1906, Helen Wills benefited from the upper-class life her father, Dr. Clarence Wills, was able to provide for his wife and daughter. She was an active girl who enjoyed horseback riding and swimming. When she turned 13, her father gave Helen her first tennis racket. She was instantly taken with the game, so Dr. Wills paid for Helen's membership at the Berkeley Tennis Club where she received private lessons with the best coaches. They were quickly impressed by Helen's persistence, often finding their young student practicing a stroke for hours.

When Helen was 14, she was introduced to Hazel Wightman, four-time U.S. national singles tennis champion. She, too, was impressed with the young Wills's talent and began working with her. Just one year later, Helen won her first U.S. junior championship. After watching the championship match between France's flamboyant tennis star Suzanne Lenglen and Norway's national champion Molla Mallory at the U.S. Women's Open, Helen was further inspired to become a great tennis player. In her autobiography, *Fifteen-Thirty,* she wrote of her experience as a spectator that day: "I knew the goal for which I hoped to aim, the kind of tennis I wanted to play."

In 1922, at the age of 17, Helen entered the first U.S. Women's Open in her career. She met Molla Mallory in the final, and lost 6-3, 6-1. The following year, Helen avenged the loss by defeating Mallory in straight sets 6-2, 6-1, becoming the youngest U.S. Women's Open champion of her day. In 1924, the two met in the final for the third straight year, with Helen defending her title in a 6-1, 6-3 victory.

The last sanctioned tennis competition at the Olympics was in 1924 at the Summer Games in Paris, France (the sport would be reinstated in 1988). Helen won a gold medal in the singles final by defeating Didi Vlastro of France in straight sets. She captured her second Olympic gold medal after winning the doubles competition with her partner and former coach, Hazel Wightman. They beat the British duo of Kitty McKane and Dorothy Covell in an exciting two-set match, 7-5, 8-6.

Helen returned to America a sports heroine. She continued her winning ways, capturing her third U.S. Open title in 1925. The following year, Helen's dominance in the sport was beginning to be challenged by another Berkeley Country Club member, Helen Jacobs. In fact, the two had met in a practice round in 1922 when Jacobs was just 14 years old. Helen disposed of the youngster in a seven-minute-set rout, 6-0. But it would only be a few more years before Jacobs would become a viable contender.

In 1926, Helen began suffering from a back injury that impaired her play. She kept the injury to herself, hoping she could play through the pain. Helen played well enough in the U.S. Open to make it to the finals against Jacobs. She lost the first set 8-6, but came back to win the next set 6-3 to even things up. Jacobs had jumped out to a commanding 3-0 lead in the third and decisive set, when Helen mumbled something to the umpire before walking off the court in mid-match. Many observers thought she was using the back injury as an excuse to avoid losing to Jacobs. However, it was later revealed that Helen had a serious spinal injury and really wasn't able to continue play that day.

Except for 1926, the mid-1920s belonged to Helen. In 1927 she won her fourth U.S. Open title after defeating Kitty McKane. McKane won the opening set 3-6, but Helen stormed back taking the next two sets 6-0, 6-2. Adding to her Grand Slam tournament titles, Helen also won the first of eight career Wimbledon singles titles, and her second of three doubles titles on the grass court surface.

In 1929, Helen married Frederick Moody, a San Francisco stockbroker. Aside from her tennis play, Helen enjoyed traveling with Frederick and writing freelance newspaper articles about fashion shows, gallery openings, and art exhibitions. She continued to win tournaments, and was ranked number one for eight years. During one stretch—from 1927 to 1933—Helen won 27 tournaments and 158 straight matches. In all, she won 19 Grand Slam titles, which ranks third in victories behind Steffi Graf (21), and Margaret Smith Court (24). Helen retired from tennis in 1938 after winning her eighth Wimbledon title, the most by any female player. The record stood until 1990, when Martina Navratilova won her ninth Wimbledon championship.

Helen's marriage ended in 1937, the same year her autobiography, *Fifteen-Thirty: The Story of a Tennis Player,* was released. She had also written a book on tennis instruction earlier in her career, and later wrote two mystery novels. In 1939, Helen married again, this time to polo player Aiden Roark. She continued to write and paint. Some of her artistic works were exhibited in galleries. For her achievements in tennis, Helen Wills Moody Roark was inducted into the International Tennis Hall of Fame in 1959. She was also named Athlete of the Year by the Associated Press in 1935. She died on January 1, 1998, and her ashes were scattered at sea.

Gertrude Ederle

1906–
Swimming

"After eight hours I knew that I would either swim it or drown."
—Gertrude Ederle on crossing the English Channel in 1926

Only five people—all of them men—had ever succeeded in doing what a 19-year-old girl from New York was attempting on the morning of August 6, 1926. When Gertrude Ederle stepped into the chilly waters of the English Channel at Cap Gris-Nez, France, the sun was out and the weather seemed fine. But because the currents of the Atlantic Ocean and the North Sea meet there, the waters of the channel can be rough, and fierce winds can whip up without warning.

The English Channel, an important waterway between the countries of France and England is about 350 miles (563 km) long. Its width varies from 100 miles (160 km) at its widest point to 21 miles (34 km) at its narrowest spot between Dover, England, and Calais, France. In this narrow stretch, called the Straits of Dover, the water is anywhere from 200 to 300 feet (60 to 90 m) deep.

People had been attempting to swim the channel for many years. Of the five men who had succeeded in crossing the channel, the first was Matthew Webb of Britain in 1875. The fastest swim up to that time was 16 hours, 33 minutes, set in 1923 by Enrique Tirabocci of Argentina. Gertrude not only wanted to be the first woman to achieve the feat, she also wanted to be the fastest swimmer.

Gertrude Caroline Ederle, born on October 23, 1906, was one of six children. Her parents were German immigrants to New York City. Her father Henry had a butcher shop on Amsterdam Avenue, and "Gertie," as she was known by her family, was a shy, good-natured girl who enjoyed helping her mother with the chores. She learned how to swim at the family's summer home in Highlands, New Jersey.

At age 12, Gertie set her first world record, swimming the 800-meter freestyle in 13 minutes, 19 seconds. She was, and still is, the youngest person, male or female, to break a world record. She enjoyed the distance swims too, and won the 3 1/2-mile (5.6-km) Manhattan Beach Joseph P. Day Cup in 1922. Gertie's win was even more impressive because she beat 51 other swimmers, including British champ Hilda James and U.S. Olympic medalist Helen Wainwright. Between 1921 and 1924, Gertie won more than 29 national titles and world records, setting most of them in 1924.

The second time women were allowed to take part in the Olympic Games, Gertrude made the U.S. women's swim team, and competed in the 1924 Olympics in Paris, France. Gertrude won two bronze medals in the 100- and

400-meter freestyle and a team gold for the 4 x 100-meter relay.

After the Olympics, Gertrude decided to turn pro and focused her attention on the longer swims. In 1925, she finished the 17 1/2-mile (29-km) swim from Lower Manhattan's Battery to Sandy Hook, New Jersey, in a record 7 hours, 11 minutes. She then decided to set her goals higher, and became the first woman to cross the English Channel—something of a novelty challenge for many in the 1920s. In August 1925, Gertrude plunged into the water, but 9 hours into the swim she got seasick and had to be pulled out of the water.

In 1926, *The New York Daily News* and *The Chicago Tribune* agreed to finance her second attempt to cross the channel. Accompanied by reporter Julia Harpman, Gertrude sailed for Europe in June and trained there for part of the summer to prepare herself for the swim. After being coated in olive oil, lanolin, and vaseline to keep warm—and fend off the stinging jellyfish—Gertrude entered the channel off the shore of Calais, France, at 7:05 AM on August 6.

Six hours into the swim, a squall churned the waters in the channel into deadly crosscurrents. After 12 hours, no one was sure Gertrude would make it, but she kept going. She made history when she stumbled onto the beach of Kingdown, Kent, after being in the water for 14 hours and 31 minutes. Not only had Gertrude Ederle become the first woman to successfully swim the English Channel, she bettered Tirabocci's time by more than two hours.

Gertrude was the toast of two continents. She spent a few weeks celebrating in Europe before coming home on the S.S. *Berengaria* to a ticker-tape parade in Manhattan, where over 2 million people welcomed home "America's Best Girl." She toured for a while with Billy Rose's Aquacade, but an injury to her back and her desire for privacy led her to move away from the show-biz spotlight. She was also suffering from a hearing loss, which was attributed to her channel swim.

In 1936, Gertrude bought a house in Flushing, New York, where she still lives rather reclusively. As she stayed out of the public eye, she found new fulfillment in teaching deaf children to swim at a local school.

Sonja Henie

1912–1969

Figure Skating

"I want to do with skates what Fred Astaire is doing with dancing."
—Sonja Henie, upon turning pro in 1936

At the first Winter Olympic Games, hosted by Chamonix, France, in 1924, 16 nations participated in 14 events. Of the 258 athletes who competed, only 13 were female—and 11-year-old Sonja Henie was among them. Though still just a child, she would be competing in the women's figure skating event. Amazingly, Sonja had already won a major title, capturing first prize in the Norwegian national championships earlier that year. Unlike the women, who were required to wear calf-length skirts during performances, the young girl appeared in a knee-length skirt.

Little Sonja charmed the judges with her moves, which included a jump into a sit spin in the "free skate" portion of her program. They were so impressed with her performance that they awarded her third place. Unfortunately, Sonja did so poorly in the compulsory figures that she finished last overall in the competition. Unfazed by her final standings, Sonja channeled all of her energy into improving her technique for the next competition.

Sonja Henie was born on April 8, 1912, in Oslo, Norway, into a family of wealth and privilege. Her father Wilhelm was a prosperous fur salesman and former amateur cycling champion whose affluence allowed Sonja the luxury of private tutors while she was training for competition. After the disappointment at Chamonix, Sonja returned to competition with a vengeance. At 14, she won her first world championship. She would win nine more before her career ended—an unprecedented 10 consecutive wins.

Sonja was only four years old when she began taking ballet lessons. Shortly after earning her first figure skating championship, she attended a performance featuring Russia's prima ballerina, Anna Pavlova. Sonja was so dazzled by Pavlova's grace and style that she decided to incorporate balletlike moves into her figure skating. Discarding the literal "figure tracing" of standard skating, she began adding dramatic jumps and spins to her routines that were previously only acceptable in male figure skating. Though she may not have realized it at the time, the young athlete was about to revolutionize the sport of figure skating.

Sonja's second Olympic experience was far more successful than her first. At the 1928 Winter Games in St. Moritz, Switzerland, the 15-year-old took home her first gold medal, becoming the youngest female ever to win the award—a record that remained unbroken for 70 years. (In 1998, 14-year-old

Tara Lipinski toppled Henie's record at the Games in Nagano, Japan.) When she was 19, Sonja won a second gold medal at the 1932 Games in Lake Placid, New York, earning standing ovations for a free skate program that included choreographed interpretations of music from popular stage shows. In her final Olympic competition at Garmisch-Partenkirchen, Germany, in 1936, Sonja won her third consecutive Olympic gold medal—a feat that remains unmatched. The only dark moment in the athlete's otherwise stellar career occurred when Sonja was photographed saluting German dictator Adolf Hitler during the Games. Four years later,

Sonja Henie performs a dance on ice in the 1943 film, Wintertime.

when the Nazis invaded and occupied Norway, the photo was widely circulated as a means of discrediting her. The image would haunt her for the remainder of her life.

That year, Sonja retired from amateur figure skating and entered the motion picture industry. Banking on her athletic success and international renown, Twentieth-Century Fox executive Darryl F. Zanuck signed her to a five-year contract, making films that were essentially vehicles for displaying her figure skating prowess. It was rumored that she was earning $150,000 for each film at a time when most people were earning less than $1500 a year. Her first film, *One in a Million,* (1936) was very well received. She made 10 more films with Twentieth-Century Fox, including *Iceland, Wintertime,* and *Sun Valley Serenade.* By 1939, Sonja Henie was the third-biggest box-office attraction in America after Clark Gable and Shirley Temple.

When the advent of television began drawing audiences away from theaters, Sonja started skating in traveling ice shows. For a time she even had her own troupe—the Hollywood Ice Revue. She continued performing in revues for 13 years. Sonja Henie became a U.S. citizen in 1941, maintaining homes in both Norway and the United States, where she lived with her third husband, Niels Onstad, after she retired in 1956.

By the time Sonja founded the Sonja Henie-Niels Onstad Arts Center near Oslo, Norway, in 1968, she had been diagnosed with leukemia. On October 12, 1969, the 57-year-old figure skating legend affectionately known as "Pavlova on ice" passed away. In her remarkable career, Sonja Henie earned more than 1,400 figure skating trophies, medals, and cups. She bequeathed her estate of $47 million, including a very valuable art collection, to her homeland—Norway. Today, more than 50 years after her last film, Sonja Henie remains the most commercially successful Olympic champion in history.

Mildred "Babe" Didrikson Zaharias

1913–1956

Track and Field, Golf

"My goal was to be the greatest athlete that ever lived. I suppose I was born with the urge to get into sports."
—Mildred "Babe" Didrikson Zaharias

Affectionately nicknamed "Babe," Mildred Zaharias was arguably the greatest female athlete of the twentieth century. There was virtually no sport in which she did not excel. Babe could fly down the track with lightning speed, hit nothing but the net with her jump shots, throw a baseball with pinpoint accuracy as hard and as fast as male ballplayers, and hit a golf ball off the tee farther than some of the men on the Professional Golf Association tour. Her flamboyant attitude was matched by her athletic skills. Once in an exhibition game, she struck out the Yankee Clipper—Joe DiMaggio, himself!

Babe's father, Ole Didriksen, emigrated from Oslo, Norway, in 1905 and settled in Port Arthur, Texas, an emerging oil town, to work as a carpenter and furniture refinisher. Ole saved money for three years before bringing his wife, Hannah Marie Olson, and their three children Ole Jr., Dora, and Esther to join him in America.

A year later, the Didriksen family began to grow. In 1909, Hannah gave birth to twins, Lillie and Louis. Another daughter, Mildred, was born on June 26, 1911 (some records show her birth year as 1913. Also, she later changed the spelling of her last name to Didrikson). Another son, Arthur, was born in 1915. During these years, Ole built a house on land he had purchased before he brought the family over from Oslo. An accomplished carpenter, Ole did most of the woodworking inside the house. Unfortunately, the house was destroyed by a flood after a hurricane swept through Port Arthur, killing 275 people.

With all of their belongings gone, the Didriksens moved 17 miles (27 km) north to Beaumont, another growing oil town supported by the Magnolia Refinery. They moved into a house on Doucette Avenue, just a block away from the refinery. Years later, the pollution became so bad there that nylon panty hose disintegrated when exposed to the air.

Unaware of the health dangers at that time, Ole built an outdoor gym for his children. Exercise and play were welcome diversions for the Didriksen kids. Though Ole struggled to provide for his family, all the children had to get jobs as soon as they were able. Babe got a job at a fig-packing plant when she was in the seventh grade. Not long after, she more than doubled her hourly wages of 30 cents an hour by taking a job at a potato-sack factory where she made a penny for every sack she sewed up.

Babe and her brothers and sisters played most kinds of sports, running races, playing baseball, swimming, and diving in the nearby Neches River. Babe credited her mother for her and her siblings' natural athletic ability—Hannah had been a successful skater and skier in Norway. The family was quite musically gifted too. Babe learned how to play the harmonica, an instrument she enjoyed throughout her life. Ole played the violin, as did one of Babe's sisters, and her brothers played the drums. Hannah sang beautifully, and many nights the Didriksens entertained their neighbors when they played out on the front porch after dinner.

When Babe entered Beaumont High School, she was encouraged to take part in many of the girl's sports, and she eagerly joined the baseball, volleyball, basketball, tennis, swimming, and golf teams. She probably would have tried out for the football squad if the school had permitted a female to play. In addition to her incredible athletic talent, Babe was a fierce competitor. She did not like to lose, and often expressed her displeasure over losing by displaying a fiery temper. She also had a cockiness about her abilities that put a lot of people off, leaving her with few friends.

Babe seemed to prefer basketball. While still in high school, she was offered a job as a stenographer for the Employers Casualty Company, who also invited her to play on their basketball team—the Dallas Cyclones. In her first game with the Cyclones, Babe outscored the entire opposing team. Babe was also a member of the company's swimming and diving teams, and she renewed her interest in track and field events. She began practicing incessantly, setting national records in women's javelin and regional records in long jump, shot put, and high jump.

At the 1932 Amateur Athletic Union (AAU) Women's Track and Field competition, Babe competed as a one-woman team in eight events, winning five of them. Her success qualified her for the 1932 Olympic Games in Los Angeles, California, where she was restricted to competing in three events: the javelin throw, the 80-meter hurdles, and the high jump. Babe won the gold medal in the first two events, but though it was initially ruled that she tied for first with Jean Shiley in the high jump, the judges later ruled her jump as illegal because she had gone over the bar headfirst. Shiley took home the gold, and the silver went to Didrikson.

Babe was named the Associated Press Woman Athlete of the Year in 1932, the first of five such awards she would receive. Following the Olympics, Babe tried to parlay her athletic success into financial gain by making personal appearances in exhibition golf games and playing briefly on a number of major baseball teams. In 1935, she won her first amateur golf championship but, after the tournament, the U.S. Golf Association revoked her amateur status, citing that she had already participated in a number of pro sports events. Babe then returned to the exhibition circuit, where in 1938 she met a wrestler named George Zaharias. The two were married by the end of the year.

Babe's marriage allowed her the financial security to re-enter the amateur golf circuit in 1943, after the U.S. Golf Association agreed to reinstate her. In typical "Babe" style, she dominated the sport throughout the 1940s, winning 17 consecutive tournaments and earning the Associated Press Athlete of the Year award three times during her long winning streak. In 1949, along with other top-notch female golfers such as Patty Berg, Louise Suggs, and Betty Jameson, Didrikson cofounded the Ladies Professional Golf Association (LPGA), an organization designed to give women the same opportunities that male golfers had.

From 1947 to 1955, Didrikson continued to play golf, becoming one of the "winningest" women in the sport and earning national recognition for the growing LPGA. In 1950, the Associated Press named her the top woman athlete of the half-century. By 1952, however, she had begun to tire frequently and consulted a doctor, who diagnosed her with rectal cancer. Vowing to return to competition, she underwent surgery for the disease in 1953. The following year she won several tournaments, including her third U.S. Women's Open championship, and her inspiring comeback earned her the Ben Hogan Award.

Determined not to let illness slow her down, Babe continued playing golf and became a spokesperson for the American Cancer Society. But when she began to suffer weakness and severe back pain, her doctors discovered that the disease had recurred. She died of cancer on September 27, 1956. In her relatively brief life, the woman some call the

"Babe" Didrikson Zaharias at a women's golf tournament in Miami, 1947

greatest all-around female athlete of the century had thrown open the doors of opportunity to women in competitive sports, leaving a lasting legacy for female athletes around the world.

Patricia Berg

1918–
Golf

"I'm very happy I gave up football, or I wouldn't be here tonight."
— Patty Berg on the eve of her induction into the LPGA Hall of Fame

Her athletic achievements in the sport of golf have earned Patricia "Patty" Berg countless honors and awards. In her career, Patty had 57 victories, including 15 major tournaments. Along with her play, Patty's contributions to golf place her in the company of such distinguished women golfers as Mildred "Babe" Didrikson, Louise Suggs, Mickey Wright, and Kathy Whitworth. Patty is one of only six women golfers to win both the U.S. Women's Amateur and U.S. Women's Open. During her career she was the recipient of three Vare Trophies, awarded annually to the woman with the lowest overall scoring average. And as winner of the *Golf Digest* Performance Average Award in 1954, 1955, and 1957, it was yet another three-time honor for Patty. However, for her pioneering efforts in promoting women's golf as well as cofounding the Ladies Professional Golf Association, Patty Berg may be one of the greatest contributors to women's sports in the twentieth century.

Even as a youngster, Patricia Jane Berg loved sports. Born on February 13, 1918, in Minneapolis, Minnesota, Patty was soon a fierce competitor, as demonstrated by her success in track and field and in speed skating, where she came in second at the national girls' championships in 1933. Another of her passions was football. Patty quarterbacked the otherwise all-boys 50th Street Tigers, a team that included her brother and future professional football star and coach Bud Wilkinson.

When Patty turned 13, her parents decided she was too old to be playing a physical contact sport with boys. They persuaded her to try the more lady-like sport of golf. Her father bought her a secondhand set of clubs and a golf membership at Interlachen Country Club in nearby Edina, Minnesota. Three years after taking up the game, Patty won the Minneapolis City Championship and reached the semifinals of the U.S. Women's Amateur tournament. This was the beginning of a seven-year run in which Patty would win more than 28 amateur championship titles including the Minnesota Women's State Amateur in 1935, 1936, and 1938.

Among her other early achievements, Patty was named to the U.S. Curtis Cup team in 1936 and 1938. This international women's amateur competition is held every two years with the United States facing a team made up of women from England, Scotland, Ireland, Northern Ireland, and Wales. The winning country takes custody of the cup until the next match is played. Patty also won the National Amateur title in 1938 at the Westmoreland Country Club in Wilmette, Illinois, and won the first of three Associated Press Athlete of the Year honors. At the age of 20, Patty had already won every major amateur title in the United States.

Despite the fact that there was still no women's organized professional golf tour, Patty turned pro in 1940. As the most recognized and successful women's golfer of her time, Patty earned money by traveling around the country giving golf clinics and exhibitions. She also signed a contract with Wilson Sporting Goods, which began manufacturing a set of golf clubs that bore her name.

In 1941, Patty was involved in a serious automobile accident and suffered injuries that sidelined her from the game for 18 months. After her recovery, Patty joined the marine corps and served as a lieutenant from 1942 to 1945 in World War II. After the war, Patty returned to golfing full-time. As though there had not been a five-year hiatus from the game, she won her first U.S. Women's Open Championship in 1946.

The first formation of the first women's professional tour (WPGA) was attempted by Hope Seignious, Betty Hicks, and Ellen Griffin shortly after the war. But the tour struggled, trying to attract players and spectators. Patty certainly was doing her part. She continued her winning ways, capturing seven titles in 1948 alone. Finally, with the additional efforts of Patty and golfers Mildred "Babe" Didrikson, Louise Suggs, and Betty Jameson, the WPGA was replaced by the creation of the Ladies Professional Golf Association (LPGA).

Patty became the LPGA's first president. Often the players worked long hours setting up the tournaments they were playing in but the LPGA's strongest assets were its players. These included Babe Didrikson, arguably the greatest female athlete of the twentieth century, as well as Louise Suggs, Betsy

Rawls, and Patty herself. For their contributions to the game, Berg, Didrikson, Suggs, and Jameson were named as the first inductees to the newly created LPGA Hall of Fame in 1951. Patty was the tour's leading money winner in 1954, 1955, and 1957.

In 1959, at the age of 41, Patty was competing in the U.S. Women's Open at the Churchill Valley Country Club in Pittsburgh. During the tournament she recorded a hole-in-one, the first woman ever to do so in a United States Golf Association event. New star players on the golf scene in the 1960s like Mickey Wright and Kathy Whitworth continued to build the LPGA's popularity, ensuring its survival. In 1963, the LPGA finally attracted television coverage of the final round of the tournament. For the female athletes, monetary rewards increased tremendously during the 1960s, with prize money tripling from $200,000 to $600,000. Women's golf had come a long way since the days when Patty began her career.

Throughout the next several years, accolades and honors continued to shower Patty for her athletic achievements. In 1963, Patty was named the winner of the Bob Jones Award, presented by the USGA to a player who demonstrates its namesakes's sportsmanship and respect for the game. As the first woman so honored, Patty was given the 1976 Humanitarian Sports Award by the United Cerebral Palsy Foundation. And as an ultimate honor, in 1978, the LPGA established the Patty Berg Award, presented to women golfers who have made outstanding contributions to the game.

Though illnesses and injuries have plagued Patty throughout her life, she has demonstrated the same resolve and determination in her recoveries that she showed in her desire to win. In 1971, Patty underwent cancer surgery; in 1980, hip surgery; and in 1989, back surgery. But none of these health problems slowed Patty down. In the summer of 1991, at the age of 73, Patty recorded yet another hole-in-one. She is the author of three books on golf, and has devoted countless hours to volunteer charity work.

In 1995, Patty was honored by the Professional Golf Association by being named their Distinguished Service Award winner. In 1996, as a Minneapolis native, Patty was named the recipient of the Minnesota Golf Association's Distinguished Service Award. Established in 1994, and named after 20-year MGA executive director Warren Rebholz, the award is presented to "individuals who through their actions have exemplified the spirit of the game at its highest level. . . ." And in May 1997, 66 years after taking up the game of golf, Patty was honored with the Spirit Lifetime Achievement Award.

Patricia Berg's legacy will live on beyond her achievements in the game of golf. In 1993, the Southwest Florida Regional Medical Center honored Patty by opening a cancer treatment clinic bearing her name. In 1995, the University of Minnesota named its athletic program the Patty Berg Foundation. A longtime resident of Fort Meyers, Florida, Patty Berg continues to lead an active life—playing golf when she can, continuing her volunteer work, and giving something back to the game she loves by teaching golf to adults and children.

Toni Stone

1921–1996
Baseball

"A woman has her dreams too. When you finish high school, they tell a boy to go out and see the world. What do they tell a girl? They tell her to go next door and marry the boy that their family's picked out for her. It wasn't right."
—Toni Stone explaining her feelings about the resistance to women in sports

In baseball's historical records, Toni Stone is documented as the first woman to play professional ball in a men's league. As noteworthy as that might be for the many women who were pioneers in their chosen sport, being first was never as important to Toni Stone as the fact that she played the game.

When Negro Leagues team owner Syd Pollack signed Toni to play for his Indianapolis Clowns, many questioned his motives. While Syd had always contended that he signed Toni because she could play ball well, others suggested that Toni was brought into the league to revive interest in the game and improve gate sales. The Negro League teams were not the only ones suffering from sagging fan attendance; the All-American Girls Baseball League as well as the minor leagues in general had also experienced a decline. By the mid-1950s, as the best black players were being signed to teams in the once all-white National Baseball League, more and more sports fans were tuning into games on television rather than going out to the ballparks.

Toni Stone got her chance to play professional baseball when she replaced the Clowns' former second baseman Henry Aaron, whose contract had been purchased by the Boston Braves. Born Marcenia Lyle in St. Paul, Minnesota, in 1921, Toni wanted to play pro ball from the time she was a child. Marcenia was one of four children and both of her parents worked. Her father was a barber and her mother was a beautician. Neither one of them ever understood their daughter's obsession with baseball, but that mattered little to Marcenia. She always found sandlot ball games to play in with the boys in her neighborhood.

Even before her teen years, Marcenia was determined to play baseball any way she could. She collected the boxtops from Wheaties breakfast cereal until she had enough to join one of their softball tournaments. Preferring baseball over school, Marcenia recognized that she was different from the other kids. She rejected the traditional "feminine" role young girls were then expected to follow.

One man who greatly influenced Marcenia's life was Gabby Street, a former big-league catcher and manager of the St. Louis Saints, a minor league team. When he opened a summer baseball camp for kids, Marcenia hung around and pestered him until he gave her a chance to show him how good she was. Gabby was so impressed with Marcenia's play that he bought her a pair of cleats and let her participate. She was the only girl who attended Gabby's camp.

When she was 15, Marcenia headed off to the San Francisco Bay area to find her sister. This relocation would set Marcenia on her path into professional baseball. When she arrived, she had no money, no job, and no place to live. Marcenia got all three before she found her sister.

Toni played American Legion ball for a while. The league was established by the American Legion in 1928 to serve as "a means of teaching practical Americanism to the youth of the country." She changed her name to Toni because she thought it sounded like "tomboy," and she wanted her name to reflect what she was all about. Toni thought she might finally have a chance to play big league ball in 1943 when the All-American Girls Baseball League was created. But instead, Toni faced the same barrier as the male black ballplayers in America—she was turned away because of her color. Not to be dissuaded, Toni joined the San Francisco Sea Lions, a barnstorming, semipro baseball team. The team traveled around the states, challenging other town's teams to games. In her first time up at the plate, Toni drove home two runs.

Toni was happy to be playing baseball, but she felt the Sea Lions owner was not paying her the money he had promised, so while barnstorming through New Orleans, Toni joined up with the Black Pelicans. She played second base with them for several seasons. In 1949, Toni joined the renowned New Orleans Creoles, a minor league team that had been around since the early 1920s. For her efforts she was paid $300 a month and steadily improved all areas of her game. Though a good hitter, batting .265, Toni was actually getting a fair amount of newspaper coverage for her fielding abilities.

During the time Toni was playing ball in the minors, she met Aurelious Alberga, a retired black officer who had served in World War I. Though Alberga was forty years older than Toni, they fell in love and married in 1950. Never a big fan of his wife playing baseball, Alberga was no more successful at getting Toni to stop playing than were her parents, or Gabby Street, or any gender barrier or color barrier that stood in her way.

Toni Stone's biggest break came in 1953 when she signed with the Indianpolis Clowns. The highlight of her career came while she was a member of the Clowns. On Easter Sunday, 1953, the Clowns were playing against the St. Louis Browns. The game was being pitched by Browns great, Satchel Paige. Toni was shaking when she got up to the batter's box, but she got a hit, right out over second base. It was the only hit the Clowns recorded against Paige the whole game—and the happiest moment of Toni's life.

Toni finished the 1953 season with the Clowns. She hit a respectable .243 and played in 50 games. The following year Pollack sold her contract to the American League champion Kansas City Monarchs. Though they were a premiere team, Toni didn't get much playing time. Disillusioned, she retired at the end of 1954. Coincidentally, the All-American Girls Baseball League folded the same year.

Even though Toni no longer played pro ball, she took part in pickup games and continued to play recreational baseball into her sixties. After she retired, Toni and her husband settled in Oakland where she worked as a nurse. When Alberga became ill, all of Toni's time was spent caring for her husband until his death in 1987. Toni and several other ballplayers were honored in 1991 by the Baseball Hall of Fame. A special honor came in 1993 when Marcenia "Toni Stone" Alberga was inducted into the Women's International Sports Hall of Fame. She now joins so many other great female athletes who, like Toni, forged their own paths in order to fulfill their dreams. Toni Stone may have been given the opportunity to play professional baseball as a draw to preserve a failing league, but she wound up leaving an indelible mark on the game, and helped pave the way for future generations of girls who also have dreams.

Althea Gibson

1927–
Tennis

"I don't consciously beat the drums for any special cause, not even the cause of the Negro in the United States, because I feel that our best chance to advance is to prove ourselves as individuals."
—Althea Gibson on racial discrimination

No one could have guessed from her outward appearance how apprehensive 23-year-old Althea Gibson was as she boarded the subway train in Harlem one cloudy morning in September 1950. Arriving at her final destination, the West Side Tennis Club in Forest Hills, was the fulfillment of a dream for Gibson. But it was also uncharted territory.

Althea Gibson is best remembered for breaking the racial barrier in tennis when she competed in the U.S. Lawn Tennis Association tournament in 1950. She was also the first African-American of either gender to win a tennis title. Gibson also changed the history of women's golf 14 years later, when she earned her player's card—and thus a membership in the previously all-white Ladies Professional Golf Association. Gibson's success encouraged and inspired other black athletes who were prevented from competing in amateur and professional sports because of their race.

Althea Gibson was born in Silver, South Carolina, on August 25, 1927. She was the first of Daniel and Annie Gibson's five children. The Gibsons were sharecroppers, like many other blacks living in the rural South during that time. Even with a good harvest, Daniel earned barely enough money to support his family. When three years of bad crops were followed by the Great Depression, Gibson, like many other southern blacks, moved north in the hope of earning a better living.

The Gibsons lived in a small apartment in New York's Harlem neighborhood. There, Althea got into mischief so often that when she was about seven, she was sent to live with an aunt in Philadelphia, Pennsylvania. The change in her surroundings did little to improve her behavior, however. She returned to New York an even more defiant nine year old. Before long, she began cutting school to go to afternoon movies. The more she was punished, the more disobedient she became. Sometimes she didn't come home for days at a time.

Althea spent those days playing basketball, baseball, and other sports in the Harlem playgrounds near her home. She knew she had a talent for athletics, and playing sports gave her a sense of self-worth that she did not find at school or at home.

One summer day in 1941, Gibson wandered into one of the "play streets" in Harlem, where the city had organized adult-supervised activities for neighborhood kids. On one play street she found a court for paddle tennis, a game similar to tennis but played with wooden paddles instead of rackets. The game instantly appealed to Gibson and before long, she was playing regular tennis. Her talent didn't go unnoticed. Some of the members at the Cosmopolitan Club, a prestigious all-black country club, sponsored her for junior membership and paid for private lessons. Since blacks were barred from white tennis clubs and from participating in white-sponsored tournaments, the Cosmopolitan and other black clubs formed their own tennis club, the American Tennis Association (ATA). They hoped a player with Althea's talent and skill could finally break the color barrier.

Althea made the most of the opportunity. She learned to curb her rebelliousness and follow court etiquette. She took the sport very seriously, and it paid off. A year after joining the club, Althea won her first major ATA tournament, the New York State Open Championship. In 1944 and 1945, she won ATA girls division titles. Her success inspired two surgeons to sponsor her tennis career if she agreed to return to high school. In 1946, the 19-year-old moved to North Carolina, where she continued to hone her tennis skills on the private court of one of her sponsors.

During Gibson's final year in high school, she played in the Eastern Indoor Championships, an all-white tennis tournament. She achieved a minor victory by reaching the quarterfinals. The following week, she again reached the quarterfinals in the National Indoor Championships of the U.S. Lawn Tennis Association (USLTA).

The former dropout graduated 10th in her class from Williston Industrial High in 1949, and received a full scholarship to Florida A&M University. She continued to play in indoor tennis tournaments, but Gibson's ultimate goal was to be invited to the USLTA-sponsored outdoor summer tournaments. Most of the outdoor tournaments were held at private, all-white country clubs, which still refused to admit blacks.

Gibson's cause was promoted by Alice Marble, a well-respected, four-time U.S. National Champion and 1939 Wimbledon champion. In a powerful editorial in the USLTA's *American Lawn Tennis Magazine,* Marble exposed the racism that pervaded amateur tennis. It was all Gibson needed. Suddenly, invitations to outdoor tournaments started rolling in. In August 1950, she was invited to play in the most prestigious tournament in the country—the U.S. National Tennis Championship in Forest Hills, New York.

Despite her good showing at Forest Hills, Althea Gibson did not become a champion. Discouraged, she competed in fewer tournaments, and even considered leaving the sport when her ranking dropped to 70th. But in 1955 an invitation to join three other American women on a goodwill tennis tour of southeast Asia revived her enthusiasm. The following year, Gibson embarked on a string of international tournaments, winning a remarkable 16 out of 18. Her winning streak was capped by a victory at the French Championships in May 1956, when she not only became the first black to win a French national championship, but also the first black in the world to win a major singles title.

In 1957, she achieved another dream, winning both singles and doubles championships at Wimbledon and the U.S. Open at Forest Hills. She repeated the feat the following year. Then, at the top of her game, she stunned the tennis world by announcing her retirement. When Althea competed, tennis wins were awarded with trophies, not money, and it was time to go out and make a living.

Gibson tested the waters in other careers, including singing and acting. She also tried the entrepreneurial route by participating in a tour with the world-famous Harlem Globetrotters. She opened the basketball games with a round of exhibition tennis. When none of these ventures was successful, she set her sites on a new sport—ladies' golf. In 1964, Gibson once again broke the racial barrier by becoming the first black woman to earn a membership card in the Ladies Professional Golf Association. LPGA members who held players' cards were essentially protected from being barred from play at individual tournaments, and exempt from having to pay the $50-$100 tournament entrance fees.

Though Gibson enjoyed the sport, she never achieved the same success in golf as she had in tennis. Throughout the 1970s and 1980s, she served as a mentor and coach for young athletes. In 1975, she accepted a job from the East Orange, New Jersey, Department of Recreation, completing the circle that began in 1941 with her own Harlem play-street supervisor Buddy Walker. In her new job, Gibson could give something back to a community of kids in need of a role model. She found tremendous satisfaction in reaching out to help the kids of East Orange, teaching them how to build self-confidence by improving their athletic talents.

Althea Gibson retired in 1992, without having earned the huge sums of money most athletes enjoy today. However, her contribution to opening up opportunities in sports for blacks, women, and other minorities, is a true testament of her indomitable spirit, one whose value is priceless.

Patricia Keller McCormick

1930–
Diving

"You can't go out now after so many years of hard work without a fight."
—Pat McCormick vying for her fourth Olympic gold medal, 1956

Eighteen-year-old Patricia McCormick arrived at the 1948 Olympic trials with the hope of winning one of the three spots on the diving team that would represent the United States at the London Games. Unfortunately, she missed making the team by less than 1/100th of a point. When teammate Victoria

Draves won the 10-meter platform and 3-meter springboard events, bringing home two Olympic gold medals, a disappointed McCormick asked her how she had accomplished such an extraordinary showing. Draves told her it was the pride she felt in representing her country. Vicki's words were all the motivation McCormick needed. She became even more determined to be an Olympic champion.

Patricia Keller was born on May 12, 1930, in the quaint seaside town of Seal Beach in southern California. She fondly recalls spending time playing in the Pacific Ocean with her older brother. The two often hung out together at "Muscle Beach," a favorite spot for weight lifting and bodybuilding enthusiasts. Although her mother complained that she wished her daughter would be more ladylike, Pat's early athletic interests helped her build the strength and endurance she would later need for her diving career.

A gifted natural athlete, Pat began competing in swimming and diving competitions when she was just 11 years old, and at 16 she became the Long Beach, California, champion. In 1947, the teenager began formal training in diving after Aileen Allen, a coach at the Los Angeles Athletic Club, watched the youngster dive. Allen invited Pat to join the prestigious club, whose members included two-time Olympic diving champion Sammy Lee. Though Pat lacked previous training, her years of bodybuilding had provided her with exceptional physical strength.

The same year, Pat met a man named Glenn McCormick, a wrestler and gymnast at the University of Southern California. Although most people assume that diving is similar to other water sports, it actually originated from gymnastics. Diving requires more body movement and agility than swimming, water polo, or other aquatic sports. Glenn helped Pat train by teaching her gymnastic form and technique, and later that year, Pat became a runner-up in the U.S. National Platform Diving Championships.

In 1948, Pat and Glenn were married. Pat's happiness was somewhat dimmed when she did not make the U.S. Olympic team that year, but what most people might view as failure was a clear sign to Pat that she was capable of becoming an Olympic athlete. From that point on, she dedicated herself to becoming a world-class diver.

Pat's punishing training schedule included 80 to 100 platform dives a day, six days a week. She avoided the graceful, acrobatic dives that then characterized women's diving and practiced the more difficult and challenging dives common among male divers. A visit to the doctor revealed so many scars, welts, lacerations, and chipped teeth that her physician quipped that he had only seen such damage where a building had collapsed. As she trained for the 1952 Olympics, she also collected several diving awards, including U.S. national championships in springboard and platform, as well as a gold medal in platform and a silver medal in springboard at the 1951 Pan American Games.

All Pat's energies were invested in the 1952 Olympics, which were held in Helsinki, Finland. The pressure she had placed on herself was intensified by the unbroken winning streak of the U.S. women's diving team—it had not lost an Olympic gold medal since 1920. This time, Pat McCormick did not disappoint. She not only beat Madeleine Moreaux of France to win the gold medal in the 3-meter springboard event, but she also took home the gold in platform diving, beating her own teammates, Paula Jean Myers and Juno Irwin.

McCormick turned down numerous offers to turn professional, deciding instead to try to repeat her achievements in the 1956 Olympics in Melbourne, Australia. Only five months before the Olympic trials, Pat gave birth to her first child—she had continued to train and swim up to two days before her son was born. She ranked first in both springboard and platform trials.

In the springboard competition, Pat won easily against fellow U.S. athlete Jeanne Stunyo, with the greatest margin of difference ever between gold and silver medalists. Winning the platform event was not so easy. Going into the final round, McCormick was in second place behind teammate Juno Irwin. To win the gold, she needed to complete her remaining two dives flawlessly.

Her final dive, a difficult full twisting one-and-a-half, was nearly perfect. Pat McCormick had won her fourth Olympic gold medal, becoming the first diver in history, male or female, to complete what is called the "double-double"—a sweep of two golds in two consecutive Olympics.

When a triumphant Pat McCormick returned home, she was recognized for her Olympic achievements by the Associated Press, which named her Female Athlete of the Year. She also became the first and only female diver to receive the Sullivan Trophy, an award given annually to the finest amateur athlete in America.

After retiring from diving, Pat McCormick received additional honors. She was inducted into the International Swimming Hall of Fame in 1965, the International Women's Sports Hall of Fame in 1984, and the U.S. Olympic Hall of Fame in 1985—an accomplishment she shares with Olympic diver Micki King.

In 1984, 28 years after Pat completed her "double-double," she carried the American flag in the opening ceremonies of the Olympic Games in Los Angeles, California. That year, her daughter, Kelly, took the silver medal in springboard, missing out on the gold by only three points. In the 1988 Olympics in Seoul, South Korea, Kelly won the bronze medal in springboard. Pat and Kelly became the only mother-daughter medal winners in Olympic history.

Today, Pat McCormick is a successful businesswoman. As chairman of Pat McCormick Enterprises, she travels throughout the United States as a motivational speaker. She has also been an NBC commentator for three Olympics, as well as a spokesperson for Kodak and for *Sports Illustrated* magazine. She has been a member of the President's Council on Physical Fitness and Sport and an international representative for the U.S. State Department. As founder of the Pat McCormick Educational Foundation, she raises funds to help underprivileged junior high students complete their education.

Larissa Latynina

1934–

Gymnastics

"I am astounded that someone remembered me. In Russia, it is very rare that they remember the veterans, and I am so very happy and appreciative to be invited to Oklahoma for this."
—Larissa Latynina at her induction into the International Gymnastics Hall of Fame

Very few American athletes will forget the boycott of the 1980 Moscow Olympic Summer Games by the United States and several other countries. The Olympic Games were being

hosted for the first time by a country ruled by a Communist government—
the Soviet Union. In 1979, the Soviet Union had invaded the neighboring
country of Afghanistan, which they would occupy for the next 10 years. In
protest, United States President Jimmy Carter made it clear that if the Soviet
Union did not withdraw its troops from Afghanistan, the United States would
not send its athletes to compete at the Moscow-hosted Games.

The 1980 Games were not the first Olympics shrouded by political con-
troversy. In 1956, the second Olympic Games in which Russia participated,
several countries, for various reasons, refused to come to the host city of
Melbourne, Australia. Egypt, Iraq, and Lebanon boycotted to protest the
Israeli-led takeover of the Suez Canal; Holland and the People's Republic of
China kept their athletes home because of the continued recognition of
Taiwan's National Olympic Committee; Spain and Switzerland did not attend
to protest the Soviet Union's invasion of Hungary. Both the Soviet Union and
Hungary were there, and unfortunately their water polo teams were matched
in the semifinals. It got very ugly, with players from both countries exchang-
ing kicks and punches. Eventually the referee stopped the match and awarded
the win to Hungary, which was leading at the time.

Amid the controversy and tension of the Games, a 22-year-old Russian
gymnast was dazzling the crowd with her athletic skills and balletlike grace-
fulness. This was the first of three Olympic Games for Larissa Latynina. Today,
she is still the most decorated Olympic athlete in the Games' 100 + year history. What's even more remarkable about Larissa's athletic accomplishments
is that her 12-year career was interrupted twice while she gave birth to her
children.

Larissa was born on December 27, 1934, in Kherson, Ukraine, then a
republic of the Soviet Union, the second largest country in Europe. As a child,
Larissa studied ballet long before she ever entered a gym. Her early training in
dance would later distinguish her performances from those of her fellow gym-

nasts, setting new standards in the sport. At age 16 she was the national school's gymnastics champion. When she arrived at Melbourne, she was a poised, mature gymnast, though she would be considered old compared with today's competitors. In Larissa's strongest event, the floor exercise, her program was so well choreographed that she appeared to move effortlessly from one element to the next. For this beautiful presentation, Larissa was awarded her first individual-event gold medal. She went on to capture a gold medal in the vault, a silver medal in the uneven bars, and a bronze in the portable-apparatus team competition. Obviously the best female gymnast at the Games, Larissa easily won the gold medal for the all-around competition. Larissa also led the Soviet women's squad to the team title, and in the process was awarded her third gold medal of the Olympics. Overall, Larissa captured six medals in her Olympic debut, and was the most decorated athlete, male or female, at the 1956 Summer Games in Melbourne.

Larissa's Olympic performance was just the beginning of her reign as the world's best female gymnast. At the European championships in 1957, Larissa set a record by winning all five individual events—and five more gold medals. She repeated the feat a year later at the world championships. In 1960, Rome played host to the Summer Olympic Games. Larissa was still at the top of her skills, and again won six medals, capturing golds in the all-around individual competition and floor exercise, and helping the Soviet women's squad to defend its team title. Larissa also won two silver medals and a bronze, earning second place in total medals won, behind the Soviet men's gymnastics star Boris Schakhin, who won seven.

By 1962, Larissa was feeling the pressure of another, younger competitor from Czechoslovakia named Vera Caslavska. At the world championships, Larissa defended her all-around title, having beaten Caslavska only by a slim margin. At the 1964 Olympic Games in Tokyo, Caslavska beat Larissa in the all-around individual competition, winning the gold medal and earning her place as the world's best female gymnast. Though 30 years old, Larissa still maintained her dominance in the floor exercise, winning her third consecutive gold medal in that event. In all, Larissa won two gold, two silver, and two bronze medals.

Larissa's last competition was the 1966 world championships. She finished 11th in the standings, and retired shortly afterward. Her contribution to Soviet sports did not end there, however. In 1967, she accepted the post as the new women's gymnastics coach. Under her direction, the Soviet women's team recaptured their place at the top of gymnastics by winning the team gold in 1972 at the Munich Olympics. After being involved in gymnastics for most of her life, Larissa retired in 1991.

In 1985, the Women's Sports Foundation inducted Larissa Latynina into its Hall of Fame. And, in perhaps the greatest honor of her athletic career, Larissa Latynina was inducted into the International Gymnastics Hall of Fame on June 26, 1998, in Oklahoma, the home of America's most decorated gymnast—Shannon Miller. Larissa still lives just outside Moscow, keeping busy these days with her great-grandchildren. Still active in sports, the tennis court outside her home now replaces the mats and other gym apparatus that were so much a part of her life.

Tenley Albright

1935–
Figure Skating

"It's the excitement of trying something, and having some little tiny success, and sort of knowing that you can do something, I think, that spurs you on."

—Tenley Albright on being successful

When Tenley Albright stepped on the ice in Cortina, Italy, to compete in the 1956 Winter Olympic Games, she had a chance to make sports history. No American woman had ever won an Olympic gold medal in figure skating. Her performance was even more remarkable because an early childhood illness had almost ended her career before it began.

Tenley Emma Albright was born on July 18, 1935, in Newton Centre, a fashionable suburb of Boston, Massachusetts. The only daughter of Hollis Albright, a prominent surgeon, and his wife Elin, young Tenley lived a life of privilege and affluence. When Tenley was seven, her parents gave her a pair of white ice hockey skates for Christmas. The following year, Tenley convinced her obliging father to flood part of their backyard so that she would have her own private rink. Soon Tenley outgrew the skates and the homemade ice rink, so she donned a real pair of figure skates and began taking lessons at the renowned Skating Club of Boston. She could get there only once a month, however, because America was then at war and gasoline was rationed. Still, every time Tenley went ice skating, she wanted to do more of it.

Clearly, she was enjoying skating, but she wasn't really applying herself to learn its technical aspects. To her, the compulsory figures (skating in a series of tight loop formations), were monotonous and uninspiring. Her coach, Maribel Vinson Owen, finally sat Tenley down and explained that as boring as it was to practice figures, she had to learn them if she intended to compete on any level. Once Tenley began to see how much discipline and focus was required to master them, she actually became intrigued with the compulsory figures. A budding young skater was beginning to emerge.

Then, in the fall of 1946, 11-year-old Tenley contracted polio. Polio is an infectious viral disease characterized by a fever, stiff neck, nausea, muscle pain, and potential limb and respiratory paralysis. Though she was not completely paralyzed, Tenley spent three weeks in the hospital. No one was quite sure whether she would ever walk again, as the polio had severely impaired her leg, back, and neck muscles. In an interview, Tenley recalled how the doctors came to her room one Monday morning and told her they would be asking her to take three steps that coming Friday. All that week, Tenley concentrated on trying to achieve that one little milestone. When Friday came, Tenley took her first steps and began her road to recovery, to everyone's delight.

During her recuperation, Tenley was encouraged by her doctors to resume skating. They thought the exercise would help her strengthen the muscles that had been weakened by the virus, particularly those in her back. The doctors were right. Remarkably, four months after being released from the hospital, Tenley felt strong enough to skate competitively. At the tender age of 12, she entered and won the Eastern United States Junior Ladies Figure Skating competition, the first major event of her career. Tenley became the teenage skating star everybody was watching.

She won her first national novice title at age 13. In 1950 she skated off with the national junior title, and the following year and, at age 16, she finished first in the Women's Senior Eastern Championship. Having been so successful thus far, it was time for Tenley to test her skills on the international level, and she qualifed to represent America at the 1952 Winter Olympic Games, held in Oslo, Norway. No one expected Tenley to win a medal; after all, she hadn't won a U.S. National Championship yet. She took to the ice and skated brilliantly, surprising everyone by winning the silver medal behind Great Britain's Jeannette Altwegg.

A month later at the U.S. Nationals, Tenley won the first of her five consecutive titles. The following year at the World Figure Skating Championship held at Davos, Switzerland, Tenley Albright, still only 17, became the first American to win the women's singles title.

Wanting to follow in the footsteps of her father by becoming a surgeon, Tenley enrolled in premed classes at Radcliffe College in Massachusetts in the fall of 1953. Gritty and determined to juggle her career and the challenges of an academic education, Tenley rose before dawn to get to skating practice before heading off to a full day of classes. In addition to her studies, she managed to skate seven hours a day and even squeezed in ballet lessons to improve the artistic expression in her figure skating.

Tenley successfully defended her U.S Nationals title in 1954 and 1955, and she also won a second world championship in 1955. With the 1956 Winter Olympics at Cortina, Italy, fast approaching, Tenley decided to take a leave of absence from Radcliffe at the end of her sophomore year to train full-time for the upcoming games.

Two weeks before the competition, disaster struck. While practicing her routines, Tenley hit a rut in the ice and fell. The blade of her left skate slashed her right ankle to the bone, severing an artery. Her father flew to Cortina immediately to personally attend to his daughter's injury. Though stiff and in pain, Tenley finished first in the compulsory figures, but with only a slight lead over her teammate Carol Heiss. To win the gold medal, Tenley would have to perform an almost flawless free skate program on an injured leg. Could that leg withstand the impact of various spins and jumps in her routine?

Tenley greeted the crowd and began her free skate program. Hiding her pain, she skated elegantly, earning top marks from 10 of the 11 judges. By winning the Olympic gold medal, Tenley had accomplished what no other American woman had before. Although Carol Heiss won the world championships later that year, Tenley succeeded in winning the U.S. National title one more time. It was the final competition of her incredible career.

In 1957, Tenley Albright entered Harvard Medical School. When she graduated in 1961, she joined her father's surgical practice in Boston. In 1979, Tenley Albright became the first woman to serve on the United States Olympic Committee. A cancer researcher, Dr. Albright has been a member of the Board of Regents of the National Library of Medicine, the American College of Sports Medicine, the President's Council on Physical Fitness and Sport, and the American Cancer Society's board of directors. In 1988, she was inducted into U.S. Olympic Hall of Fame and the U.S. Figure Skating Association's Hall of Fame.

Kathy Whitworth

1939–
Golf

"Why not continue to do what you love to do, if you're successful at it and get some enjoyment out of it? Even if you're not as successful as some people think you should be, who cares?"
—Kathy Whitworth on her lifelong commitment to the game of golf

The top women's professional golfers of today owe a debt of gratitude to pioneers like Patty Berg, Louise Suggs, and Mildred "Babe" Didrikson. The success of the Ladies Professional Golf Association (LPGA) can be traced back to the tireless efforts and sacrifices of these women to establish a woman's tour. Today, the LPGA is one of the greatest success stories in women's sports. LPGA tournaments offer over $25 million in prize money to their members, spread over 38 tour events. The LPGA also enjoys media coverage, with 26 of their events carried on national television.

Among the first wave of women golfers to benefit from the continuing growth of the LPGA was Kathy Whitworth. In a career that began in the 1950s and continued into the 1990s, Kathy compiled the most wins (88) in the history of the sport—more than Sam Snead, more than Arnold Palmer, and more than Jack Nicklaus. Kathy was also the first woman on the tour to reach the $1-million mark in earnings, which is even more remarkable because she played most of her matches before the big purses were available.

Kathrynne Ann Whitworth was born on September 27, 1939, in the rural Texas town of Monahans. While she was still a young child, the Whitworth family moved to the sprawling ranching community of Jal, New Mexico. Kathy's father opened a hardware store that serviced the petroleum and gas industries in the neighboring areas around Jal. Aside from running the business, Kathy's father also involved himself in community affairs, serving as Jal's mayor for three terms. Kathy's mother was also active in civic functions, but her primary energies were devoted to raising Kathy and her two siblings.

During an outing at the local country club when Kathy was about 15 years old, she played her first game of golf. Though considered a natural athlete, she didn't have such a great game. The fact that she hadn't played well didn't deter Kathy in the least. In fact, she enjoyed playing so much that she couldn't wait until she could play again. Golf became Kathy's obsession, and she asked her parents to help pay for lessons. Kathy trained with a professional golf instructor at the Jal Country Club for a while, and then started working with Harvey Penick, whose former students included Betsy Rawls, Ben Crenshaw, and Tom

Kite. Penick lived in Austin, so Kathy and her mom drove down from Jal periodically for a series of lessons, staying three days at a time.

Within three years of learning the game, Kathy won the Women's Amateur Championship in her home state of New Mexico. She was awarded a golf scholarship to Odessa Junior College in Texas, but stayed only for a year. Kathy felt that she couldn't afford to remain an amateur very long. Turning pro, Kathy began traveling from city to city playing golf on as many courses as she could find. Her first tournament win came in 1962 when she won the Kelley Girl. For the next 17 seasons, Kathy would win at least one tournament a year.

In her second year on the tour, Kathy earned only about $5,000, but she was attracting attention for her intense drive to be the best woman golfer. Ever the consummate professional, she was soft-spoken and rarely displayed any negative emotion. As such, Kathy was well liked by the other women on the tour, and the press. Golf rival JoAnne "Big Mama" Carner said of her colleague: "Everyone likes her, because she always treated people with such respect and worked so hard to improve the LPGA."

Kathy's breakthrough year was 1965. She won the Titleholders, her first important major tournament win. She was also awarded the Vare Trophy for having the best scoring average that year, an honor she would win a remarkable seven times before her retirement. To cap off that magnificent season, Kathy was named Associated Press Athlete of the Year.

For the rest of the 1960s, Kathy was a dominant force in women's golf. In 1966, she won her second Titleholders tournament, and went on to win three more Vare Trophies. She was named LPGA Player of the Year four times (she would earn that honor an astonishing seven times overall), and in 1967 was again named Associated Press Athlete of the Year. Her incredible run in the 1960s brought Kathy a hefty sum in prize money, and she was the LPGA's leading money winner eight times in her career.

Kathy also served as the president of the LPGA four times. She was good for the game and the women's tour. In 1975, while she was still an active player, Kathy was inducted into the LPGA Hall of Fame. To enter the Hall of Fame, a golfer must meet certain criteria. She must be a member of the LPGA for at least 10 straight years, and the winner of 30 events, including two majors—the U.S. Women's Open, the LPGA Championship, the Dinah Shore, or the du Maurier Canadian Classic.

Toward the end of the 1970s, Kathy's game tailed off and she considered leaving the tour. However, she struggled through her slump and won the Coca-Cola Classic in 1981. In the 1970s, Kathy was again at the top of her game, and the 1980s would be a decade of history-making achievement and recognition.

In 1982, at the Brookfield West Country Club in Atlanta, Georgia, Kathy won the Lady Michelob Classic, her 83rd career victory. That tournament win was significant for Kathy—she surpassed Mickey Wright's 82 career-victory total, to become the winningest woman golfer. In 1983, at the Women's Kemper Open, Kathy sank a 40-foot (12-m) putt on the 18th green to tie PGA great Sam Snead with 84 career victories. Finally, amid the increasing hype and pressure, Kathy rewrote the record books. On July 22, 1984, at the Rochester International, Kathy got her 85th win, passing Snead's record. That accomplishment made Kathy the winningest golfer—male or female—in history.

Honors continued to be showered Kathy's way. In 1986, the Golf Writer's Association presented the William Richardson Award to Kathy for her immeasurable contributions to the game of golf. Only two other female golfers—Patty Berg and Babe Didrikson—have won that award. Kathy continued to play tournament golf well into her 50s. In a display of the utmost respect and deference to one of their own, the LPGA dedicated its 1993 tournament to Kathy Whitworth. She finally retired from the tour in favor of participating in senior tournaments. She joined her generation of colleagues, becoming a teacher of the sport, in the hopes of helping the younger players of today continue to play golf in the tradition of the pioneers.

Wilma Rudolph

1940–1994
Track and Field

"I would be very sad if I was only remembered as Wilma Rudolph, the great sprinter. To me, my legacy is to the youth of America to let them know they can be anything they want to be."
—Wilma Rudolph

It would be difficult to name another champion athlete who has had to overcome as many challenges as Wilma Rudolph. At her best, no one could outrun the "Black Gazelle," the media's nickname for Wilma. But her story is not only about sprint records and Olympic medals. Before Wilma could run, she had to learn to walk—and that did not come easily.

Wilma Rudolph was born prematurely to Blanche and Ed Rudolph on June 23, 1940, in St. Bethlehem, Tennessee. She was the 20th of 22 children (including Ed's 11 children by a previous marriage). By the time she was three years old, the frail child who had weighed less than 5 pounds (2.2 kg) at birth had already battled mumps, measles, and chicken pox. When she was 4 she contracted polio, double pneumonia, and scarlet fever, any of which could have been life threatening. Wilma survived, but her bout with polio left her with limited mobility in her left leg, and her doctors doubted that she would ever walk again. Blanche Rudolph thought otherwise, and told her daughter so. Wilma decided to believe her mother.

Though the nearest therapy facility was 45 miles (72 km) away in Nashville, Blanche and Wilma rode the bus there every Saturday for Wilma's whirlpool and massage treatments. Blanche and her other children also took turns massaging Wilma's leg every day. At eight years old, Wilma was fitted with a metal brace attached to a special shoe that enabled her to take her first steps. Before long, she was able to attend school. Seeing her classmates run and play made her even more determined to exercise her leg so that she could join them. By the time Wilma was 11, she no longer needed the brace. One Sunday morning, she waited outside her church until everyone else had gone in, then took the brace off, left it on the steps, and slowly walked down the aisle to join her family. For the first time in her young life, she felt healthy.

Wilma's entry into competitive sports started at Burt High School when she made the girls' basketball team—but only because Coach Clinton Gray wanted Wilma's older sister Yvonne on the team. Ed Rudolph had insisted that both his daughters would play or neither would be allowed. Wilma was already accustomed to hours of painful exercises, and she handled the long practice sessions without fatigue. She became an all-state player by the time she was 15.

Her speed and ability to "buzz" around the court earned her the nickname "Skeeter" (short for mosquito).

Wilma was even better in track events. Her legs, once thin and frail, were now long, muscular, and strong. During basketball off-seasons, she won most of the informal track meets she competed in. The girl who couldn't even walk six years earlier was now winning sprint events.

During conference championship semifinals in Wilma's sophomore year, she met Ed Temple, the track coach at Tennessee State University (TSU) who was refereeing the playoffs. Temple had transformed TSU's women's track team, the Tigerbelles, into one of the top teams in the United States. Although Burt High lost that playoff game, Temple later invited Wilma to participate in a summer athletic camp at Tennessee State.

Temple believed in teaching mental toughness as well as running, breathing, and endurance techniques. He helped Wilma feel less intimidated by other track stars and concentrate on perfecting her own skills. The following year, she won the 75- and 100-yard dashes at the August AAU meets. She also anchored the winning relay team. But the most memorable moment of the meet for Wilma was being introduced to baseball great Jackie Robinson. The shy 16-year-old would always remember the advice he gave her that day: "You are a fascinating runner," he said. "Don't let anything or anybody keep you from running."

In 1956, Wilma traveled to Seattle, Washington, for the Olympic trials. Fellow Tigerbelle Mae Faggs, an American record-holder and two-time Olympian, provided invaluable guidance to her young teammate. At the qualifying heat of the 200-meter dash, Faggs and Wilma crossed the tape simultaneously, both earning spots on the U.S. Olympic team that would compete in Melbourne, Australia. Once in Melbourne, Wilma discovered that most of the athletes were friendly, curious, and eager to exchange souvenirs with athletes from other countries. She was gratified to learn that for the first time she was being judged not by the color of her skin but by how fast she could run.

Wilma Rudolph pushes toward her 100-meter gold-medal victory at the Rome Olympics, 1960.

Wilma made the semifinals of the 200-meter dash, but she finished third and did not advance to the finals. A few days later, as part of the U.S. women's 400-meter relay team, Wilma won a bronze medal when the team finished third behind the Australian and British teams. Inspired by the gold medal performances of track star Betty Cuthbert, she vowed to compete and win in the next Olympic Games.

In 1958, shortly after she graduated from high school, Wilma gave birth to a baby girl, Yolanda. Juggling the roles of single parent and athlete (she had earned a full athletic scholarship to TSU) was very difficult. The Rudolph family once again provided the support she needed by caring for Yolanda while Wilma attended classes and trained.

Wilma qualified for the U.S. women's track team by winning both the 100- and 200-meter dashes. Three of her college teammates also made the team, and Ed Temple was named the U.S. Olympic track team coach. Wilma was running well enough to have a chance at three Olympic gold medals. But then, just days before the Games began, she twisted her ankle.

Doctors were not sure she would be able to compete, but Wilma won the 100-meter dash easily, earning her first gold medal with a finishing time of 11.0 seconds. She also outran her competition in the 200-meter dash to win her second gold medal. In the 4 x 400-meter relay, Wilma ran the anchor leg, and although she bobbled the baton handoff, she recovered in time to reach the finish line three-tenths ahead of her competitors. The U.S. women's track team had set a new relay record. Wilma later reflected on her triple victory: "Three Olympic gold medals! I knew that was something nobody could ever take away from me, ever." She added that her favorite race was the relay, because she was joined on the medalists' platform by her Tigerbelle teammates. Later in the day, Wilma spoke to the press. In her comments she pledged to use her physical talents to "the glory of God, the best interests of my nation, and the honor of womanhood."

Though the Ku Klux Klan was still terrorizing blacks in the South, and attempting to sabotage the civil rights movement at every turn, Wilma received a hero's welcome when she returned to the United States. She was a hero—not a black hero, or a female hero, but a real American hero. President John Kennedy invited Wilma to the White House. The Associated Press (AP) named her Female Athlete of the Year.

Wilma went back to school to finish work on her degree and she continued to compete through 1962. She was named the recipient of the Sullivan Award in 1961, and earned her second AP Athlete of the Year honor. She married Robert Eldridge in 1963. They had four children, but the marriage ended in 1976. Large endorsement contracts were rarely offered to athletes at that time, so Wilma chose a different route. She became a schoolteacher and coach in Tennessee and in 1977 wrote her autobiography, *Wilma,* which was later made into a television movie.

Perhaps Wilma's greatest contribution, a lasting legacy of her desire to help others, was in establishing the Wilma Rudolph Foundation. Headquartered in Indianapolis, Indiana, the organization carries Wilma's extraordinary vision of hope for the future of America's children. The goal of the foundation is to motivate children from all walks of life through athletic participation.

In the summer of 1994, Wilma was diagnosed with brain cancer. That fall, the U.S. athletic community, and the world, lost one of the greatest athletes and humanitarian ambassadors to grace the twentieth century. On November 12, at the age of 54, Wilma Rudolph passed away, but the foundation that bears her name continues to carry on the work that she began.

Jody Conradt

1941–

Basketball coach

"We proved to a skeptical audience that women's basketball was appealing. That's a part of history no one [else] will attain because it was a first. And you can only have one first."
—Jody Conradt on her effect on women's college basketball

The Women's Sports Foundation has its own International Hall of Fame. Since its inception in 1980, the Hall of Fame members have honored 86 athletes and 12 coaches. The three categories given this well-deserved recognition are: Pioneer—those whose athletic achievements were recognized prior to 1960; Contemporary—players whose athletic achievements came after 1960; and Coaches—active and retired, a category that was added in 1990.

The Hall of Fame members, "the trailblazers who have paved the way for the [women] athletes of today and tomorrow" include tennis legends Althea Gibson and Billy Jean King, track and field stars Babe Didrikson and Wilma Rudolph, and golf greats Patty Berg, Mickey Wright, and Kathy Whitworth. Among the coaches are Tuskegee track and field Olympian Nell Jackson, Tennessee Lady Volunteers' head coach Pat Head Summitt, and 1995 inductee Jody Conradt, one of the winningest women's college basketball coaches in the game.

Jody Conradt's story begins in the small town of Goldthwaite, Texas—population 1,700. A diehard Texan, Jody was born to Charles and Ann Conradt on May 13, 1941, and has always lived and worked in Texas. As a youngster, Jody was already displaying the well-disciplined temperament that she would carry into adulthood. Excessively neat, Jody would line up her stuffed animals exactly the same way every day, and the clothes in her dresser drawers were always perfectly arranged.

Considered a "tomboy" in the neighborhood, Jody got her love of sports from her father, who had played semipro baseball at one time. Another sport—basketball—was very popular in Goldthwaite. Jody recalls how she couldn't wait to get into high school so she could try out for the girls' team. Basketball became her passion, and she decided that she wanted to be a famous basketball star when she grew up. She realized her dream of playing on the girls' team when she reached Goldthwaite High School. There, she became a key player averaging 40 points a game. The girls' basketball squad was so good that they often drew larger crowds than the boys' team.

After high school, Jody headed off to Baylor University in Waco, Texas. She played collegiate basketball while studying for her degree in physical education. When she graduated in 1963, Jody immediately accepted a job as basketball coach at Midway High School in Waco. There she taught the traditional form of basketball she had learned as an athlete—the six-player, slow-paced style. Jody coached at Midway for six years before moving up to coach college basketball at Sam Houston State in Huntsville, Texas. Though it was not a large college, it gave Jody the opportunity to work with higher-level, more accomplished players. The game was faster now too, with women playing the same five-player style as men.

In 1973, Jody was offered the position of women's athletic coordinator at the University of Texas at Arlington. Arlington had no women's basketball program, so this position was Jody's greatest challenge to date. On a shoestring $1,200 budget, Jody had to teach every women's sport. Amazingly, under her coaching, the basketball, volleyball, and softball teams all won state championships.

Jody's extraordinary success at Arlington attracted the attention of the university's athletic director at Austin, Donna Lopiano. A professional sports wannabe herself, Lopiano dreamed of pitching for the New York Yankees. As a young child, she had a complete arsenal of pitches and made her neighborhood Little League team, but she was turned away the first day of practice because she was in violation of the rules—"girls are not allowed in Little League." Lopiano went on to become one of the greatest fast-pitch softball players of all time. After assuming the coaching helm at Austin, Lopiano turned the Lady Longhorns athletic program into one of the best collegiate programs, male or female, in the United States.

Lopiano wanted Jody to come to Austin and head up the women's basketball program. It was the opportunity of a lifetime for Jody, but there were many hurdles to overcome. At first, Jody didn't even have a team—just one player. The other players had all quit in protest over their former coach being fired and Jody being hired. There was also flak about Jody's salary, $19,000 a year, which many people felt was a ridiculous amount to pay someone to coach girls' athletics.

In spite of all the controversy, Jody proceeded to build one of the most successful women's athletic programs in the United States. Her Lady Longhorn teams dominated the Southwest Conference for 13 years, including a stretch of 183 consecutive wins. When the National Collegiate Athletic Association (NCAA) inaugurated its first women's basketball tournament in 1983, Jody's Lady Longhorns were there. In fact, Jody's teams have participated in 12 NCAA tournaments, twice making it to the Final Four. During Jody's 20+ year tenure at Austin, her teams finished in the top 20 sixteen years in a row, and were first in 1984, 1985, 1986, and 1987.

The skeptics who thought women's collegiate sports programs at Austin were "silly" have been silenced by some mighty impressive statistics. From 1986 to 1991 Lady Longhorn game attendance was the nation's highest. On average in the 1988-1989 season alone, more than 8,000 spectators came to the women's games.

Perhaps one of Jody's greatest coaching achievements came in the 1985-1986 season when her Lady Longhorns went 34-0, the first women's team in history to go undefeated. They capped their incredible season by winning the national championship, defeating the University of Southern California 97-81. Jody won the National Coach of the Year honor in 1980, 1984, and 1986. There is no greater honor in women's coaching.

As U.S. National Team coach in 1987, Jody led the women's squad to a gold medal at the Pan American Games. And at the University of Texas at Austin, she has had three players on U.S. Olympic teams, and coached Kamie Ethridge whose numerous honors include the Broderick Award, the Wade Trophy, and the Frances Pomeroy Naismith Award. Jody's leadership does not end with basketball drills; more than 90 percent of her players have graduated, and she has also coached 19 all-Americans.

In 1997, Jody reached a milestone that no other women's basketball coach has achieved—she won her 700th game in front of a hometown crowd on December 18, when her Lady Longhorns defeated Northwestern. With a record of 709-210 (as of the 1998-1999 season), Jody's winning percentage of .771 makes her one of the winningest women's basketball coaches in NCAA history. Perhaps her greatest honor to date came in 1998 when she was named to the Naismith Basketball Hall of Fame. Only one other basketball coach, Margaret Wade, has ever been awarded that honor.

Despite her enormous success, Jody remains humble, often saying that records are not important to her. In an interview she said, "I always keep in mind that the game must be played by the players, not the coach." When Donna Lopiano stepped down as athletic director at Austin in 1992 to become executive director of the Women's Sports Foundation, Jody took over as Austin's athletic director. Though she faces even greater demands now, she still spends time working with charitable organizations, including the Neighborhood Longhorn program she helped establish. The goal of the program is to encourage students in the Austin area to strive to be the best they can in both academics and athletics. Jody's other passion is running a basketball camp she created for women of all ages. She has made an indelible mark in women's sports and made believers of those who didn't think women's collegiate sports were important.

Margaret Smith Court

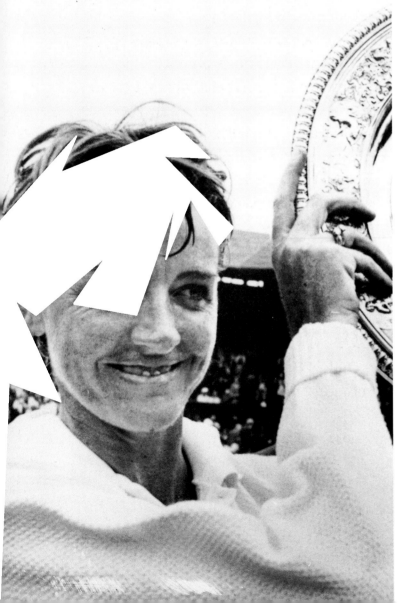

1942–
Tennis

"It was my job to stand at the net and volley back every ball. Whenever anybody tells me I can volley well, I recall those moments I had to volley or get caught."
—Margaret Smith Court on having to sneak into a tennis club to play as a child

Easily one of the most dominant tennis players in the 1960s through the mid-1970s, Margaret Smith Court won more major championships in her 18-year career than anyone else on the tennis circuit—male or female. She is also one of an elite group of five—Don Budge 1938, Maureen Connolly 1953, Rod Laver 1962, and 1969, and Steffi Graf 1988—who have completed the Grand Slam of tennis—singles wins at the Australian Open, the French Open, Wimbledon, and the U.S. Open, all in the same year. With 62 major title wins, including 24 Grand Slam singles titles, Margaret has 8 more than her nearest rival—Martina Navratilova, who won 54 major titles in her 20+ year career before she retired in 1994.

Clearly, Margaret Smith Court is one of the finest athletes the game of tennis has ever seen. She was born on July 16, 1942, in the small country town of Albury, Australia. Her father worked in a dairy-processing plant, while her mother stayed home to raise Margaret and her three siblings. Neither parent nor the other children were much interested in sports, but Margaret developed a passion for tennis at a very young age. The story goes that Margaret, along with some of the neighborhood boys, used to sneak through a hole in the fence of the local tennis club and play when a court was open. The only catch was that they had to keep the ball in the front half of the court to remain hidden from view. It was Margaret's job to stand at the net and volley every ball back. Eventually she would get caught and be thrown out of the club. This happened so many times, that the owner, Wally Rutter, finally invited Margaret to join the club and take lessons. Since she couldn't pay for the court time or the instructions, Margaret took on odd jobs such as sweeping the courts and chalking the lines.

As a teenager, Margaret's natural athletic skills began to take form. She had competed in track and field, running in the 400- and 800-meter sprints. Margaret even considered trying out for a spot on the Australian track team and competing in the Olympics. However, the more she ran, the more she lost the quickness and agility that was a critical part of her tennis game. Margaret had to choose between the two sports if she wanted to be a serious competitor in either one. So she hung up her cleats, ending her track career in favor of tennis.

To continue her training, Margaret moved to Melbourne to take lessons at a club owned by Frank Sedgman, a former number one-ranked men's world champion. She worked in Sedgman's office as a receptionist to help cover her expenses. The countless hours of practice and the sacrifices made to train in Melbourne paid off when Margaret won her first Grand Slam title—the Australian Open, in 1960. It was the first of seven consecutive championships she would win in her home country. And, before her career was over, Margaret would win an unprecedented 11 Australian Open singles titles.

After defending her Australian Open title in 1961, the 18-year-old joined the international tour. Despite her athletic accomplishments, Margaret was still a young, shy teenager, often having to fight off bouts of nervousness before her matches. Once her anxiety was under control, however, Margaret was a formidable opponent. She won the Kent All-Comers Championship, and reached the semifinals at the Italian Open and the quarterfinals of the French Open and Wimbledon.

By 1962, Margaret decided it was time for her to travel independently of her country's national team. This proved to be a good decision for her as she matured, gaining confidence and poise with every match she played. She won her third straight Australian Open, as well as the French and U.S. Opens. Ranked number one, Margaret entered as the top seed at Wimbledon. Only Billy Jean King, another tennis player on the rise, thwarted Margaret's shot at her first Grand Slam. The two met in the first round where King stunned Margaret by winning the match. It was the first time in the history of Wimbledon that a number one seed lost in the first round of competition. This encounter between the two was just the first of many in their great rivalry at the top of women's tennis.

The following year it was Margaret who beat King at Wimbledon. Unlike their 1962 match, the two women met in the final. Margaret won the match, earning the first of her three Wimbledon singles titles, and remained at number one. Over the next few years, Margaret's play was not as spectacular as it had been earlier in her career but she did win the U.S. Open in 1965, and reached the final round at Wimbledon the following year. However, Margaret had become exhausted from all the travel and the extensive practice necessary to stay on top of her game. She announced her retirement to the press at the end of the 1966 season, explaining that she now wanted time to do some other things with her life.

Back home in Australia, Margaret opened a boutique in Perth. In 1967 she married Barry Court, a successful wool broker, and the two settled into a quiet life together. However, it wasn't long before Margaret began missing competitive tennis. With Barry's encouragement, Margaret came out of retirement in 1968. This time, Margaret would not be touring alone. Barry was happy to accompany his wife on the tennis circuit.

Margaret worked hard, putting in long, grueling hours of practice to get back on top of her game. In 1969, she won all the Grand Slam tournaments except one—Wimbledon. Twice in her career, Margaret had come within one tournament of becoming only the second woman in tennis history to complete the Grand Slam. In 1970, the greatest of her career, Margaret won it all. The most memorable of those matches was Wimbledon, where she met her old nemesis Billie Jean King in the final. Playing on a sprained ankle, Margaret met King volley for volley, in a record-setting 46-game battle. In the end, Margaret prevailed 14-12, 11-9. What a comeback Margaret had accomplished!

In 1971, Margaret took time off to have a child. Back on the tour in 1973, she came within one win of completing her second Grand Slam. Her efforts were thwarted by Chris Evert, who defeated Margaret in the semifinals of the U.S. Open. This was also the year that Margaret unwisely accepted the challenge of a one-on-one match with the self-professed male chauvinist tennis star Bobby Riggs. Exploiting Margaret's well-known pre-match nervousness, Riggs beat her in straight sets. It was the only negative moment in an otherwise brilliant season.

Over her career, Margaret Smith Court achieved the number one ranking seven times. She won her first major tournament in 1960, and fifteen years later in doubles competition at the U.S. Open, she won her last. Her 24 Grand Slam tournament wins included 11 Australian Opens, 5 U.S. Opens, 5 French Opens, and 3 Wimbledon championships. She was a pioneer in the women's movement, too, having interrupted her career twice to have children, each time resuming her career. She played competitively until her retirement in 1977, and was honored for her achievements with her induction into the Tennis Hall of Fame in 1979. Seven years later, Margaret Smith Court joined many other successful women athletes with her induction into the International Women's Sports Hall of Fame.

The Girls of Summer

*"One thing about our league: it gave a lot of us
the courage to go on to professional careers at
a time when women didn't do things like that."*
— Dorothy Kamenshek, Rockford Peaches, AAGBL

Whan Japanese fighter planes bombed the United States Naval Base at Pearl Harbor, Hawaii, on the morning of December 7, 1941, the attack catapulted America into World War II. Over the next several days, military recruiting offices all over the country were flooded with men wanting to enlist in the army, navy, air force, and marines. The time had come for America to help its allies defeat those who were threatening democracy around the world.

With so many men heading off to war, many jobs needed to be filled to keep the country going. As a result, women began to appear in jobs traditionally held by men. Many women went to work in converted factories, assisting in the assembly of military equipment, such as guns, ammunition, aircraft, and ships. The war effort also affected America's leisure activities and entertainment industry. Many performers donated their time and talents, selling war bonds, creating training films, and traveling around the globe to entertain U.S. troops. America's favorite pastime—baseball—lost many of its top players as they were pressed into service to fight the war.

In an effort to keep America interested in baseball until the war was over and ballplayers could resume their careers, an enterprising businessman came

The manager of the Rockford Peaches gives players a pep talk.

up with an idea—a temporary all-women's baseball league. The All-American Girls Baseball League was the brainchild of Philip K. Wrigley, the chewing-gum magnate who owned the Chicago Cubs baseball team. Wrigley had good reason to believe a woman's league might be successful. At the time, more than 40,000 women were already playing softball in amateur and semipro leagues around the United States.

Actually, women began playing baseball in 1866 when students at Vassar, a noted all-women's college, formed two baseball teams. At first, their "uniforms" were cumbersome and restrictive—long-sleeved blouses with high necklines, ankle-length skirts, and high button shoes. Then Amelia Bloomer, a pioneer in the women's movement, designed a pair of baggy trousers that came to be known as "bloomers."

Baseball's popularity continued to grow and, by the 1890s, women were playing a more professional style of game. The teams were called Bloomer Girls, after the trousers they wore. Many teams came and went over the next 50 years, but overall there was enough excitement in the women's games to keep the fans coming. Many women of that era who excelled in the game are remembered for their pioneering efforts to promote baseball—including the versatile Maud Nelson. She gave 40 years of her life to the game—pitching, playing third base, and owning and managing "bloomer clubs." In the early 1930s, Virne "Jackie" Mitchell pitched in an exhibition game against the Yankees and struck out Babe Ruth and Lou Gehrig! Women were knocking at the door, and a professional, organized, and well-funded women's league was about to be born.

From its creation in 1943 until it folded in 1954, the All-American Girls Baseball League underwent many changes—in its name, in the way the game was played, and in who played. Initially, the women played with a 12-inch (30-cm) softball. The distance to the pitcher's mound and between the basepads was slightly longer than standard softball-field measurements. Though runners were allowed to steal bases, which is not normally allowed in softball, the fans wanted to see the game played with the livelier, smaller hardball, which traveled farther and faster off the bat. Soon the ballfield configuration matched that of a baseball diamond, and the softball was replaced by the smaller 9 1/4 inch (23.4-cm) hardball.

The league played only in the Midwest, but hundreds of women traveled to Chicago from all parts of the country in May 1943 to participate in the first tryouts. They came from all walks of life—teachers, secretaries, clerks, and housewives. Initially, four teams were organized—the Rockford (IL) Peaches, the Racine (WI) Belles, the Kenosha (WI) Comets, and the South Bend (IN)

Blue Sox. Eventually, the AAGBL expanded to 10 teams, with several hundred women playing in the league over the course of its 11-year existence.

Though the women who played in the league were all great athletes, Wrigley felt that beauty and charm weighed as heavily as athletic ability. He sent all the players to "charm school" to learn how to walk, stand, and sit correctly. Off the field and on, the women were required to wear skirts and make-up, and have long hair. Any violation of the dress code resulted in a fine. Imagine trying to slide into base in a skirt! Many of the players wound up with nasty, painful abrasions and bruises on their legs. But the women figured the discomfort was worth it because it gave them the chance to play professional baseball.

In the first few years of the AAGBL, huge crowds turned out to see the games. At its peak in popularity in 1948, the AAGBL attracted over a million fans to its games. In the bleachers, spectators cheered the efforts of such extraordinary players as Dottie Kamenshek, Connie Wisniewski, Sophie Kurys, and Rose Gacioch. The league even had its own All-Star Game and its equivalent of the NBL World Series—the Shaughnessy Series. Though the Rockford Peaches dominated the league with four pennants (three in a row from 1948-1950), five other teams also won the crown before the league folded in 1954.

Many explanations have been offered to explain the demise of the AAGBL. Some suggest that the rise in TV coverage of major sports reduced interest in smaller professional and semiprofessional sporting events. Others blame mismanagement of the league in later years when the franchise owners cut back funds on spring training, promotion, and publicity. For the women who played in the first and only women's professional baseball league, however, the experience made their lives richer and more complete. Many went on to become doctors, lawyers, and other professionals. Before the league, many women felt those opportunities were beyond their reach.

Some of the AAGBL women left lasting legacies to the game of baseball. Minneapolis Millerette Annabelle Lee taught her nephew how to pitch. Bill

Madonna at bat (left), with Tom Hanks and Geena Davis cheering from the dugout in the 1992 film, A League of Their Own

"Spaceman" Lee became a pitcher and was a member of the NBL Montreal Expos and Boston Red Sox teams in the 1970s and 1980s. And outfielder Helen Callaghan's son Kelly Canaele wrote the novel *A League of Their Own.* The book inspired actress and director Penny Marshall to turn it into a successful Hollywood film, ensuring that the league and its players would not be forgotten. In 1988, Bill Lee accompanied his aunt Annabelle to the Baseball Hall of Fame in Cooperstown, New York, to see a new exhibit established in recognition of the All-American Girls Baseball League.

Billie Jean King

1943–
Tennis

"I knew at 12 years old that I wanted to change things. The first day I had a free group lesson I knew I wanted to play, and it was about a year after that, sitting at the Los Angeles Tennis Club, looking at a really blue sky, that I knew I'd like to change my sport, make it more hospitable. It was very stodgy and elitist and went against everything I believed in.
—Billie Jean King

In 1990, *Life* magazine published their picks of the "100 Most Important Americans of the 20th Century." None of the 18 U.S. presidents who served in this century made the list, but four athletes did. Three of them were male—Babe Ruth, Jackie Robinson, and Muhammad Ali. The lone female athlete—chosen because of her tireless efforts to advance the women's sports movement in America—was Billie Jean King. Though most people might think of her as one of tennis's all-time great players, Billie Jean was, and is, so much more than that.

Born Billie Jean Moffitt on November 22, 1943, in Long Beach, California, she showed her love of sports at an early age. She often hit baseballs with her father Bill and her brother Randy, who went on to pitch in the major leagues for the San Francisco Giants. When she was 10 years old, Billie Jean won a softball championship. She also liked to rough it up playing football with the neighborhood kids, but her mother Betty began encouraging her daughter to participate in sports that were less physical and less prone to injuries.

When she was 12, Billie Jean signed up for free tennis lessons being offered by Clyde Walker, the recreation coach at the local municipal courts. Years later, in her autobiography, *Billie Jean,* she described her introduction to tennis: "That first day I really fell in love with tennis. . . . I stayed out there a couple of hours and was completely enthralled." When she got home, Billie Jean excitedly told Betty that she wanted to play the game forever, and had set a goal for herself: to rank number one in the world.

As Billie Jean continued to learn the game, she realized that tennis was traditionally a sport of the elite. She wanted to make the sport accessible to everyone interested in playing the game, not just those who could afford expensive country-club membership fees. As she grew older, she became a stronger and more vocal advocate on issues related to equality for women sports professionals.

Billie Jean really wasn't your typical tennis player anyway. Short and somewhat stout, she was not the typical, long-legged, and graceful player. She also suffered from allergies and asthma, and often had difficulty breathing after she'd been running around on the court for a while, so her play appeared to be labored. Her vision was so bad that she had to wear thick prescription glasses in order to see anything, including a fast-approaching tennis ball. She didn't even dress "right" for the sport. On one occasion, Billie Jean was plucked out of a team photo because she was wearing shorts and a T-shirt instead of a tennis dress. But despite her nonconformity, there was no denying that Billie Jean could play tennis.

Billie Jean breezed through her teen years, winning most of her matches on the junior tennis circuit. As a high school senior, Billie Jean was ranked number four among all women players in the United States. At just 17, Billie Jean entered her first Wimbledon tournament. She lost in her first round singles match, but when she paired with Karen Hantze in the doubles competition the unseeded duo shocked everybody by beating Margaret Smith Court and Jan Lehane in the finals to win the coveted All-England Lawn Tennis Championship trophy.

In 1961, college athletic scholarships were not yet available for women, so Billie Jean had to pay her own way through Los Angeles State College. Tennis did not pay much back then as it does today, so Billie had to get a job to make ends meet. Though she only played tennis part-time, in the spring and summer, Billie Jean continued to compete at Wimbledon and in grass-court matches in the United States.

In 1964, after much encouragement from Larry King, a college student she'd been dating for two years, Billie Jean traveled to Australia to train with tennis great Mervyn Rose. By the time she returned, her game had risen to a new level. By 1965 she was playing so well that she reached the semifinals at Wimbledon and the finals of the U.S. National Championships. When the season concluded, Billie Jean and Larry married. Since professional (paying) tennis didn't exist for women in the 1960s, the Kings had to manage on Billie Jean's tennis instructor's salary—$32 a week.

Billie Jean finally realized her dream of being number one in 1966. After beating her old nemesis, Margaret Smith Court, in the semifinal match at Wimbledon, Billie Jean defeated three-time Wimbledon champ Maria Bueno of Brazil in the final. It was the first of six singles titles she would win in her career. Her prize? A £50 gift voucher for tennis attire and half a dozen Mars candy bars her fellow players left in her room as a congratulatory gift.

When prize money was finally introduced in the era of Open tournaments, Billie Jean was outraged to discover the huge difference between men's and women's checks. While the men were awarded $3,500 for first place at the Italian Open, for example, their female counterparts received only $600. Billie Jean became openly vocal about the situation, and challenged the unfairness of the organizers and promoters. When her outspokenness failed to bring about any changes, Billie Jean acted on her protests. In 1970, she organized a women's pro tour, convincing cigarette manufacturer Virginia Slims to sponsor the first event. Eight other women joined Billie Jean on the tour, including Americans Rosie Casals, Peaches Bartkowitz, Julie Heldman, Kristy Pigeon, Nancy Richie, and Val Zeigenfuss. They were joined by two Australian players, Judy Dalton and Kerry Melville. All nine women were threatened with suspension by the United States Lawn Tennis Association (USLTA). By 1971, the Virginia Slims Tour was running almost 30 tournaments a year, with total prize money of at least $10,000 guaranteed for each event.

Throughout this upheaval, Billie Jean was playing great tennis. In the first 3 1/2 months of the Slims tour, she won 8 tournaments and earned $37,000 in prize money. She also beat Rosie Casals at the U.S. Open to win her second Open title. That fall, Billie Jean won 11 more Slims tournaments and became the first woman athlete to earn $100,000 in one year.

In 1972, after a slow start, Billie Jean won her first French Open, her fourth Wimbledon singles title, and her third U.S. Open championship. For her tremendous season as a player and her tireless efforts in promoting women's tennis, *Sports Illustrated* magazine broke tradition by naming Billie Jean the first woman Sportsperson of the Year.

Not everyone was happy about the women's successes. Many male tennis players felt that the women's game was inferior and that they shouldn't be earning equal prize money. One of the most out-

Billie Jean King brings women's equal pay issues to the table at Wimbledon, 1975.

spoken opponents was 55-year-old Bobby Riggs. In his career, he had won Wimbledon and the U.S. National Championship. Flamboyant, egotistical, and a great self-promoter, Bobby tried to get Billie Jean to agree to a one-on-one match. By beating her, Bobby aimed to put to rest any more "nonsense" about women's tennis being on a par with men's tennis. At first Billie Jean turned him down, but after Bobby soundly defeated Margaret Smith Court, Billie Jean felt she had no choice but to play him.

The "Battle of the Sexes" match was played in the Houston Astrodome before a crowd of more than 30,000, with another 50 million viewers tuning in to the ABC live telecast. At stake was more than a tennis match—Billie Jean felt that the credibility of women's tennis rested squarely on her shoulders. Though she later recalled feeling an overwhelming sense of responsibility, she didn't show it in her play during the match. People today still talk about that historic event, in which Billie Jean beat Bobby Riggs in straight sets 6-4, 6-3,

6-3. For Billie Jean, her victory proved that women had earned respect for their own athletic abilities.

The "battle" sparked a flurry of interest in women's tennis. To strengthen their position, the women formed their own union, called the Women's Tennis Association (WTA), and Billie Jean was elected its first president. She continued to play tennis through the 1970s before retiring from active play in 1984. Along the way, Billie Jean captured a few more Grand Slam titles, and in 1979, she teamed with Martina Navratilova to win her 10th Wimbledon doubles championship. More significant than the win itself was the fact that Billie Jean had now won 20 Wimbledon titles, surpassing Elizabeth Ryan's 45-year record of 19 wins. During her career, which spanned three decades, Billie Jean won a total of 37 major tournament titles in singles, doubles, and mixed doubles competition.

And Billie Jean has been just as busy off the court. In addition to serving twice as president of the WTA, Billie Jean helped found the Women's Sports Foundation in 1974, and the first sports magazine devoted to women— *Women's Sport & Fitness.* She has coached such tennis greats as Tim Mayotte and Martina Navratilova. In addition, she coached the 1996 gold-medal U.S. Olympic Tennis team, and serves as director of World Team Tennis (which she also cofounded). Showing no signs of slowing down, Billie Jean works as a tennis commentator for Home Box Office. It is easy to understand how her contributions to women's sports and women's rights have earned her a place among the 100 most important Americans of the twentieth century. Countless people have already benefited from Billie Jean King's pioneering efforts, and her work will undoubtedly continue to reap benefits for women in the years to come.

The Battle of the Sexes

"No person in the United States shall, on the basis of sex, be excluded from participation in, be denied the benefits of, be treated differently from another person or otherwise be discriminated against in any interscholastic intercollegiate club or intramural athletics."
—Title IX, section 106.41- Athletics, 1972

The 1970s saw many social changes in America. After over a decade of protests, marches, and clashes with the police and the national guard over U.S. involvement in the Vietnam War, American soldiers came home for good. The Supreme Court, in its landmark ruling in *Roe* vs *Wade,* declared that any restrictions on abortions in the first trimester of a pregnancy were unconstitutional. With feminist Gloria Steinem at the editorial helm, *Ms.* magazine made its debut. It was the first magazine created by an all-woman staff, and it covered women's concerns as human beings, not only in their roles as wife and mother. For the first time, women competed in the Boston Marathon. And on June 23, 1972, President Richard Nixon signed Title IX, a law that prohibited sex discrimination in all federally funded educational institutions. In effect, the most important piece of legislation for women at that time, it found its way to the Congress of the United States.

The amendment was introduced by Indiana Senator Birch Bayh. He remembers fondly the words of Congresswoman Shirley Chisolm, the leadoff witness at the hearings—"Gentlemen, you all are aware that I have been discriminated against because I'm black, but let me tell you from the bottom of my heart, not nearly as much as I have been discriminated against because I'm a woman." So how did Title IX change things for young girls and women in America? The law now required any school or educational institution receiving federal funding to give girls the same opportunities as boys. This included sports programs and also required that scholarship dollars be proportional to the number of males and females in athletic programs. Finally, more money would have to be provided for athletic-related costs—uniforms, sports equipment, coaches, practice times, and sports facilities. Schoolboys and schoolgirls must receive the same benefits under the law.

How important was the passage of Title IX? Christine Grant, the women's athletic director at the University of Iowa says: "It's clearly the most important thing that has ever happened to women in sports in this century. Without Title IX, I don't think we would have seen one-hundredth of the progress we have made." Before 1972, there were no athletic college scholarships for women. Only 1 percent of all the intercollegiate athletics budgets in the country were allocated to women's programs, the other 99 percent funded the men's programs.

Title IX clearly had an impact on athletic opportunities in high school and college for women across America. In 1971, according to a research study conducted by the Women's Sports Foundation, only 294,015 girls participated in high school sports. Just one year later the number jumped to 817,073, an increase of over 275 percent. By the end of the decade, more than 2 million high school girls were enjoying a variety of sports.

For some time, American women had been expressing displeasure with their role in society, including their marriages. By the 1960s, expressions over the social and political conditions in America were beginning to change from underlying rumblings to louder and more visible demonstrations. At issue was everything from rock and roll music and the use of drugs, to protests over the draft and U.S. involvement in the Vietnam War. The civil rights movement was gaining momentum and the women's rights movement was emerging. In 1966, feminist Betty Friedan founded the National Organization for Women (NOW), whose main objective was to ensure equality for women "in a truly equal partnership with men."

Men were not happy about this invasion into their "male-dominated" world. Why should women be given management positions? Hadn't they always assumed the role of administrative support? Hadn't they always assumed the role of the diminutive "weaker sex"? The workforce was not the only area of society where women faced glaring inequities such as lower pay than men for the same job; women were also being shortchanged in educational and athletic opportunities.

By the early 1970s, the two genders were at odds with each other. Women wanted more, and men didn't want to relinquish what they had. Many men, often called "male chauvinist pigs," believed that women were inferior, and therefore didn't deserve equal rights. Some professional male athletes felt that women couldn't compete as well as men could. Some were quite noisy about such opinions.

In 1973, Bobby Riggs appointed himself the champion of the cause for men's tennis. He said that women's tennis was not as interesting as men's, and felt that women shouldn't earn as much in the game as men because they couldn't win against a man. Known for his outspokenness and bravado, the former Wimbledon and U.S. Open champion was always making outrageous challenges. In one match, he placed chairs on his side of the court as a stunt to handicap himself against what he believed was a lesser opponent. Another time he actually played while holding a dog on a leash.

Finally, Riggs challenged tennis star Billie Jean King to a one-on-one match. Even though he was 26 years older than King, Riggs believed he could defeat any female opponent, and would prove once and for all that men were the superior sex, putting to rest any further debate on that issue. Unfortunately, King turned him down. She was busy fighting for women tennis players to earn equal prize money in matches and working hard to establish a tennis circuit for women. Riggs went looking for another opponent. He found her in Margaret Smith Court, only the second woman to achieve the Grand Slam of tennis.

Warming up for their "Battle of the Sexes" match, Bobby Riggs arm wrestles Billie Jean King at the press announcement.

In a game known as the "Mother's Day Massacre," Riggs soundly defeated Court 6-2, 6-1. When King heard the results of that match she knew there was too much at stake for the future of women's tennis. She had to play Riggs.

The two set the date for their match—September 20, 1973. At a press conference before the match, Riggs said: "She [Billie Jean King] says they're gonna scrape me off the court of the Astrodome and I claim it's gonna be her they're gonna scrape off so that's what it's all about and it is gonna be the battle of the sexes. Don't let anybody tell you it's any different."

Dubbed the "Battle of the Sexes," Riggs and King met at the Houston Astrodome to play in front of 30,000 spectators and the 50 million viewers who tuned in to the prime-time telecast on ABC. Amid the circuslike atmosphere, six male athletes dressed like gladiators carried King into the stadium on a regal chair adorned with feathers. Riggs came into the stadium in a carriage pulled by six very scantily dressed female models. The crowd was split in its support. Men wore signs that read "Whiskey, Women, and Riggs," women wore "Libber over Lobber." There were those who lifted homemade signs that read "I Love Bobby Riggs," and "I Love Billie Jean King."

Riggs leaps over the net to congratulate Billie Jean.

Once the match was underway, the fanfare disappeared and King got down to business. She played a serve-and-volley game, and ran Riggs all over the court. She won the first set 6-4. Riggs was showing signs of fatigue in the second set. Again, King won, 6-3. By the third set, Riggs was exhausted. King beat him 6-3, with the final point won when Riggs's return shot hit the net and dropped harmlessly at his feet. King, exalted, threw her racket up in the air. Trying to show some bounce of energy left in his legs, Riggs managed to hop over the net and meet King there.

Before the match, King had felt a tremendous weight of responsibility on her shoulders. She believed that the match was forcing people to think a little bit differently about things for the first time. Later, tennis star Martina Navratilova had this to say about King's win over Riggs: "She [King] transcended the sport and made women think they can do this. They can go to the boardroom and be strong and speak their mind and believe in themselves on a par with men." Clearly, this event had not been just a tennis match.

As for Billie Jean King, she knew how important that evening in the Astrodome had been. "It was vindicating, a very deeply held belief by all women that they were just as good as men. And women of my era are still talking about it. I don't think they realized this little tennis match was going to do that to them. It wasn't about *tennis*, it was about *social* change and I knew that going in. I knew it."

Peggy Fleming

1948–
Figure Skating

"My dad taught me to always do my best. Tomorrow night, I'm going to give it all I've got."
—Peggy Fleming before her free skate at the 1968 Olympics

The members and coaches of the 1961 United States Figure Skating team boarded a plane bound for Prague, Czechoslovakia, to compete in the world championships. William Kipp, one of the top skating coaches in America, had also been working with a young 11-year-old who had fallen in love with the sport from the moment she laced up her first pair of ice skates at age 9. Something about the quietness and graceful feel of gliding around the ice appealed to Peggy Fleming.

Because her family moved quite a bit when she was just beginning to skate, Peggy had to change coaches several times. When she met Kipp, she liked him instantly, and her skating quickly improved. Unfortunately, she didn't have the chance to work with Kipp for long. The plane never made it to Prague, and the U.S. team never had the chance to compete in the world championships. The plane crashed just outside Brussels, Belgium, killing everyone on board. Now young Peggy Fleming would share in the responsibility of rebuilding the figure-skating program for America.

Peggy Gale Fleming was born in San Jose, California, on July 27, 1948. When she was nine, Peggy, and sisters Janice, Maureen, and Cathy, moved to Ohio where her father Albert had accepted a job as a newspaper pressman at the *Cleveland Plain Dealer*. As a preteen, Peggy had enjoyed outdoor activities in the mild San Jose climate, playing baseball, climbing trees, and roller skating. It wasn't until she got to Ohio that she tried ice skating. According to her sister Janice, Peggy was a natural from the minute she first stepped on the ice. She passed her Preliminary and First USFSA tests in 1957. Moving back to California in 1958, Peggy joined the St. Moritz Ice Skating Club and won her first competition, capturing the Pacific Coast Juvenile Girls title a year later.

By 1960, the Flemings were living in the Los Angeles, California, area, where Albert worked for the *Los Angeles Times*. Having become quite proficient in her age group, Peggy quickly rose up in the amateur ranks. Between 1960 and 1963, she had won all of the regional titles (Juvenile, Novice, Junior and Senior). In her first U.S. Championships appearance in 1962, she won the silver medal in the Novice division. Competing again in 1963, she moved up to the Junior Ladies class, and won the bronze.

The entire Fleming family supported Peggy's skating, and some sacrifices had to be made. Since skating lessons and rink time for practice sessions were very expensive, Peggy's father took on part-time jobs, even learning how to operate the Zamboni machine to clean the ice at the rink. To defray some of the costs, her mother Doris made all the outfits Peggy wore in her competition appearances, including the Olympics. Even Peggy's sisters pitched in— cooking dinners, mowing the lawn, and helping with household chores.

The 1960s would be Peggy's decade. She continued to mature as a world figure skating competitor. In 1964, she won the U.S. Nationals, becoming the youngest skater to win that championship. After earning a spot on the women's Olympic team, she came in a respectable sixth at the Winter Games in Innsbruck, Austria. At the world championships, she came in seventh, and continued to tour Europe with many of the top female skaters. However, after receiving word that her father had suffered a major heart attack, Peggy and her mother returned home. Though Albert recovered, he had to take it easy for a while.

The following year, Peggy successfully defended her U.S. national title at Lake Placid. Though exhausted from competing in Colorado's high altitude, she came in third at the world championships in Colorado Springs. With the next Worlds being held in the high altitude of Davos, Switzerland, Peggy and her family decided to move to Colorado Springs. There she could adapt to the thinner air, and train with the world-renowned figure skating coach, Carlo Fassi.

Under Fassi's guidance, Peggy was doing her best skating. She won her third straight U.S. national title, and went to Davos skating with greatly improved compulsory figures. Peggy scored extraordinarily well in the compulsories, leading Canadian defending champion Petra Burka by 49 points. Only four people had ever defeated a reigning champion, and Peggy became number five. After skating a clean free skate program the next night, she won the title by 63 points over Gabrielle Seyfert of East Germany.

After the Worlds, Peggy again toured Europe, taking a break to skate in a

Peggy Fleming (center) receives her gold medal at the 1968 Olympics, Grenoble, France.

special exhibition in Boston. As a surprise, Albert drove all the way from Colorado just to see his daughter perform. Sadly, it was the last time Peggy ever saw her father. Shortly after she returned to Europe to rejoin the tour, Albert Fleming had another heart attack and died before he got back to Colorado. After her father's funeral, Peggy thought about giving up her skating career. The sacrifices her family had made on her behalf meant the world to her, but she couldn't imagine how she could earn enough money to continue her training for the Olympic Games in Grenoble, France, just two years away. But her mother and sisters would hear nothing of it. They had come this far with Peggy, and they were going to see that she got to Grenoble.

Peggy successfully defended her U.S. national title for an unprecedented fourth time in Omaha, Nebraska, in 1967, and won her second straight world title in Vienna, Austria. The stage was set for the competitions in 1968. Peggy was heavily favored to win her fifth national title, and she did not disappoint her fans in Philadelphia, Pennsylvania. Undoubtedly the favorite to win a gold medal at Grenoble, Peggy's performance would be seen live and in color by millions, for the first time.

Leading by 77 points after the compulsory figures, Peggy stepped on the ice to perform her free skate program. She was dressed in a yellowish-green skirted leotard accented with rhinestones—a costume Doris had made for her daughter for these 1968 Olympic Games. Captivating the judges and the audience with the artistry and graceful skating style that had become her trademark, Peggy won the gold medal. In fact, it was the only gold medal the United States took home from Grenoble. She skated off the ice filled with tears of joy, and hugged her mother and Coach Fassi.

After the Olympics, Peggy went on to Geneva, Switzerland, where she won her third straight World title. Going out on a positive note, Peggy decided to turn professional. She signed a four-year contract to skate with the Ice Follies, a contract to do six TV specials, and several contracts for commercials. After all the years of struggling, money would never again be a problem.

Peggy's professional career has been as bright and successful as her amateur skating career. She won two Emmys for her Sun Valley TV special, and she launched an acting career, appearing on *Diagnosis Murder* and *Newhart*. Peggy also hosted a special on animal poaching in East Africa, and has worked for 18 years as an on-air sports analyst for ABC, covering national, world, and Olympic events. Ever involved in charitable causes, Peggy has served as the honorary chairman for Easter Seals, and is the national spokesperson for the National Osteoporosis Foundation.

Perhaps Peggy faced her greatest personal challenge in 1998, when she discovered a lump in her left breast. It was cancerous, but a type that responds well to lumpectomy and radiation therapy. She decided to share the experience with the public, appearing on *20/20* and *Oprah,* in the hopes of educating other women about the disease and demonstrating the inner strength she has found to battle it. She is quick to point out what is truly important in life—not medals and the glory, but family and friends. Peggy is richly rewarded in that part of her life, receiving the love and support of her husband Dr. Greg Jenkins, and her sons, Andy and Todd. The image of her gold medal free skate performance in 1968 will serve as a lasting reminder of her grace, style, and dignity, both on and off the ice.

Sheila Young

1950–

Speed Skating, Cycling

"I wish my sports were bigger here, but not for the glory. I wish they were recognized more because people are missing a chance to see how exciting they are."
—Sheila Young on the lesser-known sports of speed skating and cycling

When Sheila first became involved in speed skating it was outshone in the United States by more popular winter sports such as skiing and figure skating.

As a result, the name Sheila Young is not as instantly recognizable as Kristi Yamaguchi, Michelle Kwan, or Picabo Street, for example. However, that takes nothing away from Sheila's remarkable accomplishments as both a champion speed skater and a cyclist. Sheila is one of an elite group of athletes who have simultaneously and successfully competed in more than one sport.

Born on October 14, 1950, in the Detroit suburb of Birmingham, Michigan, Sheila's initial entry into sports was limited at best. She didn't particularly care for winter sports. As a four year old, Sheila's most sports-related activity was learning how to ride her two-wheeler bike. However, she was born into a family of sports enthusiasts. Both of her parents loved ice skating and cycling, and encouraged their children in these activities. Besides, as her father explained, "I couldn't afford a baby-sitter, so everybody had to come along." By age nine, Sheila began to enjoy ice skating. Her older sister was a speed skater, and the two girls often skated on the frozen lakes and rinks in and around Birmingham.

Though Sheila was raised in a loving and supportive family, her preteen world changed dramatically when her mother became ill. Unable to win her battle against cancer, her mother died when Sheila was 12 years old. Shortly after, the family moved to Detroit, where Sheila's father had accepted a new job. These two major events—her mother's death and the move to Detroit—had a tremendous impact on Sheila. Uncomfortable in her new surroundings and trying to adjust to life without her mother, Sheila began spending more and more time on the ice.

With her father's coaching, and many long hours of practice, Sheila got better and better. Soon, she was entering and winning speed skating meets. In 1972, Sheila made the U.S. Olympic team and traveled to Sapporo, Japan, to compete in the 500-meter sprint event. She missed winning a bronze medal by 8/100 second.

Having done well in international competition, Sheila wanted to continue training and improve her performance even more. She began working with Peter Schotting, one of the best speed skating coaches in the sport. Schotting was so impressed with Sheila's abilities that he predicted she would become a world champion after working with him for a year. It was Schotting who introduced Sheila to another sport—cycling. Since it was difficult to find rinks to train in all year round, cycling was another way to build up the leg strength and endurance speed skating required.

Schotting was a demanding coach and he designed a rigorous training program for Sheila, including body conditioning, and long hours of skating, running, and cycling. In 1973, all the hard work paid off. Sheila won the 500-, the 1,000-, and the 1,500-meter events at the U.S. Championships. Though she had been viewed as primarily a sprint skater, Sheila's first-place finishes in the longer races showed how versatile she had become. She capped off a great year by setting a world record in the 500-meters later in the season, and returned home from the World Championships with the gold medal in the 500-meter race.

When the skating season was over, Sheila turned her attention to competitive cycling. She had always enjoyed bike riding for fun, and had been including cycling in her training for a few years. Now she was interested in testing her skills in world-class competition. Surprisingly, Sheila qualified for the world cycling track championships in Sebastian, Spain. While she was confident and relaxed in speed skating events, Sheila was nervous and anxious about her first major cycling competition. She crashed a few times in the preliminary heats—in one of her falls she was injured so severely that the doctors suggested she withdraw from the final. But Sheila refused to quit. Her final race was against the heavily favored Soviet cyclist Galina Ermolasva. Cuts, bruises, and all, Sheila went out and stunned everybody by winning the race. Sheila had become the first American—male or female—to win a cycling track championship. Even more impressive was the fact that Sheila had achieved something no other American athlete had—she was world champion in two entirely different sports.

Determined to continue her winning ways, Sheila went right back to work—training on the ice for the new season. She won the World Championship title again in the 500-meter sprints in 1975, and then focused all her energies on making the Olympic team and the trip to Innsbruck, Austria, for the 1976 Winter Games. Though she had missed out on a medal four years earlier, Sheila was not to be denied this time around. In all, she won three medals—a gold in the 500-, a silver in the 1,500-, and a bronze in the 1,000-meter race. By capturing three Olympic medals, Sheila had also accomplished what no other American had done before her.

It was unfortunate for Sheila Young to come along before speed skating received the attention that it enjoys today. Her feats are even more remarkable given the lack of top training facilities and monetary support that were available for skaters like Bonnie Blair and Beth Heiden a decade later. As for cycling, it wasn't even a women's Olympic event when Sheila was at her peak. Fortunately for female athletes, both of these sports now have many fans as well as the organizational support that no doubt would have benefited Sheila Young. Even so, her accomplishments in speed skating and cycling will probably remain unsurpassed for years to come.

Anita DeFrantz

1952–

Rowing, Sports Administration

"My approach to discrimination is that I don't see obstacles, I see goals. I would not let anything deter me."
—Anita DeFrantz on dealing with discrimination in sports and life

Seotember 4, 1997, was a historic day in Lausanne, Switzerland, where the 106th session of the International Olympic Committee (IOC) had convened. By acclamation, United States Olympic Committee (USOC) member Anita DeFrantz became the first female vice president of the prestigious umbrella organization of the Olympic movement. It was a remarkable achievement for the 44-year-old African-American. A descendant of slaves, social activism is as much a part of Anita's life as athletics.

Anita DeFrantz's great-great-grandfather was a Louisiana plantation owner who emigrated to America from the Alsace-Lorraine region of France. He fathered a son, named Alonzo David DeFrantz, by one of his female slaves, who had been taken from her home on Africa's Gold Coast. Though Alonzo was born a slave, he was later freed by his father. As a free man, he joined Benjamin "Pap" Singleton in 1877 to help organize other newly freed blacks in a move to the prairies of Kansas.

Years later, one of Alonzo's sons, Fayburn Edward DeFrantz, became director of the YMCA in Indianapolis, Indiana. Nicknamed the "Big Chief," Fayburn, Anita's grandfather, was active not only in athletics, but also in the black community. He arranged for some of the most prominent African-Americans of the time, including W. E. B. Du Bois, Langston Hughes, Paul Robeson, and Walter White, to speak at the local church after Sunday services.

Fayburn's son, Robert David DeFrantz, was also active in working for black equality. As a student at Indiana University, Robert headed the school's chapter of the National Association for the Advancement of Colored People (NAACP). There Robert met his future wife Anita, who was one of the first African-American women to integrate on-campus housing at Indiana.

Robert and Anita married and had four children: three boys and a girl, named after her mother. Anita Luceete DeFrantz was born on October 4, 1952, in Philadelphia, Pennsylvania, but she was raised in Indianapolis. By the time Anita reached adolescence, her parents had become actively involved in the civil rights movement of the 1960s. Up until that time, African-Americans were forbidden to send their children to schools attended by white children, or enter theaters, restaurants, or public restrooms patronized by whites, or even drink from the same water fountains. And even African-Americans who were qualified for better positions were limited to low-level, low-paying jobs.

Because Anita was not only black but also female, she faced discrimination on two fronts. She had been born long before the enactment of Title IX—a law that forbids discrimination based on sex in any federally funded school or institution—so, like other female athletes, her opportunities were very limited. For exercise, she swam at the Frederick Douglass Park pool, where a coach had put together a competitive swim team for the neighborhood kids. But when the coach moved away, the team foundered.

At Shortridge High School, where the DeFrantz children were students, there were plenty of athletic opportunities—for the boys. Here was a girl who had grown up in the heart of basketball country and who desperately wanted to dribble and shoot baskets, yet she had to settle for sitting in the bleachers, cheering for her brothers. The only "sport" open to Anita was playing in the woodwind section of the school's marching band.

When Anita headed off to Connecticut College in 1970 on an academic scholarship, she hadn't forgotten the disappointment and frustration she'd felt in high school. She played a little basketball, but she was already a sophomore when she stumbled onto a sport she knew nothing about—rowing. As she walked across the campus one day, she noticed a man carrying a long, narrow boat over his shoulder. The man was Connecticut's rowing coach, Bart Gulong. He told Anita that her height and build made her perfect for the sport. Anita seized the opportunity to join the rowing team.

Before long, Anita was among the best women rowers at the college. When she found out that rowing was an Olympic sport, she set a new goal: to make the American team and compete in the 1976 Olympics in Montreal, Canada. By the time Anita was ready to graduate, she had been accepted into law school at the University of Pennsylvania and had also been offered a CORO Public Affairs Fellowship in Los Angeles, California. She ultimately chose to attend the University of Pennsylvania, but her primary motivation was not just to study law. Anita really wanted to train at the prestigious Vesper Boat Club in Philadelphia. Only a few years before, the boat club had become the first men's rowing club to organize a women's rowing team.

Under Coach John Hooten, Anita became a great rower. When the members of the 1976 U.S. Olympic rowing team were selected, Hooten said, "She was the best starboard in the country. She was in the seventh seat [of an eight-oared shell with coxswain], which is very difficult because it requires you to be very smart and precise but also very aggressive." Along with her teammates, Anita won a bronze medal, coming in third behind the East German and Soviet teams. For Anita the victory was particularly significant—she was the first black ever to win an Olympic medal in rowing.

Upon her return from Montreal, Anita set two more goals. She was determined to earn a law degree and to win a gold medal at the 1980 Olympics in Moscow. In 1977, she was admitted to the Pennsylvania State Bar, but her second goal, however, would never materialize. She had a heavy schedule of commitments, including working as an attorney for the Juvenile Law Center, serving on the boards of directors of the Vesper Boat Club and the U.S. Rowing Association, and acting as an athlete's representative for the United States Olympic Committee—all while training for the rowing trials for the Moscow Games. Coach Hooten, who had already expressed concern about her difficult schedule, recalled a time when Anita told him she had to miss a practice so that she could testify before the U.S. Senate for the passage of the Amateur Sports Act of 1978.

Anita DeFrantz's dream of returning to the Olympics ended in January 1980 when the USOC boycotted the Summer Games to protest the Soviet Union's invasion of Afghanistan. At first stunned and then enraged, Anita asserted, "[The Games] don't belong to a country. They're a celebration in a country, but they belong to the world. [President Jimmy Carter] reduced the Olympics to the status of a trade embargo." Anita filed a lawsuit against the

USOC, and though she lost the suit, she did make the 1980 Olympic rowing team. They would never compete at Moscow, however.

Anita DeFrantz's passionate support of athletes' rights earned her a different kind of Olympic honor: the IOC presented her with the bronze medal of the Olympic Order, the organization's highest award. It is bestowed on individuals who "achieve remarkable merit" or contribute to the development of sport.

Anita also attracted the attention of Peter Ueberroth, the organizer for the 1984 Summer Olympic Games in Los Angeles, who invited her to join his committee as a vice president. After the 1984 games ended, she joined the Amateur Athletic Foundation of Los Angeles, of which she would later become president. In 1986, IOC President Juan Antonio Samaranch tapped her to succeed American IOC member Julian Roosevelt, who had passed away that year. She became the first black from a non-African country to be elected to the committee.

Although a strong advocate for athletes, Anita DeFrantz has little tolerance for unfairness in competition. In 1988, when Canadian sprinter Ben Johnson was stripped of a gold medal after testing positive for steroids, Anita DeFrantz denounced his behavior, calling Johnson "a cheat and a coward." Since then she has been a strong proponent of the IOC's campaign against banned substances. She has also been instrumental in lobbying for a number of women's sports, such as softball and soccer, to be added as sanctioned Olympic events.

In 1992, Anita was elected to the IOC's executive board. In 1997 she became the most powerful woman in amateur athletics when she was elected vice president of the IOC, the first woman in the organization's 103-year history to attain this position. Anita's deep commitment to athletics and community work leaves her little personal time. She is not married and has no children. But these facts don't bother Anita. "I don't believe people make sacrifices," she says. "People make choices. That's the approach I take. I made a decision to do these things. I believed I could make a difference. I find it fulfilling to work with children. I love kids. I have 3 million of them in Los Angeles."

Chris Evert

1954–
Tennis

"I was the ice queen and [fans] wanted to see me melt. They wanted to see me cry, probably show some emotion. But I carried it inside myself."
—Chris Evert on her "Ice Maiden" image

The U.S. Open, traditionally held at the National Tennis Center in Flushing Meadows Park, New York, is considered the grand finale of the season, the last of the four tournaments that comprise the Grand Slam title of tennis. In 1989, the fans witnessed what was to be Chris Evert's last professional tournament play. After losing to Zina Garrison in the quarterfinal round on September 5, Chris met Garrison at the net, shook hands, and said a final goodbye to the fans. Having been on top for more than 10 years, Chris was retiring from the game she helped elevate to the next level for women in the 1970s and 1980s. The crowd cheered as Chris left the court for the last time. Zina Garrison was so moved by this extraordinary moment in tennis, she began to cry.

Christine Marie Evert, the second of five children, was born in Fort Lauderdale, Florida, on December 21, 1954. There was never any doubt that Chris would play tennis, as it was an all-family event for the Evert clan. Chris joined her two brothers and two sisters, who were all playing by the time they reached their sixth birthdays. Her father Jimmy divided his time between working as a teaching pro and managing the Holiday Park Tennis Center. A University of Notre Dame graduate, Jimmy had attended on a tennis scholarship. He won some impressive tournaments in his own playing days, including the 1940 U.S. National Indoor Championship and the Canadian Singles title in 1947.

Unlike other champions who remember having a burning passion as children for their sport, Chrissie didn't feel that way about tennis. Mostly, she played because her father took her to the courts with him. Though she was not particularly athletic, her calm demeanor suited the traditional style of the game. Chrissie's steady temperament gave her the patience to practice for endless hours. Her even-keeled personality also helped Chrissie reach a level of maturity that would be an asset as she began moving up in the ranks.

Having been coached by a professional from the time she was old enough to swing a tennis racket, Chrissie's game was quite good by the time she turned 15 in 1969. The following year, the junior tennis champion captured her first big victory and stunned the tennis world by defeating Grand Slam champion Margaret Smith Court, whom many considered the greatest tennis player in the world.

The most significant match of Chrissie's early career, the one that catapulted her into the spotlight, came while she was still playing as an amateur. In her first appearance at the U.S. Open, she played the kind of tennis that foreshadowed a legendary career. Chrissie had all the assets of a true champion—the poise, grace, and mental toughness.

After winning her first match easily over Edda Buding 6-1, 6-0, the ponytailed blonde, blue-eyed teen met Mary Ann Eisel, who was ranked number four in America. Eisel won the first set 6-4, and was serving 40-love ahead in the second set 6-5. Down triple-match point, Chrissie dug in and responded to the challenge. After saving six match points and evening up the set 6-6, Chrissie won the tiebreaker 5-1, sending the match into a third and decisive set. A newly invigorated Chrissie went on to rout Eisel 6-1 in the final set, and the crowd gave the new teen sensation a resounding ovation as she left the court. Chris's fairy-tale tournament ended when she was defeated in the semifinal round by Billie Jean King, unquestionably the most formidable player in American women's tennis at that time. In fact, King went on to win the U.S. Open women's singles title.

When Chrissie turned pro on her 18th birthday, she was still methodical in her approach to the game. Reserved on and off the court, Chrissie showed little emotion. Many people mistook her demeanor as snobbishness and unfriendliness. The crowd-pleasing teen of 1970–1971 was now being referred to by the press as the "Little Ice Maiden." Years later, Chrissie reflected on those early years, explaining that she's never really been "one of the girls," and was too shy to seek out friendships. As far as her on-court demeanor was concerned, Chris believes her father instilled that poker-faced approach to her matches. "Don't show any emotion: it will be to your advantage because your opponent will be frustrated."

While competing at Wimbledon in 1973, Chrissie fell in love with Jimmy Connors, a young, brash tennis star. Their relationship blossomed and the happy couple announced their engagement toward the end of the year. The following year was an exciting one for Chrissie. She won her first two Grand Slam tournaments—the French Open and Wimbledon. With Margaret Smith Court absent and Billie Jean King and Evonne Goolagong losing in the early rounds, Chrissie breezed through the tournament, beating Olga Morozova 6-0, 6-4 in the final. At age 19, Chrissie was the second-youngest player to win the title. The next day, Connors claimed the men's title. By year's end, Chrissie had achieved the women's number one ranking in the United States.

As the year ended, Chris and Jimmy realized that they just weren't ready for marriage. Both were touring, often in different circuits, and neither wanted to stop playing tennis. In January 1975, just a few weeks after Chrissie turned 20, the couple called off the engagement. Though Chrissie may have been saddened by the breakup of her relationship with Connors, she showed no signs of what she might be feeling in public. She continued to play great tennis, and became the number one ranked player in the world. She stayed on top through 1977, and never dropped below number four in her 17-year career.

After victories in both Wimbledon and the U.S. Open in 1976, Chrissie was named Sportswoman of the Year by *Sports Illustrated*. She also reached the $1-million mark in career prize money, becoming the first woman to do so in tennis. Between 1974 and 1986 Chris won at least one Grand Slam title. Having reached at least the semifinal round in 52 of her 56 Grand Slam matches per year, Chris has the distinction of being one of the all-time best Grand Slam players. In all, Chris won 18 major titles: 7 French Opens, 6 U.S. Opens, 3 Wimbledon, and 2 Australian Opens. She also became the first player to win 1,000 matches and 157 tournaments. Her .900 career-winning percentage (1,309 victories versus 146 losses) is still the best in the history of professional tennis.

Perhaps the most exciting moments in Chrissie's career came in play against another superstar on the women's tour—Martina Navratilova. Their rivalry was one of the most intense ever, and it helped the women's tour rise to a new level. Martina got the better of their head-to-head competitions, holding a 43–37 edge overall, but Chris had a few thrilling wins against Martina. Playing on the clay courts (her best surface) at Roland Garros at the French Open, Chrissie registered exhaustive three-set victories over Martina in 1985 and 1986.

When Chris retired after her quarterfinal match loss to Garrison, she set to work on fulfilling a lifetime goal—establishing Chris Evert Charities, Inc. The organization does not just bear her name; she devotes a tremendous amount of her time to overseeing most aspects of raising money to fight drug abuse and assist drug-exposed, neglected, and abused children. The inaugural event in 1989 helped raise the money needed to open a drug treatment facility in an impoverished south Florida neighborhood. So far, in events like the Chris Evert Pro-Celebrity Tennis Classic, the charity has raised more than $5.5 million. Chris's celebrity support is a Who's Who of virtually every area of sports and entertainment. Whitney Houston sang at the Gala Black-Tie Dinner Dance. Don Johnson, Brooke Shields, Alan King, and pals Martina Navratilova and Billie Jean King have also donated their time and efforts to make the annual weekend event unforgettable and successful.

In retirement, Chris has little idle time. She works as a TV sports analyst for NBC. In 1988, she married former two-time Olympic downhill skier Andy Mill (Chris was also briefly married to tennis pro John Lloyd). They have three sons, Alexander, Nicholas, and Colton. Among Chris's many honors are being named the Greatest Woman Athlete of the Last 25 Years by the Woman's Sports Foundation in 1985, and being unanimously elected into the International Tennis Association Hall of Fame in 1995. The four-time Associated Press Athlete of the Year, and ranked number 50 on the list of the top 100 athletes of the twentieth century, Chris has everything in perspective. "Being a mother . . . having Andy as my husband . . . doing broadcasting and fulfilling my endorsements is definitely enough for me."

Olga Korbut

1955–

Gymnastics

"I am not the pigtailed girl anymore. But I hold her dear to my heart."
—Olga Korbut in 1991, after seeing her 1972 Olympic performance

The last time Germany had played host to the Olympics, Adolf Hitler was Führer. Those were the 1936 Games where Hitler boasted of Aryan superiority, and left the stadium humiliated when African-American Jesse Owens walked away with four gold medals. Soon after, the world was plunged into war, with freedom and democracy at stake.

The opening ceremonies at the 1972 Summer Olympic Games in Munich, West Germany, welcomed over 7,000 athletes representing 121 nations for two weeks of rousing competition. They included a bubbly teenager from Belarus, Russia, standing only 4 feet 11 inches (150 cm) tall and weighing 90 pounds (41 kg) who turned in one of the most memorable performances of those Games. Unfortunately, the 1972 Olympics will forever be shrouded in sadness and horror by the murder of 11 members of the Israeli team by Palestinian terrorists.

Olga Korbut was born on May 16, 1955, in the town of Grodno, not far from the capital city of Minsk in what is now Belarus, a country in eastern Europe. At that time it was part of the Soviet Union called Byelorussia. Olga was the younger of two daughters—her father was an engineer and her mother was a cook. Seventeen years later, she flashed a beaming smile and waved to the crowd as she entered the Olympics gymnastics competition in Munich.

Olga began her training early, wanting to follow the lead of her older sister. When she turned 11, Olga began attending one of the Soviet Union's sports schools, which were funded and run by the government. She started training with coaches Yelena Volchetskaya and Renald Knysh, who worked Olga hard to see just how much she was capable of achieving. Because of her young age and small size, Olga became quite successful at some daring acrobatic routines on the balance beam and the uneven parallel bars. In just a few short years, Olga was competing on the national level.

In 1969, she finished in fifth place at the Soviet Union's national championships, and in 1970 she won her first national title on the vaulting horse. Though Olga earned a spot on the Soviet national team, she suffered a setback in her budding career when she became ill following an injury. After the break in her training, Olga had to work hard to regain the skills that had helped her shine in her sport.

Olga made the Soviet Olympic team in 1972, earning the last spot by coming in third in overall performance. Along with teammates Lyudmila Tourischeva and Tamara Lazakovitch, Olga went to Munich to win gold for her country. Dressed in her red leotards with matching bows on her pigtails, Olga dazzled the crowd by doing the first-ever back somersault on the balance beam. Her youthful exuberance was infectious and the crowd loved her. As Bela Karolyi, the famous Romanian gymnastics coach explained, Olga had the four elements necessary to impress the judges: a difficult routine, apparent enjoyment of the event, artistic presentation, and the support and enthusiasm of the crowd.

In the team competition, Olga went on to win the gold medal along with Tourischeva and Lazakovitch. Two nights later, while performing on those same bars, she fell, eliminating any chance to win the gold medal in the women's all-around competition. As the audience had shared her successes earlier in the competition, waving and smiling back at the "pixie" from Byelorussia, so too did they share in her sadness as she broke into tears when she returned to her seat. The following night, having pulled herself together, Olga won two gold medals—on the beam and in the floor exercise, along with a silver for the uneven parallel bars in the individual apparatus events.

Overnight, it seemed, Olga had single-handedly transformed the sport of gymnastics. Before the Munich Games, there were about 15,000 female gymnasts in the United States. Just two short years later, the number exploded to more than 50,000. Olga was voted the Female Athlete of the Year by the Associated Press, was invited to the White House to meet President Nixon, and made a trip to Disneyland before returning to her family in Grodno.

The light had shone brightest for Olga at the 1972 Olympics. She returned to competition, winning a gold medal on the vault at the World Championships in 1974. By 1976, though she earned a spot on the Soviet team and competed in the Olympics in Montreal, Canada, a new star captured the

The amazing maneuver performed by gold-medalist Olga Korbut at the 1972 Munich Olympics

crowd—a 14-year-old Romanian named Nadia Comaneci. Olga had matured in those four years, from a cute 17-year-old to a 21-year-old woman. Still, she won another silver medal in the balance beam, where she amazed the audience when she pressed her chest and body lengthwise against the 4-inch (10-cm) wide beam, brought her legs over her head, and rested her toes on the beam in front of her. Her final medal was another gold as a member of the winning Soviet team.

When she returned to Byelorussia, Olga married Russian folk-rock musician Leonid Bortkevich. In 1979, she gave birth to a son, Richard. After years of athletic competition, Olga was happy to settle into a quiet private life with her husband and son. However, on April 26, 1986, one of the nuclear reactors at the Chernobyl power plant, just 180 miles (290 km) from Grodno, exploded, sending radioactive debris thousands of miles over a large area of the Soviet Union and Europe.

After participating in a gymnastics tour in the United States in 1989, Olga discovered that she was suffering from a thyroid problem related to radiation poisoning. Like many of her neighbors and other residents in Byelorussia, Olga had been exposed to the radiation fallout from the Chernobyl accident. Wanting to be involved in educating others about the aftereffects just beginning to surface, and anxious to help other victims, especially children, Olga became a spokesperson for the Emergency Help for Children Foundation in 1990.

When Soviet-American relations appeared to be moving in a more friendly direction, Olga, Leonid, and Richard moved to the United States and decided to settle in Atlanta, Georgia. Today, well past the age when most young gymnasts compete, Olga is happy with her new life in America. She teaches gymnastics in Atlanta, and has remained actively involved in helping to raise money for the sick and needy Chernobyl victims in her homeland. As for gymnastics, Olga has often expressed how nice it would be to establish competitions for women who no longer do the acrobatic feats of youth, but can still turn in a performance full of the same grace and beauty as ballet.

Martina Navratilova

1956–
Tennis

The moment I stepped onto that crunchy red clay, felt the grit under my sneakers, felt the joy of smacking the ball over the net, I knew I was in the right place."
—Martina Navratilova on her lifelong love affair with tennis

She was half of one of the greatest rivalries ever seen in the sport of tennis. Martina Navratilova, one of the most dominant players in the women's circuit in the 1970s and 1980s, squared off against Chris Evert on the courts for 10 years, battling back and forth for the coveted number one ranking. The two could not have been more opposite in personality—and in play. Chrissie was right-handed, Martina was a leftie; Chrissie preferred to stay back and play a baseline game while Martina loved to charge the net, attacking every ball hit her way. Chrissie was blonde and feminine, Martina had a muscular physique; Chrissie was quiet and methodical in her play, Martina was explosive, vocal, and passionate about her game. Over the long haul, it was Martina who got the better of their head-to-head competitions, winning 10 of 14 Grand Slam finals against Evert.

The huge contract endorsements should have come to Martina, but instead they went to Chrissie and other women on the tour. Instead of being embraced by America, Martina was ostracized by sponsors and fans after disclosing her homosexuality. It would take years and continuous extraordinary play before the fans and her fellow athletes embraced the Czech-born defector in her adopted homeland.

The Czech Republic (formerly known as Czechoslovakia) is a small central European country bordered by Germany, Poland, Austria, and Hungary. Shortly after the end of World War II, the Communist Party gained control of the government. With Communist rule came harsh conditions—the government controlled almost every aspect of its citizens' lives, restricting travel and other basic freedoms. Food and water were almost always in short supply, and life in Czechoslovakia was a poor existence at best.

Martina Subertova was born on October 18, 1956, in Prague, Czechoslovakia. Her parents—Miroslav Subert and Jana Subertova (Czech wives add "ova" to their husband's last name)—were both avid skiers. Miroslav worked as a ski patrolman, and Jana taught the sport for a living. Martina was actually named after a lodge her parents lived in after they got married. It was called *Martinovka,* (Martin's Place).

Unfortunately, Martina's parents divorced when she was just three years old, and Jana took her young daughter and moved into a one-room home in Revnice. From the window, you could peer down on a tennis court below. Already showing signs of athletic talent, little Martina put on a pair of skis almost as soon as she could walk. She began to ski with her mother, and enjoyed participating in other sports such as soccer and hockey. When ski season was over, Jana began playing tennis with Mirek Navratil, who gave lessons and maintained the courts. Mirek was a warm and caring man, and Jana enjoyed his company. Soon, they fell in love and married in 1962.

It was Mirek who taught his young stepdaughter how to play tennis. When Martina was about six years old, she borrowed her grandmother's old racket—she had been a member of the Czech national tennis team before World War II—and began hitting the ball against a wall. Soon, Mirek was working with Martina on the courts, volleying balls back and forth to let her get a feel for the game. Mirek was so impressed with Martina's progress that he took her to Prague to meet the Czech Tennis Federation coach, George Parma. Though she was only nine years old at the time, Parma, too, was impressed with Martina's skills. Martina began taking lessons with Parma, traveling back and forth to Prague once a week.

When she was 12, Martina was permitted to travel to a tennis tournament in West Germany. Under Communism, it was a rare privilege to travel outside Czechoslovakia, and even more rare to go to countries outside the Iron Curtain, the ideological barrier that separated countries controlled by the Soviet Union from the West. In 1972, Martina captured the Czech national title, and earned the right to travel and compete in matches in foreign countries including the United States.

Martina made her first trip to America in 1973. An excited seventeen year old, she loved everything about the United States, including its fast foods. She enjoyed eating junk food like pizza and hamburgers, and developed a passion for pancakes. In just eight short weeks in America, Martina gained 25 pounds

(11.3 kg). Overweight and sluggish, Martina lost her first-ever match with Chris Evert. There would be many duels ahead in the years to come.

She returned again in 1974, slimmer and faster, and was ranked 10th in the world. Martina began beating the high-ranked women on the circuit including Margaret Smith Court. For her greatly improved tennis play, she was named Rookie of the Year. Most of her prize money went to the Czech Federation Team, and Martina began to feel very stifled and restricted by the government's control over her career. In one of the toughest decisions in her young life, Martina decided to defect, or leave the country illegally. She planned to defect to the United States at the end of the 1975 tournament season. By doing so, she could not return to her country, and did not know when, or if, she would ever see her family again.

Professionally, 1975 had been the best year of Martina's career so far. She reached the finals of three of the four Grand Slam events, and beat Chris Evert twice. After Chrissie asked Martina to be her doubles partner, they won four tournaments together. It had also been a financially lucrative year—Martina earned over $200,000. Now able to come and go as she pleased, Martina "went wild" with her newfound freedom. She went on shopping sprees, buying expensive jewelry, cars, and clothes She also went on eating binges, downing a quart of ice cream and a whole pizza in one sitting. She slacked off in practice and it showed in her matches. When Martina lost in the first round of the U.S. Open in 1976, she realized that she needed someone to help her stick to a disciplined exercise and diet regimen.

With the help of companion Sandra Haynie, Martina began a strict workout that included lifting weights and running sprints. Her revolutionary fitness program changed the way other women athletes approached their training. The changes paid off. In 1978, Martina won both the French Open and Wimbledon, beating Chris Evert and gaining her first Wimbledon title. She also solidified her number one ranking.

As Martina continued to shine in her professional career, her personal life began to come under public scrutiny. Having left Sandra Haynie, Martina had a new love—author and gay-rights advocate Rita Mae Brown. Though they were only together for about a year, Martina's celebrity status made it difficult to hide her involvement in a lesbian relationship. It is estimated that Martina lost millions of dollars in endorsements by "coming out" and acknowledging her homosexuality. However, she became a hero in the gay rights movement.

Martina was victorious at Wimbledon in 1979.

Martina was one of the greatest players to ever grace the courts. Before she retired from a phenomenal 20-year career in 1994, Martina compiled one of the most extraordinary records in the game. Her nine singles Wimbledon championships (six in a row) is the all-time record on the grass courts of England. Her record of winning 74 matches in a row is the longest streak in women's tennis. She won a total of 54 Grand Slam titles (singles, doubles, and mixed doubles), second only to Margaret Smith Court's total of 62. She also has two French Open titles, three Australian Open titles, and four U.S. Open championships. In her best season, 1983-1984, Martina won six consecutive Grand Slam titles, more than any other male or female in the history of tennis.

Martina's list of honors is as impressive as her stats. She was named Female Athlete of the Decade for the 1980s by both the Associated Press and United Press International. While still an active player, she was inducted into the International Women's Sports Hall of Fame in 1984. Perhaps the honor that pleases her most is her United States citizenship, which she received on July 21, 1981.

Nancy Lopez Knight

1957–
Golf

"My greatest strength has always been my mind. . . . I've always been able to play myself around the course mentally. . . . I've always been able to substitute a negative thought with a positive one."
—Nancy Lopez on her biggest strength on the golf course

Upon her induction into the Ladies Professional Golf Association (LPGA) Hall of Fame in 1987, Nancy Lopez said it was an honor to be among such greats as Patty Berg (1951), Mildred

"Babe" Didrikson Zaharias (1951), Mickey Wright (1964), and Kathy Whitworth (1975). But many of Nancy's colleagues in the Hall of Fame are saying the same thing about her—the youngest woman ever to be inducted into the Hall of Fame. Nancy never believed that such an honor was attainable, but her incredible stats as an amateur and pro golfer prove that she has earned her place in the history of the sport.

The younger of two daughters of Mexican-American parents, Nancy Marie Lopez was born on January 6, 1957, in Torrance, California. The family lived in Roswell, New Mexico, where her father Domingo repaired cars at his East Second Body Shop. Her mother Marina devoted her time to raising Nancy and her older sister Delma.

Nancy learned how to play golf from her father Domingo, who had been a pretty good amateur player himself. After her mother Marina became ill with a lung disorder, the doctor recommended that she take up walking to help strengthen her lungs. Domingo thought golfing might be the perfect way for his wife to exercise, and the couple took Nancy with them whenever they went to the local course.

By the time Nancy was about seven years old, she was practicing golf almost daily. She learned how to handle rough terrain and sand hazards by playing at the local golf course, which wasn't as carefully trimmed and groomed as most private courses. Nancy was just 12 years old when she won the New Mexico Women's Amateur Championship. After winning it again the following year, she began competing on a national level. By 1972 she had twice won the United States Golf Association Junior Girls Championship, the most important teen tournament in the country. As a student at Goddard High School, Nancy was so good that she was permitted to play on the boys' golf team and became one of its top players. The team won the state championship in 1972. In her senior year, Nancy entered the U.S. Women's Open and stunned her competitors and the crowds by tying for second place behind Sandra Palmer.

Nancy accepted a golf scholarship to the University of Tulsa, where she planned to earn a degree in engineering. She played golf for two years, winning the Association of Intercollegiate Athletics for Women (AIAW) Championship while still a freshman. In 1976, she was named All-American and the university's Female Athlete of the Year. In 1977, Realizing that she was better at golf than academics, Nancy decided to turn pro. At 19, she joined the LPGA and came in second in the Women's Open, her first pro tournament. She repeated her success in the next two tournaments, taking second place in both.

At 20, Nancy was chosen Woman Rookie of the Year.

Nancy's fledgling career almost ended in late September 1977, when her mother died suddenly after surgery for appendicitis. Devastated by her mother's death, Nancy temporarily quit the tour. Five months passed before she would compete in another tournament.

Nancy had a phenomenal year in 1978, however. Having dedicated the season to her mother, she won eight tournaments, including a record-breaking five-tournament streak beginning with the Bent Tree Ladies' Classic in February. She went on to win the Sun Star Classic, the Greater Baltimore Classic, the LPGA Championship, the Nabisco Dinah Shore, the U.S. Women's Open, the du Maurier Classic in Canada, and the Baker's Trust Classic—an especially exciting come-from-behind win. In addition to her stunning successes, she was named LPGA Rookie of the Year and Player of the Year and received the Vare Trophy, awarded each season to the player with the best overall scoring average.

Nancy's youth, personality, and athletic skills gave a much-needed lift to the LPGA's image. In 1979, she won 8 of 22 tournaments and placed in the top ten in 14 others. She was named Pro Golf Player of the Year and earned her second Vare Trophy. Her total winnings for the season exceeded $200,000.

That year, she met and married a Pennsylvania sportscaster named Tim Melton but unfortunately, the marriage did not last long. Through Melton she met Ray Knight, third baseman for the Cincinnati Reds. Some years later, after Nancy and Ray had both divorced, they resumed their friendship and eventually started dating. They were married on October 29, 1982. Nancy played very little golf in the first two years of her marriage to Ray. In November 1983, she gave birth to her first child, Ashley. With Ray's support, Nancy got her career back on track, and in 1985 she won five tournaments, including the LPGA Championship—at times with her toddler in tow. In the Henredon Classic that year, she finished an amazing 20 strokes under par, setting a record that remains unbroken. She was named 1985 Athlete of the Year by the Associated Press; she also won her third Vare Trophy and was named Player of the Year for a third season.

Nancy sat out the 1986 season to have her second child, Erinn Shea, but returned to the pro circuit in 1987 with both of her children and a nanny. That year she completed one of the most successful seasons of her career. She was named Golfer of the Decade by *Golf Magazine* and, at age 30, she was inducted as the 11th member of the elite LPGA Hall of Fame—an honor bestowed only on those who have been an LPGA member for at least 10 years and have achieved a record of 30 tournament wins, including two major titles.

Nancy and Ray's third child, Torri Heather, was born in 1991. When Ray was named manager of the Cincinnati Reds in 1993, the family's busy schedule became hectic. Nancy relishes motherhood, and dislikes being away from her children for more than a few days at a time. She considers it a treat to watch them perform in school plays, or to accompany them on Halloween night.

At the end of 1999, Nancy was just two tournaments short of reaching a milestone of 50 career victories. But she is not ready to retire yet; she vows to play the sport she loves for as long as she can. Nancy Lopez Knight has learned that being a professional golfer is less a job than a game. Fellow Hall-of-Famer Carol Mann Hardy says of Nancy: "She plays by feel. All her senses come into play. That's when golf is an art."

Joan Benoit Samuelson

1957–

Marathon

"Winning is neither everything nor the only thing. It is one of many things."
—Joan Benoit Samuelson on balancing a career with life's other demands

At the 1928 Amsterdam Olympics, several women collapsed from exhaustion after the 800-meter race, leading the International Amateur Athletic Federation to restrict women to shorter races. That ruling stood for 56 years. The grueling 26-mile (42-km) women's marathon did not make its Olympic debut until 1984, during the Summer Games in Los Angeles, California.

A great deal had changed in the interim. Women were competing in sports previously open only to men, not only long-distance running events like the Boston Marathon, but also team sports such as soccer and basketball. Competing in the first Olympic marathon in 1984 offered the best women runners a chance to make history. But for American long-distance runner Joan Benoit, it was almost a lost opportunity. Just weeks before the trials, her right knee became inflamed and locked up, threatening to keep her out of the Games entirely.

Born to Andre and Nancy Benoit on May 16, 1957, Joan was raised in the New England town of Cape Elizabeth, Maine, best known for its picturesque lighthouse, which sits atop a craggy hill overlooking the Atlantic Ocean. On weekends, the Benoit family loaded up the car and headed to Sugarloaf Mountain to indulge in their favorite activity—skiing. Joan and her three brothers, Andre Jr., Peter, and John, all loved the sport, but Joan was so taken with it that she decided she wanted to be a champion skier.

In an effort to keep pace with her older brothers, Andre and Peter, Joan became very competitive. She often pushed to get one more run on the slopes before darkness descended. On one such occasion in September 1973, squeezing in that final run on the slalom course proved very costly—Joan crashed into a gate and broke her leg.

Once the cast came off, Joan began to run as part of her rehabilitation program. A shy teen, Joan enjoyed the solitude and quiet of running alone. She competed only against herself, and the more she ran, the more she enjoyed it. At first she was embarrassed by her newfound joy: if a car passed her on the road, she would stop running and pretend to be looking at flowers.

In high school, Joan became a competitive middle- and long-distance runner and she continued to run while attending Maine's Bowdoin College (her father's alma mater). Joan joined several athletic clubs so that she would be able to compete in approved events, and her times continued to improve. In January 1979, she finished second in a marathon in Bermuda at 2:50:54. Her results earned her a spot in the prestigious Boston Marathon, held on April 16 that year.

The 1979 Boston Marathon was Joan's first, and only the seventh such race in which women were officially allowed to compete. She won it easily, with a posted time of 2:35:15, setting a new U.S. record and a Boston Marathon record for women, beating the previous record-holder's time by almost 10 minutes. The victory thrust the shy runner into the public eye, and the adulation and attention she received almost made her give up running.

After graduating from Bowdoin, Joan continued to compete in running events of different lengths to increase her endurance and strengthen her technique. In 1981, she had surgery on her Achilles' tendons due to a heel injury sustained in the Bermuda Marathon three years earlier. But after recovering, Joan came back stronger than ever. By the mid-1980s, she was arguably the finest marathoner in the world.

Joan's performance in her second Boston Marathon in 1983 was even better than her first. At 2:22:42, she broke the world record by almost three minutes. The win secured her place at the qualifying trials for the 1984 Summer Olympics held in Los Angeles. She had missed an opportunity to compete in the Olympics four years earlier, when the Soviet invasion of Afghanistan prompted the United States and several other countries to boycott the Games. For an athlete, four years can be half a lifetime of competition, and this time Joan did not intend to miss her chance.

In March 1984, while training for the Olympic trials, Joan's right knee began giving her pain. By April, she was told that she needed arthroscopic surgery to remove the plica, a fold of skin in her knee that had become inflamed, but that might mean giving up her chance at the Olympics. Joan decided to take the gamble, and she had the surgery on April 25, just 17 days before the trials were scheduled to begin. She wasted no time getting back to her training, determined to make at least a showing at the trials. To Joan's surprise, she completed the first 20 miles (32 km) without difficulty, pulling ahead of many of her competitors. In what is still one of the most remarkable individual athletic achievements ever, Joan crossed the finish line first, posting a time of 2:31:41.

On the morning of August 5, Joan stood at the starting line as a competitor in the Olympic women's marathon. She took the lead after 3 miles (5 km) and never relinquished it. At 13 miles (21 km), she held a 90-second lead over her nearest competitor. As Joan neared the Los Angeles Coliseum where the marathon ended, she entered a tunnel. Alone in the tunnel and aware that she was going to win the gold medal, Joan told herself that her life would never be the same after that moment. She emerged to a cheering "home-team" crowd, and won the marathon in 2:24:52.

Shortly after her Olympic triumph, Joan married her college boyfriend, Scott Samuelson. In 1985, she achieved a record-breaking victory in America's Marathon in Chicago, Illinois, posting the second-fastest time ever run—a record that still stands. Joan continued to run after her Chicago victory, although less frequently. She competed in the 1987 Boston Marathon while three months pregnant with daughter Abby, her first child. Her second child, Anders, was born two years later. Declaring that she divides her running career into "B.C." (before children) and "A.D." (after diapers), Joan stayed home during the 1988 Olympics to spend time with her children. A back injury sidelined her for the 1992 Games. However, by 1996, Joan was ready to shoot for the gold again, but she finished 13th in the trials and did not make the U.S. team.

Today, Joan Benoit Samuelson still runs in master's competitions for athletes over 40. She is also involved in charity fund-raising and public speaking.

Having published her autobiography, *Running Tide,* in 1987, she completed a second book, *Running for Women,* in 1995. At home, she's still just mom, however. She likes to tell the story of how her daughter came home from school during the 1994 Winter Games and asked her mother whether she knew any Olympians. Joan may carpool the kids to soccer practice today, but the Olympic gold medalist's 20-year career has secured her place in sports history.

Nancy Lieberman-Cline

1958_
Basketball

"What I think would be the coolest thing for me is when this kid is working on his game and one day someone says, 'Hey, nice shot. Who taught you that?' And he says, 'My mom.'"
—Nancy Lieberman-Cline, referring to her son, Timothy

Coach and general manager Nancy Lieberman-Cline headed for the locker room. Her team, the Detroit Shock, had just beaten the New York Liberty 82–68 in the last game of their 1998 debut season, and the 16,246 hometown fans at the Palace were still cheering. Nancy's biggest fan, her four-year-old son T. J., met her in the tunnel to give her a congratulatory hug and kiss.

It had been a year that exceeded Nancy's expectations, but she was already thinking in "what ifs"—what if the Shock, who finished the season with a winning record of 17–13, had won just one more game? Ever the competitor, she was already thinking about the following season.

As a young girl living in Far Rockaway, New York, Nancy played just about every sport, starting with tackle-football games with the neighborhood boys. Born on July 1, 1958, in Brooklyn, New York, Nancy became involved in athletics as a way of asserting her individuality and escaping the pain of a broken home. Her father had left the family, and finally divorced Nancy's mother, Renee, when Nancy was 12. While her older brother, Cliff, was an A student who had set his sights on becoming a doctor, Nancy dedicated herself to honing her athletic skills.

Renee strongly disapproved of her daughter's preoccupation with sports. Mother and daughter often had heated arguments in which Renee would plead with Nancy to stop acting "like a tomboy." But her mother's displeasure only made Nancy more rebellious—and more determined.

Basketball became her deepest passion. She shot hoops in pickup games played on neighborhood courts, where she acquired the mental and physical toughness required to be a successful competitive player. At just 5 feet 10 inches (178 cm) tall, Nancy's jumping ability was one of her assets. Patterning herself after Walt Frazier and Willis Reed, Nancy practiced her jumps for hours, slapping the wall over and over, determined that each leap would exceed the last.

Nancy's high school basketball team made it all the way to city finals in her sophomore year. When she was a junior, her skills drew the attention of LaVozier LaMar, the coach of the New York Chuckles, an Amateur Athletic Union (AAU) boys' team in Harlem. LaMar invited Nancy to play for the

Chuckles. Though she was a white female traveling into a gritty, predominantly black neighborhood, she had no qualms about playing with and against the neighborhood kids. Nancy's gutsy, aggressive playing style earned her the nickname "Fire," and her color-blindness quickly won the respect of her teammates and opponents. Said Nancy, "I was a redheaded, white Jewish tomboy. How could you expect me to understand prejudice?"

Nancy had already begun winning trophies and MVP awards, seemingly without effort, by the time she was 14. In 1973, at 15, Nancy was one of 40 women selected to join the training squad of the U.S. women's basketball team. Although she sustained fractured ribs and an enlarged spleen when she was elbowed by another player, she had made a name for herself as one of the best female basketball players in America.

The following year, Nancy made the squad of the USA team for the Pan-American Games, held in Mexico City. In 1976, playing for the USA team in the first-ever women's basketball tournament in the Olympics, Nancy and her teammates—including future Hall-of-Famer Ann Meyers—took home silver medals. Nancy herself became the youngest basketball player in Olympic history, male or female, to win a medal.

At Old Dominion University in Norfolk, Virginia, Nancy Lieberman led the Lady Monarchs to 125 wins and two AIAW (Association of Intercollegiate Athletics for Women) national championships. She was a three-time all-American, won the Broderick Cup for America's top female athlete, and received the Wade Trophy for Collegiate Player of the Year in 1979 and 1980—the only player to win the award twice. In her four years at Old Dominion, she scored 2,430 points, averaging slightly more than 18 points per game, and compiled a school record of 512 steals.

Nancy's next goal was to lead the USA women's Olympic team to a gold medal at the 1980 games in Moscow. But after the Soviets invaded Afghanistan, several countries, including the United States, boycotted the Games in protest.

Rather than play basketball abroad in the European leagues, as many of her colleagues had done, Nancy searched for opportunities in the United States. Fortunately for her, the professional Women's Basketball League (WBL), which was established in 1980, recruited her and "Lady Magic," as Nancy came to be called, led her team to the playoffs. Unfortunately, the WBL quickly folded due to lack of support.

For a while, Nancy became a conditioning coach for tennis star Martina Navratilova, and she has since been credited with turning around Martina's lagging career. But the lure of basketball was strong, and she returned to the game in 1984, signing on with the Dallas Diamonds in the Women's American Basketball League for an unprecedented $60,000 a year. Two years later, in 1986, the United States Basketball League drafted Nancy to play with the all-male Springfield Fame. In her debut game, she came off the bench with four minutes left in the first quarter, scoring 4 points and landing a steal. Though other women, including Ann Meyers, had tried out with NBA teams, none had ever played regularly in a men's pro league. Nancy had achieved another first.

Over the next few years, Nancy played briefly with the Washington Generals, the team that plays against the show-business Harlem Globetrotters. But when the 34-year-old tried out for the 1992 women's Olympic team, several younger players got the nod instead. Turning her attention away from playing but not away from basketball, she formed a sports marketing firm called Events Marketing, Inc. She also launched a broadcasting career as a color analyst for several networks, including ESPN.

When the WNBA, a new women's professional league, was launched in 1997, Nancy came out of retirement to play one season for the Phoenix Mercury. In 1998, she was named general manager and head coach of the newly franchised Detroit Shock.

Aside from handling administrative and coaching responsibilities, Nancy also juggles the roles of wife and mother. She married former teammate Tim

Cline in 1988, and in 1994 she gave birth to a son, Timothy Joseph Cline. A recent member of the Women's Basketball Hall of Fame, Nancy joined other greats, including Ann Meyers-Drysdale, Cheryl Miller, and Pat Head Summitt.

Coming off a winning record in her first year leading the Shock, Nancy Lieberman-Cline has even higher goals and expectations for the upcoming season. Perhaps a WNBA Championship will be the crowning achievement of her remarkable career.

Florence Griffith Joyner

1959–1998
Track and Field

"What exactly is a role model? Is it someone that is trying to set positive examples for kids? Then that's what I'm trying to do. I'm very happy to have that title."
—Florence Griffith Joyner

When Florence Griffith Joyner stepped on the track for the 100-meter dash at the July 1988 Olympic trials in Indianapolis, she turned more than a few heads. At 5 feet 8 inches (cm) tall and weighing 130 pounds (59 kg), Florence was stunning to begin with. But her flowing black hair and six-inch (15-cm) polished fingernails made "FloJo" seem more like a fashion model than a champion sprinter. On this day, her track clothes suited her style—the first of many costumes she wore was a bright green bodysuit with only the left leg bare to the hip. (Florence, who called this outfit the "one-legger," declared that it had occurred by accident earlier in the year, when one leg of her suit caught on the spikes of her running shoes and she tore it off.) Before the day was over, however, Florence Griffith Joyner would prove her flash in a far more important way—she became the fastest woman sprinter in history.

Born to Robert and Florence Griffith on December 21, 1959, in Los Angeles, California, Florence Delorez Griffith was the seventh of 11 children. Her mother had traveled to California from North Carolina hoping to establish a career in modeling, but ended up marrying Robert, an airline electronics engineer. When Flo was just five years old, her mother left Robert and moved with her children to the tough Watts section of south central Los Angeles, where she took a job as a seamstress.

Determined to keep her children in line despite their poverty and lack of a father figure, the single mother did not allow her children to watch television during the week, and insisted they be home and in bed by 10:00 p.m., even when they were in high school. Flo and her siblings listened to their mother recite daily from the Bible, and they all went to church on Sundays. What Florence lacked in monetary wealth, she made up for by giving her children the richness of a supportive and loving home.

As part of a large family, Flo discovered ways to express her individuality early on. She experimented with hairstyles—once braiding her hair straight up from her head. She also kept a journal, read poetry, and liked unusual pets—instead of adopting a puppy or kitten, Flo once brought home a boa constrictor!

Flo was only about seven when she began competing in races at the Sugar Ray Robinson Youth Foundation. She often joked that she developed her speed by chasing after jackrabbits in the Mojave Desert when she visited her father. By the time Florence entered Jordan High School, she was a star athlete. In 1973 and 1974, she won the annual Jesse Owens National Youth Games, and as the anchor of her high school's 440-yard relay, she won the race with the fastest time in the country. By the time she graduated from Jordan High, she had several of the school's track records in sprint and long jump competitions.

Setting her sights on a business degree, Florence enrolled at California State University in the fall of 1978. In her freshman year, she joined the track team and competed in the 200- and 400-meter races. But though her grades were good and her track skills were superb, Florence had to drop out when she ran out of money. Fortunately, Cal State sprint coach Bobby Kersee helped her find financial aid and continue to attend college. (Bobby Kersee would become her brother-in-law when he married Jackie Joyner, the sister of Flo's husband.)

In 1980, Kersee became the track coach at the University of California at Los Angeles, and Flo transferred so that she could work with him. She missed qualifying for the 1980 Olympics in Moscow but, in any case, the United States boycotted those Games to protest the Soviet invasion of Afghanistan.

Flo had better luck in 1982 at the NCAA Championships, where she won the 200-meter race in 22:39 seconds. At the championships the following year, she won the 400-meters. In her first Olympics in Los Angeles in 1984, Flo took the silver medal in the 200-meter race, missing a world record by only 1/100th of a second—but she missed out on the team gold in the women's relays. Judges had ruled her long fingernails a hazard to the other competitors.

After the Olympics, Flo got a job as a hairdresser. She grew lax with her fitness regimen and was no longer in competitive shape when she met Al Joyner, the 1984 Olympic gold medal winner of the triple jump. After the two began to date, Al convinced Flo to return to training. She began running competitively again in 1986, and the following year she took second place in the 200-meter race at the world championships in Rome. That October, Florence Griffith and Al Joyner were married.

From that point, "FloJo," as she became known, embarked on an intensive training schedule to prepare for the 1988 Olympics. Her daily workout in-cluded a 3 1/2-mile

FloJo wins the 100-meter dash at the 1988 Olympics in Seoul, South Korea.

(5.6-km) run with Al each morning, weight training that focused on her legs, and 1,000 sit-ups each evening. By the time of the Olympic trials, FloJo was in top physical and mental shape.

Sporting fingernails decorated with red, white, and blue decals and gold Olympic rings, FloJo streaked through the 100-meter dash, setting a world record of 10:49 seconds that has yet to be broken. (She would set an American record in the 200-meter dash during the same trials.) At the 1988 Games in Seoul, South Korea, FloJo sprinted to victory in both the 100- and 200-meter races and captured a third gold as part of the 4 x 100-meter relay team. In the 4 x 400-meter race, she and her teammates won the silver, coming in just behind the Soviet team. Her Olympic conquests earned FloJo the Jesse Owens Award and the 1988 Sullivan Award (awarded annually to the top U.S. amateur athlete). She was also named Athlete of the Year by the Associated Press.

Florence Griffith Joyner's stunning victories at the Seoul Olympics were somewhat overshadowed by an allegation that she had used illegal performance-enhancing drugs—a charge she vehemently denied, pointing out that she had passed every drug test administered to competing athletes. Even after the 29-year-old retired from competition following the 1988 Games, the controversy continued to plague her.

FloJo's busy post-Olympic career included writing children's books and designing uniforms for the Indiana Pacers. She also served as co-chair of the President's Council on Physical Fitness and did a stint as a fitness columnist for *USA Today*. In 1991, FloJo gave birth to a daughter, Mary Ruth. She was inducted into the U.S. Track and Field Hall of Fame in 1995, and although she tried to make a comeback in time for the 1996 Olympics, an old injury of her Achilles' tendon kept her sidelined.

In 1996, FloJo suffered what she called "seizurelike symptoms" while flying to St. Louis, Missouri, with her family, and she was briefly hospitalized. On the morning of September 21, 1998, the Orange County sheriff's office received an emergency call from FloJo's husband, Al. He told them that his wife was unresponsive and not breathing. The world-record athlete had apparently passed away in her sleep. An autopsy revealed that FloJo had a congenital brain disorder that had caused her seizures. Tragically, it was only after the autopsy that the persistent allegations of steroid abuse were finally put to rest.

After her death, President Bill Clinton said of Florence Griffith Joyner, "We were dazzled by her speed, humbled by her talent, and captivated by her style. Though she rose to the pinnacle of the world of sports, she never forgot where she came from, devoting time and resources to helping children—especially those growing up in our most devastated neighborhoods—make the most of their own talents."

Nadia Comaneci

1961–
Gymnastics

"On the uneven bars, she whirls as easily as a sparrow fluttering from limb to limb on a tree; on the balance beam, clings to it as surely as a squirrel would; on the vault, lands as softly as a sea gull on the beach. . . ."
—*New York Times* columnist Dave Anderson describing Nadia's gymnastics style

Almost lost in the excitement over Nadia Comaneci's spectacular string of seven perfect scores in the 1976 Summer

Olympic Games was the fact that Nadia was also the first Romanian in history to win an Olympic gold medal in gymnastics. She awed the crowds who had come to watch the women's competition by performing a flawless routine on the uneven bars—so flawless that the scoreboard could not register the first perfect 10.0 score ever awarded in an Olympic gymnastics event. The board first flashed 0.00, until a "1" was manually placed in front of it. This graceful, 86-pound (39-kg) 14-year-old had stunned the gymnastics world and made history.

Born behind the Iron Curtain in the small town of Onesti, Romania, on November 12, 1961, Nadia lived a very different kind of life from her Western gymnastics counterparts. Romania was one of the Soviet Union's satellite states and followed its rigid Communist ideals. Many of the people of Romania and other Soviet bloc countries such as Czechoslovakia, Hungary, Lithuania, and Yugoslavia were poor and lived under meager circumstances. As a child, however, Nadia was hardly aware of the oppressive conditions that gripped her homeland. She was a typical carefree youngster who enjoyed running, jumping, and playing with her friends.

When Nadia was six years old, she was spotted at her kindergarten playground by Romanian national gymnastics coach Bela Karolyi. Bela and his wife Martha had been scouting many schools in search of six- and seven-year-olds to include in a gymnastics team. Bela approached Nadia and asked if she would like to come to his school to learn gymnastics. With her parents' permission, Nadia joined several other young girls at the Karolyi school.

Nadia's parents did not have to shoulder the tremendous financial burden that their daughter's athletic training would cost in the West, however. As a prospective national gymnast, all of Nadia's needs, including coaching, room and board, costumes, and travel expenses were paid for by the Romanian government. Bela was immediately impressed with his new student. Nadia demonstrated mental toughness, fierce determination, and a maturity beyond her years. She was fearless on the various apparatus, eager to experiment with new moves, twists and turns, and daring dismounts. One of her dismounts, a twisting back-somersault from the uneven bars, was named the "Salto Comaneci" after her.

The Karolyis enjoyed great success with their new gymnastics team. Women's gymnastics, once dominated by the Soviet Union and its satellites, was gaining strength in other countries. Nadia was only nine years old when, in 1970, she won her first Romanian national junior championship. She would own the title for an incredible five years before moving up to senior level international competitions. By 1975, Nadia was well known throughout the gymnastics world for her daring acrobatic feats and amazing athletic skills.

At the European championships, 13-year-old Nadia shocked spectators and competitors by walking away with the gold medal in the all-around competition. She would win the title again in the next two years, the only woman gymnast ever to do so. By the end of the 1975 European Championships, Nadia won three more gold medals—for the vault, uneven parallel bars, and balance beam. She finished second in the floor exercise, earning a silver medal.

In 1976, during the American Cup competition at New York City's Madison Square Garden, Nadia made her first appearance in front of an American audience—and won. After joining the men's winner, American Bart Conner, on the podium, Nadia was encouraged to give Conner a kiss on the cheek for photographers. The two teenagers little realized that their paths would cross years later in a much different way.

When the Romanian team arrived at the Olympics in Montreal in the summer of 1976, three Soviet women gymnasts—Olga Korbut, Nelli Kim, and defending champ Lyudmila Tourischeva—were favored to win the all-around gold medal. But 4-foot 11-inch (150 cm) Nadia had other plans. She upset defending champion Tourischeva, and Nadia's performances over the course of the women's competition astonished everyone and landed her in the Olympic history books. Nadia took home three gold medals, a bronze, and a team silver. She earned an unprecedented seven perfect 10s, and her 79.275 accumulated average score was the highest ever achieved in Olympic overall competition.

Nadia and her teammates were welcomed back to Romania at the airport in Bucharest by crowds of her very proud countrymen. Nadia was named a Hero of Socialist Labor and received a gold medal. Shortly after returning from Montreal, Nadia and most of her teammates moved to Bucharest. This began an unhappy period in Nadia's life. Though she successfully defended her European gymnastics title in 1977, her parents had decided to divorce that same year. And, since Bela Karolyi had stayed in Onesti, Nadia was assigned new coaches. By year's end, a depressed and unmotivated Nadia had gained 40 pounds (18 kg) and was no longer in shape to compete. She sought out her old coach, and with his help she was ready to compete in two important international events that year. The Romanian team made a good showing, coming in second place at the Worlds, and Nadia performed well at the European championships in Copenhagen, winning three gold medals, including one for the all-around competition.

Once more under pressure, Nadia returned to Bucharest to train younger gymnastic hopefuls. Eventually, however, she teamed up with Karolyi again, hoping for one more Olympics appearance at the 1980 Moscow Games. Although several Western countries, including the United States, boycotted those Games to protest the Soviet Union's invasion of Afghanistan, Nadia did not disappoint the crowds who did attend. She won two more gold and two more silver medals—her last Olympic medals.

At age 19, Nadia announced her retirement from competitive gymnastics. Fearful that Nadia might try to defect, the Romanian government restricted her travel and assigned her once more to coach state-subsidized gymnastics. Rumors developed that Nadia was involved with Nicu Ceausescu, the son of

Romanian dictator Nicholai. Unable to bear the attention and the restrictions placed on her, Nadia began planning to defect. With the help of Constantin Panait, a Romanian roofer living in the United States, Nadia traveled one night on foot with six other defectors into Hungary, where Panait met her. The next day, Nadia escaped to Austria where she was given asylum at the U.S. Embassy. On November 28, 1989, Nadia Comaneci stepped onto U.S. soil at JFK Airport in New York.

Today, Nadia focuses on coaching and fund-raising.

Shortly after her arrival in the United States, Nadia became reacquainted with gymnast Bart Conner. The two became close friends and began performing together in 1990. The friendship blossomed into romance, and on Nadia's 33rd birthday, Bart proposed to her. After Nicholai Ceausescu was overthrown, Nadia returned to her native country with her fiancé. The two were married in a civil ceremony on August 26, 1996, and participated in a religious ceremony the following day in the Casin Orthodox monastery in Bucharest.

Today, Nadia and Bart run a gymnastics school in Norman, Oklahoma. The two still perform together in exhibitions and are actively involved in charitable fund-raising events. Most recently, Nadia joined sports greats Chris Evert, Nancy Lopez, and Jackie Joyner-Kersee when she became the 1998 recipient of the Flo Hyman Award, "presented to the athlete who exemplifies the same dignity, spirit, and commitment to excellence as the late Flo Hyman, captain of the 1984 U.S. Olympic volleyball team."

Jackie Joyner-Kersee

1962–

Track and Field

"Someday this girl will be the first lady of something."
— Jackie Joyner's grandmother's explanation for naming her after Jacqueline Kennedy

Like the great Babe Didrikson, Jackie Joyner-Kersee demonstrated her exceptional multievent capabilities on the track oval. Her specialty, the heptathlon, is a grueling two-day, seven-event competition that tests the player's all-around athletic ability. Each event is scored individually, and the points are cumulative. At the end of the competition, the person with the highest overall point total wins the heptathlon. On the first day, four events are run: the 100-meter hurdles, the high jump, the shot put, and the 200-meter dash. Day two consists of the long jump, the javelin throw, and the 800-meter race. Jackie may not have participated in as many different sports as Babe, but her extraordinary athletic accomplishments have been among the best of the century.

In the midst of the drug- and crime-infested streets of East St. Louis, Illinois, Jacqueline Joyner was born on March 3, 1962. Her parents, Alfred and Mary, still in their early teens, married before Mary gave birth to their first child, Alfred Erick. Two more daughters, Angela and Debra were born shortly after Jackie.

East St. Louis had fallen on hard times before Jackie was born. Unemployment was high, and without even a high school diploma, it was hard for her father to find work. The family lived in a tiny wooden house, where the kitchen stove served as the only source of heat. There was little or no food, and clothing and shoes were in short supply.

Mary and Alfred were strict, hardworking parents, and they instilled in their children the importance of getting a good education and staying out of trouble. Fortunately there was a place for the kids to go—the Mary E. Brown Community Center was right around the corner from the Joyner home. There Jackie and her brother Al first developed their athletic talents.

Jackie loved the center and she and Al took advantage of the recreational activities offered there. Al initially gravitated toward swimming and diving, but later acquired his sister's enthusiasm for track and field. Jackie also participated in other sports like basketball and volleyball. They both began working with the center's coach, Nino Fennoy, a former member of the Lincoln High School track team.

Jackie, now a lanky 10 year old, had just the right physique for track and field but it was her warm personality that captured Fennoy's attention. Jackie had a radiant smile, and it was obvious that she derived great pleasure from just being at the center. Fennoy had Jackie working on the 400-meter run, but she also had her eye on another event—the long jump. Often, Jackie had to sit around and wait for Coach Fennoy to finish with his long jump athletes. One day when one of the girls was late for practice, Jackie just got up, ran down the runway, leaped into the air, and landed in the sand pit having jumped 17 feet (5.1 m). Jackie had jumped as far as a high school athlete.

Fennoy saw that Jackie was naturally gifted and could apply her skills to various events. He decided to introduce her to the pentathlon, an individual competition consisting of five separate events: the 800-meter race, shot put, long jump, high jump, and hurdles. It was in the pentathlon that Jackie was able to capitalize on her running and jumping abilities.

She won her first National Junior Olympics Pentathlon championship when she was 14. She won the next three years as well, establishing herself as a consistent, talented competitor. She continued her track and field training with Coach Fennoy when she entered Lincoln High School in 1977. Jackie also won a spot on the basketball and volleyball teams, and in her senior year led the Lincoln girls to the state basketball championship.

Jackie graduated from Lincoln High in the top 10 percent of her class. She accepted a basketball scholarship from the University of California at Los Angeles (UCLA), but convinced UCLA basketball coach Billie Moore to let her go out for track and field too. The competition was a lot tougher than it had been at Lincoln High, and Jackie suddenly found herself just one of the crowd on the track. Far from discouraged, Jackie went out on the track and simply practiced the long jump by herself. And her hard work did not go unnoticed.

Bob Kersee had come to UCLA in 1980 as the new assistant track coach of the college's women sprinters and hurdlers. He convinced Jackie and the UCLA athletic department brass that her future was not in basketball, but in track and field, and the two began working together. Bobby started training Jackie in the multievent heptathlon. It would be introduced as an Olympic event at the 1984 Games in Los Angeles, and Jackie wanted to be there.

The beginning of 1981 should have been exciting for Jackie. Unfortunately, it began tragically, when her beloved mother Mary died suddenly of meningitis. Jackie was devastated, but kept her emotions tucked away when she returned to school. Comfort came from an unexpected place—Bobby Kersee. As Jackie threw her energies into mastering the heptathlon events, Bobby was there to guide and comfort her.

Though she picked up the events quickly, Jackie began suffering from shortness of breath, dizziness, and fatigue. Incredibly, she was suffering from exercise-induced asthma, but even that could not hold her back. Less than a year after taking up the heptathlon, Jackie won the NCAA championship with a record-setting 6,099 points. She also secured her place as the best heptathlete in America when she won the USA national championship.

By her junior year, Jackie had earned more awards and honors than she could keep up with. She was named Most Valuable Player on her UCLA Bruins basketball team and the women's track team; she was named All-University Athlete in basketball and track for the second straight year; and she won her second Broderick Award as the nation's top collegiate athlete.

Jackie never lost sight of the ultimate goal—to make it to the 1984 Olympics. Her brother Al, a triple-jump star athlete at Arkansas State University, also had his mind set on the Olympics. And in true Joyner determination, they both made it. In her first Olympic heptathlon, Jackie won the silver medal. Brother Al won the gold in the triple jump, the first American to do so in 80 years. They were also the first brother and sister to win Olympic medals in track and field, and they did it on the same day!

Jackie, not content to settle for the silver medal, went to work to prepare for the 1988 Olympics in Seoul, South Korea. She ended her five-year career at UCLA, leaving with several records in track and basketball. The following summer, Jackie competed in the National Sports Festival (now called the Olympic Festival), winning all seven events of the heptathlon. Aside from her athletic success, things had been changing in her relationship with Bobby. Realizing that they were attracted to each other, they began dating that summer. On January 11, 1986, Bobby and Jackie were married.

What a year 1986 was for the Kersees. At the Goodwill Games in Moscow that July, Jackie smashed the world heptathlon record by finishing with 7,148 points, besting the old record by 202 points. It was the first time in over 50 years that an American held the world record in a multievent. A few weeks later, Jackie broke her own record by 10 points. In temperatures of 126° F (52° C) at the U.S. Sports Festival in Houston, Jackie accumulated 7,158 points, leaving sports journalists speechless.

For her phenomenal year, Jackie received the Jesse Owens Memorial Award given to the top track and field athlete; she was named Sportswoman of the Year by the U.S. Olympic Committee and became only the eighth woman in 67 years to win the prestigious Sullivan Award, beating out David Robinson and Heisman Trophy winner Vinny Testaverde.

In August of 1987, Jackie not only won the heptathlon at the Pan-American Games, but also tied the world long jump record of 24 feet 5 1/2 inches (7.45 m). With this achievement, Jackie Joyner-Kersee became the only American woman ever to hold world records in a multievent and a single event simultaneously. Later at the world championships in Rome, Jackie won gold medals in both the heptathlon and the long jump, becoming the first to capture golds in multi and single events at the Worlds. She was named AP Female Athlete of the Year, and received her second Jesse Owens Award.

The 1988 Seoul Olympics was the Summer Games of the Joyner-Kersee family. Al had married fellow track star Florence Griffith, and along with Jackie she had made the U.S. Olympic team. What unfolded during the competitions

Jackie clears the high jump, the second event in the heptathlon at the 1990 Goodwill Games in Seattle.

on the Olympic Oval can only be described as unbelievable. Florence set a new world record in the 100-meter dash, earning the title "the Fastest Woman in the World," and came away with three gold medals. For Jackie, it was just another day (or two) at the track. She won the gold medal in the heptathlon, setting another new world record of 7,291 points. In the long jump competition, she not only won the gold, but set a new Olympic record with a jump of 24 feet 3 1/2 inches (7 m).

Jackie continued to dominate the heptathlon for the next several years. At the 1992 Goodwill Games, she again won gold medals in the heptathlon and the long jump. Later that summer at the Olympics in Barcelona, Spain, she took the gold in the heptathlon and a bronze in the long jump. At the conclusion of the games, 1976 Olympic decathlon champion Bruce Jenner called Jackie "the greatest multievent athlete ever, man or woman."

Wanting to end her Olympic career in America on the same soil where it began, Jackie decided to try to make the Summer Games one last time. At age 34, competitions had worn down her body and she was plagued with injuries. She also continued to struggle to control her asthma. She made it to Atlanta anyway, perhaps on sheer desire alone. Unfortunately, after completing the first event of the heptathlon, Jackie pulled a hamstring muscle and had to withdraw. Having the heart of a champion, she tried to compete in the long jump. In sixth place with one jump to go, Jackie stood at the start line, her leg heavily taped. Letting it all go, she raced down the runway, went airborne, and nailed a 22 foot 11 inch (6.9 m) jump. It was good enough to win the bronze medal. With six Olympic medals in all, Jackie Joyner-Kersee is the winningest American female track and field Olympian.

Injuries and age are athlete's enemies. In 1998, Jackie decided it was time to retire from track and field competition. But even in the final "lap" of her incredible career, she had some records to set. On July 23, she won her fourth consecutive heptathlon gold medal at the Goodwill Games. Three days later, she competed in her final competition. Billed as "Track and Field's Farewell to Jackie Joyner-Kersee," the event was held in Edwardsville, Illinois, just 20 miles (32 km) from where she grew up. There were no miracles this night—Jackie finished sixth in the long jump. The world's greatest female athlete had stopped running and jumping for the first time in her 18-year career. Through tears, Jackie thanked the 9,000-plus crowd for their support. Fittingly, among the crowd were 3,000 kids from poverty-plagued East St. Louis.

There is plenty to keep Jackie busy in her retirement. So far more than $7 million has been raised to build a new community center where the Mary E. Brown Center once stood. Aside from all the records, trophies, and medals, Jackie Joyner-Kersee leaves track and field with another kind of honor—her own. Her grace, integrity, sportsmanship, and concern for those less fortunate are just as beautiful a legacy as her athletic achievements.

Paula Newby-Fraser

1962–
Triathlon

"I became involved in the sport and stayed involved because it is a lifestyle—a lifestyle of health, fun, and fitness."
—Paula Newby-Fraser on the benefits of being a triathlete

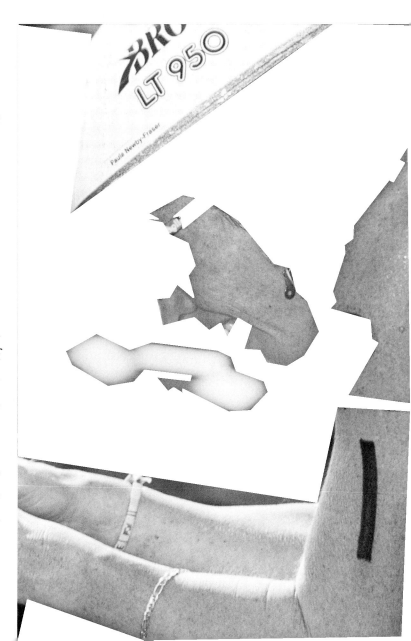

The very name "Ironman Triathlon" evokes an image of the ultimate challenge in athletic endurance, and certainly not a competition for the weak, frail, or delicate of mind and body. The grueling three-part race with no breaks tests the mettle of the very best—a 2.4-mile (4-

km) swim, followed by a bike race covering 112 miles (180 km), and finishing off with a 26-mile (42 km) marathon run. Whoever crosses the finish line first, wins.

For some, just finishing the race is reward enough. The word *Ironman* might suggest that this competition is for only the strongest, fittest male athletes. That was true at a time when women were restricted from participation in events like the Boston Marathon, or in track and field races longer than 400 meters at the Olympics. Today, there are no such barriers. As a result, one of the world's best Ironman triathletes in the world is a woman.

Paula Newby-Fraser was born in Harare, Zimbabwe, on June 2, 1962, and raised in Durban, South Africa. The youngest of two children, Paula grew up in affluent surroundings. Her father's industrial paint manufacturing plant was the second largest of its kind in the country. As a youngster Paula was a good student and enjoyed many activities, especially those that allowed her to excel as an individual, such as ballet and swimming. By the time she reached her teens, Paula was a nationally ranked swimmer, and was offered a college swimming scholarship. As a talented ballet dancer, she could have also opted to join a local dance company. Feeling athletic burnout, Paula dropped out of sports altogether. Instead she attended the University of Natal, spending most of her time just "hanging out"—sunbathing at the beach and partying with her friends.

Despite her easygoing attitude, Paula graduated from college in 1984, and went to work at an office. Paula had put on some weight from all her partying, so she began working out at a local gym and jogging with her boyfriend. Bitten by the training bug once more, Paula added aerobics and weight lifting to her workout routine.

Toward the end of that year, Paula, her boyfriend, and several friends happened to watch a qualifying race for the Ironman Triathlon World Championships. The winners would earn a free trip to Hawaii to compete in the championship final. On a whim, Paula's boyfriend suggested that they train and enter one of the qualifying races. The next day they bought bikes and began a daily routine of running and riding. Just eight weeks later, Paula took her first plunge into triathlon competition, finishing first in course-record time among the women, and tenth overall.

Having earned her trip to Hawaii, Paula came in third in the women's division, quite a feat for her debut in this world-class event. Paula felt that competition was a turning point for her because she finished only a few minutes behind women who had been training and competing much longer than she had. With her family's blessing, and only $1500 in her pocket, Paula moved to southern California—triathlon country—where she trained more rigorously than ever.

Paula entered several triathlon events in her first year in America, and won more than $25,000 in prize money. She began training with fellow triathlete Paul Huddle to prepare for the 1986 Hawaii Ironman Triathlon. Paul's help paid big dividends—Paula came in second behind Patricia Puntous of Canada. Officials later disqualified Patricia after they realized she had drafted during the bike racing segment of the competition. (Drafting is riding behind someone to take advantage of the reduced air pressure.) Paula was then declared the winner and collected the $17,000 first prize. Endorsement contracts and corporate sponsorships soon followed.

In 1987, Paula finished third in both the Hawaiian Ironman and the Ironman World Championships. Unflapped by coming in third, Paula went back to her grueling training program, working through strenuous periods off and on throughout a ten-hour day. In 1988 she captured the second of eight Ironman Triathlon World Championships. Her eleventh-place finish *overall* at the 1988 Worlds in a time of 9:01:01 stunned the endurance community. It was no fluke. The next year, Paula missed breaking the nine hour barrier by just 56 seconds.

Paula Newby-Fraser crosses the finish line at her Hawaii Ironman 1991 first-place victory.

The most incredible year in Paula's triathlete career was 1992. She won her fourth Nice International Triathlon, her fourth Ironman Japan, and her first Ironman European Championship, setting a new Ironman world record of 8:55:00. But the most coveted win came in Hawaii. Not only did Paula win her fifth Ironman title, she did it in 8:55:24, a record that remains unbroken.

Though a stress fracture in her ankle forced Paula to sit out most of the 1993 season, she continued to stay in shape. In August the doctors gave her a clean bill of health and she went right back to training for the Ironman Hawaii, just eight weeks away. Most of the triathlete women had written Paula off as a serious contender, but they shouldn't have. Erin Baker, a chief rival of Paula's, as much as announced that she would beat the five-time champion. Paula's answer was to turn in the second-best performance of her career, finishing the race in 8:58:00, three minutes off her 1992 world-record time.

In a career that has spanned two decades, Paula has won an unprecedented 21 Ironman Triathlons. That's more than twice as many as her nearest triathlete rivals—Mark Allen and Erin Baker (8) and Dave Scott (7). Paula's domination in the sport has brought her much attention and many awards. In 1989, both the *Los Angeles Times* and ABC's *Wide World of Sports* dubbed Paula "The Greatest All-Around Female Athlete in the World." A year later, though up against such finalists as Steffi Graf and Beth Daniel, Paula was named the Professional Sportswoman of the Year by the Women's Sports Foundation. It is the most prestigious international award presented to female athletes each year.

At the Hawaii Ironman in 1995, Paula announced that it would be her last appearance. The race took its toll on Paula, who was severely dehydrated and exhausted as she headed down the stretch to the finish line. She collapsed 200 feet (60 m) short, and stayed down for more than 20 minutes. Finally, Paula picked herself up and staggered across the finish line, winding up in fourth place. And though the Ironman Triathlon made its debut at the 1996 Olympic Games in Atlanta, Paula did not compete. Though she has wound down her racing career, Paula Newby-Fraser will forever remain one of the greatest triathletes the sport has ever seen.

Tracy Caulkins

1963–
Swimming

"I know a lot of people think it's monotonous down the black lines over and over, but it's not monotonous if you're enjoying what you're doing with forty others who are enjoying it."
—Tracy Caulkins on competitive swimming

When the Soviet Union invaded Afghanistan in late December 1979, it hoped to prevent the Communist government in place there from being toppled. U.S. president Jimmy

Carter threatened to order the U.S. Olympic team to boycott the upcoming Summer Games being hosted by Moscow, unless the Russians withdrew their troops. The Russians refused, so at the opening ceremonies of the Summer Olympics on July 19, 1980, several countries were noticeably absent, including Japan, West Germany, Canada, the People's Republic of China, and the United States. For amateur athletes in their prime, like hurdler Renaldo Nehemiah, gymnast Kurt Thomas, basketball player Isiah Thomas, and swimming sensation Tracy Caulkins, it was devastating—a lost opportunity to compete for the prized gold medals they had trained so long and so hard to try to win.

From the time Tracy Caulkins first hit the water to keep up with her brother Tim and sister Amy at the local swim club, she was a natural. Well, almost. At first Tracy didn't like putting her face in the water, preferring to swim the backstroke. Soon, she was swimming every type of stroke and competing—and winning—meets in her age group.

Tracy was born on January 11, 1963, in Winona, Minnesota. However, she was raised in Nashville, Tennessee, where she attended private school at Harpeth Hall Academy. She began training in Nashville with Paul Bergen, who saw great potential in the young swimmer. By the time Tracy was 14 years old, she had already won several American championships including the 100- and 200-yard breaststroke as well as the 200- and 400-meter individual medley. According to Bergen, Tracy was comfortable with all four types of swimming strokes: freestyle, butterfly, breaststroke, and backstroke. This talent also made Tracy a great competitor in the individual medley, which requires all four strokes.

Tracy was fully prepared to make the necessary sacrifices to become a champion swimmer, rising before dawn to practice at the Vanderbilt University pool before heading off to school for a full day of classes. Before her day was over, Tracy had another two-hour practice session. Many nights she didn't get home until after 10 o'clock.

All her hard work and dedication paid off. When Tracy was just 15 years old, she won five gold medals and one silver at the world championships in West Berlin in 1978. Tracy was honored by being awarded the Sullivan Trophy as the year's top amateur athlete. She is also the youngest recipient in history. The following year, Tracy won two more gold medals and another silver at the Pan American Games, a competition that was supposed to be a warm-up for the 1980 Olympics in Moscow.

Expectations were high that Tracy might win as many as five gold medals at the Summer Games, but we will never know what she might have accomplished. The United States boycott of the Games ended any opportunity for Tracy and many other American athletes to compete. Though deeply disappointed, Tracy just kept focused, and continued to compete, looking ahead to the 1984 Olympics, which would be hosted by Los Angeles. It might even be more exciting to compete as a citizen of the host country.

In 1981, while waiting for her next chance to make it to the Olympics, Tracy enrolled at the University of Florida. In her four years there, Tracy's performances made her arguably the best swimmer in the country. She earned the Broderick Cup as the outstanding college female athlete of the year in 1983 and again in 1984.

The best year of Tracy's career came in 1984, when she set NCAA records in all four individual swim events, and helped her Florida team to win both the 400-meter and 800-meter relays with record-setting times. As a 21-year-old Olympic competitor, Tracy had already amassed quite a few records for the sports history books. She had set 59 American records and won 48 national titles, surpassing swimming legend Johnny Weismuller's 36-title record when she was 19. She is also the only swimmer of either gender to set American records in all four strokes.

To prepare for the Olympics, Tracy set up a rigorous training schedule, swimming at least five hours a day. She qualified at the U.S. Olympic Trials and went to Los Angeles a very determined competitor. Tracy turned in a spectacular performance, winning the 200- and 400-meter individual medleys. In her 200-meter race, she swam a 2:12.64, setting an Olympic record. She won a third gold medal as a member of the 400-meter relay team.

At the conclusion of the games, Tracy received an unexpected honor from the United States Olympic Committee. Recognizing not only her Olympic performance, but her other accomplishments in 1984, they named her Female Athlete of the Year. Though only 21, Tracy retired from swimming. In 1986, she was inducted into the Women's Sports Foundation's International Women's Sports Hall of Fame along with tennis great Margaret Court Smith and volleyball legend Flo Hyman. A final amateur athletic honor came in 1990, when Tracy was also inducted into the International Swimming Hall of Fame. At her alma mater, the University of Florida, Tracy's accomplishments live on. The university has established a double swimming scholarship in her name, as well as the Tracy Caulkins Award, given annually to Florida's best female swimmer.

Cynthia Cooper

1963–
Basketball

*"I'm living the dream. . . .
I never thought I would ever
play basketball at the level I
am playing at now, at home,
in front of family and friends."*
—Cynthia Cooper on playing in
the WNBA

In its debut season, the Women's National Basketball Association (WNBA) crowned its first championship team on August 30, 1997 at the Houston Summitt, in front of 16,285 hometown fans. Cynthia Cooper—the 5-foot 10-inch (178-cm), 150-pound

(68-kg) guard of the Houston Comets—stood on the court with the rest of her teammates celebrating their places in basketball history. Many of the players had waited years for the chance to play in an American women's professional basketball league. For Cynthia, at age 34, this moment was the stuff dreams are made of.

Though she was born in Chicago, Illinois, on April 14, 1963, Cynthia Cooper grew up in Watts, a rough inner-city neighborhood in Los Angeles, California. She was the fifth of eight children born to Everett Cooper and Mary Cobbs. When her parents divorced when Cynthia was six years old, Mary was suddenly burdened with the responsibility of supporting the family alone. Times were hard raising eight children, and Mary often worked two jobs to make ends meet. Through all the hardships, however, Mary's steely determination kept the family together.

As a youngster, Cynthia ran track, played volleyball, badminton, and softball. But it wasn't until she was about 15 years old that she discovered basketball. While a ninth grader at Locke High School, Cynthia saw a girl playing basketball in the gymnasium. She watched in utter fascination as the girl dribbled down the court, put the ball behind her back, and laid it up and into the basket. Cynthia thought that was "cool," and she wanted to learn how to do it.

A quick study, Cynthia became one of the best high school players in the state, averaging 45 points per game by the time she was a senior. Her talent and budding skills were strong enough to earn Cynthia an athletic scholarship to the University of Southern California. Led by teammate Cheryl Miller, Cynthia and the USC Trojans won back-to-back NCAA championships in 1983 and 1984. By the time she left USC in 1986, Cynthia had compiled some impressive career statistics, scoring 1,599 points, with 381 assists, and 256 steals.

Since there were no professional opportunities for women in basketball in America, Cynthia did what most American women did who wanted to continue to play—she moved to Europe, playing her first season for Segovia, in Spain. In 1987, she moved to Italy, where she played for the next ten years for

Parma (1987-1994, 1996-1997) and Alcamo (1994-1996).

While playing competitively in the European league, Cynthia earned a spot on the 1988 U.S. Women's basketball squad at the Olympic Games in Seoul, South Korea. Along with Teresa Edwards and Anne Donovan, two of the members of the winning team at the1984 Olympics, Cynthia Cooper won her first Olympic gold medal. On September 29, she presented the medal to her mom Mary on her birthday. At the 1992 Summer Olympic Games in Barcelona, Spain, Cynthia added a bronze medal to her ever-growing collection of awards and trophies.

The big break in her professional career came on January 22, 1997, when she was assigned to the Houston Comets, one of the eight teams comprising the new Women's National Basketball Association. It was actually Cynthia's good fortune that Texas Tech great Sheryl Swoopes wouldn't be able to start the season because she was pregnant. Cynthia was to make the most of her "dream come true" opportunity. Having established herself as a premiere player in Europe, she took the new American league by storm. In July of 1997, Cynthia was chosen WNBA Player of the Week two weeks in a row, after she set two WNBA single-game scoring records. On July 22 against Phoenix, she scored 32 points, and topped that performance two nights later when she scored 44 points against Sacramento.

In her first season with the Comets, Cynthia led the league in scoring, and ranked in the top ten in assists (4.7 per game), field goal percentage (.470), three-point field goal percentage (.414), free throw percentage (.864), steals (59), and minutes played per game (35.1). After winning the first WNBA championship against the New York Liberty, Cynthia was named the series Most Valuable Player (MVP). Earlier in the playoffs, Cynthia had also been awarded the league's MVP trophy. It was an especially heartfelt moment, as her mom was in the stands to watch, one of the first opportunities she'd had since being diagnosed with breast cancer in February.

The year 1998 was just as exciting for Cynthia Cooper and the Houston

Comets. They cruised through the regular season with a 27-3 record, and Cynthia was again honored as the WNBA's MVP. After losing the first game in the championship series final against the Phoenix Mercury, and winning "a must" game two in overtime to even the series, the Comets repeated as champions in 1998, winning game three 80-71 in front of a sold-out crowd at the Houston Compaq Center. Cynthia was awarded her second trophy as series MVP.

Cynthia's dream to play in America, and to excel in the sport she loves, has been fulfilled. But she has never lost sight of what's most important in life—helping family, friends, and those less fortuante. Since her mother was diagnosed with breast cancer, Cynthia has devoted much of her off-court time to speaking on behalf of organizations such as Concept: Cure, The Race for the Cure, and the Susan G. Komen Foundation to raise funds for research and to educate women about cancer. In 1998, Cynthia founded her own organization—Coop Hoops for Kids—which raises money to help inner-city children.

At home in the Houston suburb of Sugar Land, Cynthia is surrogate mother to seven nieces and nephews: Brenda is 18, and with her aunt's help is now a pre-med student at Texas Southern. She also cares for four of her sister Lisa's children: Tyrone, 12, Antonisha, 11, Anthony, 5, and Tyquon, 4. Cynthia has been taking care of Tyquon since he was 5 months old, and she is in the process of adopting him. Cynthia has two of her brother Kenneth's kids, Kenneth, 7, and Denecheo, 5.

Juggling so many schedules and extracurricular activities is a challenge, but Cynthia welcomes it. She says gangs and drugs have been at the root of her siblings' difficulties: Cynthia's brother Everett was killed in a gang-related incident while Cynthia was a high school student. Her tireless commitment and devotion to helping her family was firmly instilled in her by her own mother. Cynthia Cooper now wants others to have the chance to dream their dreams, set their own goals, and then realize those dreams, just as she has.

Shooting Stars: Women in Basketball Today

"I've been extremely lucky. . .I have a gift to play the game, and I didn't believe God would have given me one piece of the puzzle and not the other. Every time it appeared there was no more, I kept working and there was another opportunity. The WNBA continues that pattern."

—Lynette Woodard

"*We Got Next*" is street talk—a familiar phrase around the urban black-top courts of community and recreation centers. It means the speakers are next in line to play the winners of whatever basketball game is in progress. It announces their intention to play next—"It's our turn next; we've got the court next." At least that's what the phrase meant until 1997 when the Women's National Basketball Association (WNBA) adopted the slogan for its inaugural season. Women have been struggling for their rightful place in sports for centuries, and perhaps when the WNBA players embraced "We Got Next," it may have been their way of saying "Hey guys, we're here. We have a pro league too, and we intend to *play* basketball."

The WNBA, however, is not the first women's basketball league. The now-defunct American Basketball League (ABL) tipped off its inaugural game on

Ann Meyers holds up her Indiana Pacers jersey after signing a contract to play for the team in September 1979.

October 18, 1996. And even that was not the debut of a women's professional basketball league. The evolution of women's basketball in America has been slow, and partly because of the gradual development of women's sports in general. Prior to the passage of Title IX, there were no athletic college scholarships for women in any sport. In 1974, Ann Meyers became the first woman to receive such a scholarship from UCLA. Two years later, Nancy Lieberman became the second. Her scholarship came from Old Dominion. And both women led their college teams to championships.

Meyers and Lieberman were also pioneers in professional basketball. When these women were in the prime of their playing careers, there were only a few pro options, and those disappeared almost as quickly as they came. The Women's Basketball League managed only three seasons from 1978-1981; the Liberty Basketball Association folded after one exhibition game in 1991; and the Women's World Basketball Association, which came a year after the LBA, was gone after just three seasons. For other early college stars like Delta State University center Lusia Harris, Montclair State star Carol "the Blaze" Blazejowski, and USC Lady Trojan standout Cheryl Miller, the only real option was to play in the European leagues. Harris had actually been the first woman drafted by the NBA New Orleans (now Utah) Jazz in 1977, but she decided not to accept.

In 1996, Sheryl Swoopes led the U.S. team against Cuba at the Providence Civic Center, Rhode Island.

Meyers became the first woman to sign an NBA contract (with the Indiana Pacers), but was cut three days after training camp began. Lieberman actually played on three professional men's teams—the Springfield Fame and Long Island Knights of the U.S. Basketball League, and the Washington Generals, the team that travels with the famed Harlem Globetrotters.

Women's basketball didn't debut in the Olympics until 1976. Members of that silver medal-winning team included Harris, Lieberman, Meyers, and the University of Tennessee Lady Volunteers outstanding head coach Pat Summitt. The success of the Olympic team and the budding popularity and amateur athletic recognition of women's college basketball were helping to build the foundation for the stars on the horizon—the players of the 1990s.

Perhaps the greatest boost for women's basketball came in 1993 at the women's National Collegiate Athletic Association (NCAA) tournament. Once again lagging behind the NCAA men whose tournaments were enjoying tremendous fan and televison network support, the women's NCAA championship needed something big to draw attention to their play. It came from Sheryl Swoopes, a Texas Tech senior, whose 47 points helped defeat Ohio State for the NCAA title. Swoopes's 47 points was the highest amount in an NCAA championship game by any player, male or female. Still, after college, Sheryl wound up going to Europe to play in the Italian League. But the women were knocking at the door.

Women's basketball finally exploded in 1995. Again, its extraordinary popularity was fueled by the play of the women's NCAA. The University of Connecticut Lady Huskies dribbled, shot, and dunked their way through a fairy-tale undefeated 35-0 season, including the NCAA championship. They were led by the charismatic Rebecca Lobo, a 6-foot 4-inch (193-cm) center/forward, whose poise and exuberance on the court made her a popular topic for the media. She was able to juggle her game with her studies, while also providing Rock of Gibraltar support to her mother Ruthann Lobo, who was battling breast cancer.

By 1996, several NCAA teams were enjoying winning seasons and playing exciting basketball. At the University of Tennessee, a freshman was setting game statistics on fire. In front of 23,291 fans (the largest crowd ever at a women's NCAA final), Chamique Holdsclaw led the Lady Vols to their fourth championship. The following year, the Lady Vols repeated as champs and head coach Pat Summitt was swarmed by the media. With her fifth national championship, Summitt had coached more winning teams than any other coach, male or female, except the legendary UCLA men's coach John Wooden, who won ten. Holdsclaw, a sophomore, was selected as the Outstanding Player in the Final Four tournament.

The time for another go at launching a women's pro baseball league was almost ripe. The women put together their own "Dream Team" (fashioned after the 1992 U.S. Men's Olympic gold medal team where NBA superstars Magic Johnson, Michael Jordan, Karl Malone, and others showcased their pro talent) to compete in the 1996 Olympic Games in Atlanta, Georgia. The team was made up of 12 players including three-time Olympian Teresa Edwards, 1987 Coaches Player of the Year Katrina McClain, Auburn sensation Ruthie Bolton-Holifield, 1990 Wade Trophy recipient Jennifer Azzi, 1991 Wade

Trophy winner Dawn Staley, 6-foot 5-inch (195-cm) USC All-American and professional model Lisa Leslie, Texas Tech superstar Sheryl Swoopes, and UConn's standout Rebecca Lobo.

Led by Stanford head coach Tara VanDerveer, the USA women's Olympic basketball team embarked on a nine-month, 100,000-mile (161,000-km) world tour, playing teams both in America and around the world to prepare for the Atlanta Games. Given time to mesh as a unit, the USA women's team had the perfect mix—youth, experience, and a hunger for winning. At the end of the grueling tour—the women were away from home 240 days—they had compiled a record of 52 consecutive wins, and had attracted more than 160,000 fans in cities all around the United States. The "Dream Team" even garnered support from an unlikely source—the broadcast media, as ten of their games were televised live.

The 1996 Summer Games in Atlanta opened on July 19, 1996. The opening day celebrations were held in the stadium of the University of Georgia. Teresa Edwards, who had grown up not far from the Georgia stadium, took the Olympic Oath for all participating athletes. It was her 32nd birthday. With balanced scoring from Edwards, Swoopes, and Leslie, the U.S. women's team was undefeated in its first four games, and halfway to the gold medal.

In the medal round, the United States beat South Korea, Japan, and Australia to move into the gold medal game against Brazil. Though the Brazilians had beaten America in the 1994 world championships, the American women would not be denied. They shot an unbelievable 66 percent from the floor, and beat Brazil convincingly 111-87. Lisa Leslie led the way with 29 points, but everyone on the team contributed to the gold medal victory. After the medal award ceremony, Lisa Leslie said: "We accomplished what we set out to do. We tried to get women's basketball to the next level." Indeed they had.

Riding on the success of the Olympic performance, two women's pro basketball leagues were established. The two leagues, the ABL and the WNBA, had the same goal—to bring the best women's basketball to the arenas of America. They also wanted to bring affordable entertainment back into professional sports. Ticket prices averaged between $10-$25, a far cry from the exorbitant price of tickets at men's pro sports. The structure of the leagues, however, differed. The ABL set a 40-game season that coincided with the NBA. The WNBA (which began a year later) played a 28-game schedule during the summer months when the men's and ABL seasons were over so they wouldn't be competing for fan attendance.

Lynette Woodard traveled with the Harlem Globetrotters during the 1980s.

The ABL didn't get the large corporate sponsorships, televised network commitment, or advertising revenues, but was able to sign several members from the Olympic squad, including Jennifer Azzi, Teresa Edwards, and Dawn Staley. Though the WNBA (the NBA's sister league) had the better financial, corporate, and broadcast support, it lagged a year behind the ABL's start. However, Lisa Leslie, Sheryl Swoopes, and Rebecca Lobo joined the WNBA. Veteran players like Lynette Woodard and Nancy Lieberman also signed up. Former USC star Cheryl Miller accepted the head coaching job with the Phoenix Mercury. The WNBA's biggest coup may have been in signing Cynthia Cooper. The Los Angeles native spent years playing basketball in Europe, never giving up hope that someday she would come home and play in an American pro league.

The WNBA has been the more successful of the two leagues. After two seasons, the ABL declared bankruptcy and dissolved the league. In 14 attempts, no women's pro league has survived more than three seasons. The ABL's loss, however, is the WNBA's gain. Several players from the ABL have been absorbed by the WNBA, including Azzi, Staley, former Stanford star Val Whiting, UConn greats Kara Wolters and Jennifer Rizzotti, to name a few.

The most exciting news for the 1999 WNBA season was the debut of former Lady Volunteers superstar Chamique Holdsclaw. Drafted by the 3-27 Washington Mystics, Holdsclaw (who wears number 23) is being touted as the Michael Jordan (who also wore number 23) of women's pro basketball. She led Tennessee to three NCAA national championships, was only the fourth four-time Kodak All-American (honoring the finest NCAA Division I student-athletes), and finished her college career as the all-time leading scorer (3,025) and rebounder (1,295) in Tennessee basketball history. Holdsclaw also made amateur athletic history in the 1998-1999 season when she became the first women's college basketball player to win the James E. Sullivan Award.

The WNBA is counting on building upon its previous two seasons' momentum. With the fusion of the two leagues and its players, 1999 was the best year yet for women's professional basketball. And four cities have been awarded new franchise teams for the summer of 2000.

One final positive sign of the health of the women's game is the realization of the Women's Basketball Hall of Fame, which held its ribbon-cutting ceremony on June 5, 1999, in Knoxville, Tennessee. It is the only Hall of Fame devoted exclusively to women's sports and the achievements of its many participants. The inaugural class of 25 inductees included Senda Berenson Abbott, considered the founder of women's basketball. Also well represented are WNBA-affiliated inductees Cheryl Miller (coach, Phoenix Mercury), Nancy Lieberman-Cline (GM & coach Detroit Shock), Carol Blazejowski (VP/GM NY Liberty), and Ann Meyers-Drysdale (WNBA TV analyst). Do the women "Got Next?" For now, at least, it appears that way.

Bonnie Blair

1964–

Speed Skating

"If I put in the physical work and my competitor does the same kind of training, but doesn't have the strong positive mental outlook that I do, then she's going to be beaten."
—Bonnie Blair on having a positive mental attitude

The first thing that strikes you when you meet Bonnie Blair is her warm, engaging personality. Despite her athletic achievements, she remains humble, preferring to share her lively enthusiasm for the sport she genuinely loves—

speed skating—instead of her countless medals and trophies. Highest among her many awards are five Olympic gold medals and one bronze, the most won by any American in the Winter Games.

The youngest of six children born to Charlie and Eleanor Blair, Bonnie was born on March 18, 1964, in Cornwall, New York. On the day of her birth, four of Bonnie's siblings had already become proficient skaters. While Eleanor was in labor, Charlie took the other five kids to a local skating meet, where he was working as the timekeeper. He learned of his daughter's birth when the public-address announcer told the crowd that "It looks like Charlie's family has just added another skater." The way Bonnie tells the story, she was just a few hours old when she got her first loudspeaker announcement.

Most of Bonnie's early childhood memories involve skating—watching her siblings speed skating on the ice, or skating herself. Bonnie's feet were so tiny that she had to wear shoes inside the smallest pair of skates her mother Eleanor could find for her. She was also so young when she put on her first pair of skates, she has no memory of learning how to skate. By the time she was two years old, Bonnie was skating as though it was as natural for her as walking. And at the tender age of four, she was already competing in speed skating races.

When Bonnie was still in grade school, the Blair family moved to the Midwest, settling in Champaign, Illinois. Her first big win in speed skating came at age seven when she won the Illinois state championship. Though her older brothers and sisters started to move away from speed skating and on to other interests, Bonnie's passion remained so strong that she decided to dedicate all her energies to the sport. She began serious training with Cathy Priestner, a former Canadian Olympic silver medalist. It was Priestner who worked with Bonnie to change from the "pack-race" style she had been using, to the competitive Olympic speed skating form. Priestner made arrangements with the University of Illinois for Bonnie to use their ice rink for 6 A.M. practice sessions.

At 5 feet 4 inches (162 cm) tall and weighing 130 pounds (58 kg), Bonnie was much smaller and lighter than most of the competition she would face on the international level, so she was not going to win races on physical strength. Instead of trying to overpower her opponents, she would have to focus on mastering speed skating technique.

Bonnie entered her first Olympic-style competition at age 16. She was skating a qualifying meet, just to make the trials for the 1980 Winter Games in Lake Placid, New York. She was understandably nervous. She was the last to compete, and the best time posted for the 500-meter race was 47 seconds. In order to advance she would have to skate faster than that. When her opponent didn't show up, Bonnie had the added pressure of having to race without a competitor to gauge her time against. Having had the values of approaching life's challenges with a positive attitude—instilled in her by her parents from the time she was a toddler—Bonnie focused her thoughts, settled in, and skated as hard and as fast as she could. When she crossed the line, her time was 46.7 seconds. She had done it. Though she was later eliminated at the Olympic trials, she was not discouraged. Bonnie simply set her sights on making the team for the 1984 Winter Games in Sarajevo, Yugoslavia.

Bonnie's enthusiasm and dedication to her sport, along with her exuberant personality, was contagious. She had 100 percent support from her family and friends. What she didn't have was the money to meet the enormous expenses amateur athletes face while training and traveling to compete. Help came from an unusual source—the Champaign, Illinois, police department. To raise money for Bonnie's expenses, the Champaign officers sold bumper stickers and T-shirts. With this financial support, Bonnie left for Butte, Montana, to train with the men's speed skating squad for Sarajevo.

It was at the 1984 Winter Games that a tradition began for Bonnie. Having made the U.S. Olympic team, Bonnie made her first appearance as a 19-year-old unknown. Though she finished eighth in the 500-meter competition, it was a good experience for Bonnie. More importantly, her mother Eleanor and two sisters had been able to be there every step of the way to cheer her on. Bonnie would enjoy this network of support through her successive Olympic, national, and world competitions. Known as the "Blair Bunch," those who came out to see her skate included not only the immediate Blair clan, but also other family members and friends. And they did so at their own expense.

Determined to make it to the 1988 Olympics in Calgary, Canada, Bonnie set up an even more demanding workout and training schedule. Her routines included biking, running, and weightlifting, and her efforts proved most beneficial. She won her first U.S. Sprint Championship in 1985 and she repeated as champion for the next five years. The ultimate challenge still lay ahead in Canada.

By the time the 1988 Winter Olympic Games opened, women's speed skating was dominated by the East Germans. Christa Rothenburger, who had won the gold medal in the 500-meter race in Sarajevo, was on target to repeat her performance in Calgary. Skating in the second pairing, Christa broke her own world record, posting a time of 39.12 seconds. Just two pairings later, Bonnie set herself at the start line. With about 30 of the "Blair Bunch" in the stands, Bonnie sped around the rink, finishing the race in 39.10 seconds. She had won the gold medal and set a new world record, breaking Christa's world record by just 2/100 second. The moment was particularly moving for the Blairs. Though fighting cancer, Bonnie's father Charlie had made the trip. Unfortunately, Charlie lost his battle and died shortly after the Games ended, but he was there to see his daughter become an Olympic champion. It was a special moment for them all. A few days later, Bonnie completed her Olympic performance by taking the bronze medal in the 1,000-meter race. In honor of her performance at the Games, the U.S. Olympic team asked Bonnie to carry the American flag at the closing ceremonies.

The following year, Bonnie won her first World Sprint Championship. Next it was on to the 1992 Winter Games in Albertville, France. Clearly at the top of her sport, Bonnie Blair was the favorite to win another gold medal in the 500-meter sprints. With the ever-growing "Blair Bunch" up to about 45 spectators, Bonnie won not only the 500-meter gold, but also the gold in the 1,000-meter race. For her achievements in 1992, Bonnie was also awarded the Sullivan Trophy as top U.S. amateur athlete.

With the Olympics changing from both Winter and Summer Games every four years to alternating every two years, the next Winter Olympics were just two short years away. Lillehammer, Norway, was the host country for the 1994 Games. If Bonnie could repeat her gold medal performance from Albertville, she would make history. No one, male or female, had ever won gold medals at three consecutive Olympics.

Sixty of Bonnie's family and friends made the trip to Norway. Bonnie did not disappoint, winning the 500-meter competition easily with a time of 39.25 seconds, 36/100 second ahead of her nearest opponent. In the last race of her incredible Olympic career, Bonnie won the gold medal in the 1,000-meter sprints by the largest margin in Olympic history. Her win earned Bonnie the distinction of becoming the first American woman to win five Olympic gold medals. With the bronze medal from the 1988 Games, Bonnie Blair has won more Olympic medals in the Winter Games than any other American.

Bonnie had one more goal to achieve—she wanted to become the first woman to break the 39-second barrier in the 500-meter sprint. In March 1994, she did just that, posting a 38.99 in Calgary. The Associated Press named Bonnie Athlete of the Year. On February 12, 1995, she even bested the 1994 record by skating 38.69 seconds.

The day after her 31st birthday, Bonnie Blair retired from competition. Now married to Dave Cruikshank, a fellow Olympic athlete, she divides her time between coaching and traveling around the country as a motivational speaker. Through her Bonnie Blair Charitable Fund, she also donates her time to a number of charity organizations.

Katarina Witt

1965–
Figure Skating

"Skating should be more than skate-jump, skate-jump, skate-jump. I'm a performer. There are things you learn and things you just have that come from the inside."
—Katarina Witt on incorporating style and expression in her skating

In the early morning hours of August 13, 1961, a convoy of soldiers and military vehicles rolled through the streets of East Berlin. By the time most German citizens awakened, the soldiers had already erected a 27-

mile (43-km) stretch of barbed wire that cut through the city, separating the communist East from the democratic West. Very soon after, the barbed wire was replaced by flood-lit concrete walls and electrified fences that were patrolled by East German armed guards twenty-four hours a day. To further discourage its East German citizens from attempting to escape to the West, landmines were strategically placed in the surrounding grounds. The Berlin Wall had ostensibly cut off German from German, forcing its Eastern citizens to live under oppressive rule while its Western neighbors lived in democratic freedom. And it remained in place for the next 28 years.

The Communist bloc countries were known for financing their amateur athletes and starting their training very young. Amateur athletes considered it an honor to represent their country. East Germany had four major sports schools for training athletes who perhaps one day would bring honor to the German Democratic Republic. As a five year old, Katarina Witt walked past the Kuchwald ice arena on her way home from kindergarten. She often lingered to watch the skaters gliding so beautifully and gracefully around the rink. She began to think she would like to learn skating too.

Born on December 3, 1965, Katarina Witt never knew East Germany before the construction of the Berlin Wall. Even the name of the city where she lived with her parents and older brother had been changed. Originally called Chemnitz, the name was changed to Karl-Marx-Stadt after the Soviet Army occupied the city at the end of World War II. It was Karl Marx who developed the ideology of a communist society. Behind the Iron Curtain—the term used by the West to describe the countries ruled by the Soviet Union—the government directed the lives of its citizens. There was no such thing as freedom.

Katarina's father Manfred managed a factory that produced plants and seeds for farming, and her mother Kathe was a physical therapist. Axel, Katarina's older brother, played soccer and went to Leipzig to study physical education, preparing for a career in sports. Ironically, Axel would marry Anett Pötzsch, a figure skater who trained under the scrutinizing eye of coach Jutta Mueller. Anett won a gold medal at the 1980 Winter Olympics in Lake Placid, New York.

The more young Katarina watched the skaters on her way home from school, the more she wanted to learn skating. After begging her parents for weeks to at least let her try, they finally agreed. On one such occasion, while Katarina was just gliding around on the rink, she caught the attention of Bernd Egert, who ran the Karl-Marx-Stadt sports club, one of the four sports schools in East Germany. He convinced Manfred and Kathe Witt to let their daughter try out for his school. Egert also explained that though the training was free, the program was very hard and the trainers very strict with their students.

Katarina would have to overcome her first obstacle before she began—half of the training program was already over, so Katarina would have to learn twice as much in half the time to catch up. Remarkably, she did. By the time she was nine, Katarina was so good that she was assigned a new coach—Jutta Mueller, one of the top ice skating coaches in the world. Mueller would teach Katarina the athletic moves necessary to be a world competitor, but she would learn so much more. Mueller taught Katarina how to perform, how to get the audience behind her, how to "work the crowd." She worked on Katarina's appearance, picking appropriate costumes for competition, showing her how to wear her hair, and how to put on makeup.

Because Katarina lived nearby, she did not have to live at Karl-Marx-Stadt school. However, she practiced several hours a day, in between her other classes, and spent a lot of time with Mueller. Katarina developed quickly under her new coach. At age 11, she landed her first triple jump. When she was 14, she finished tenth in the world championships. Two years later, she finished second to American Elaine Zayak. In 1983, now a major world contender, Katarina won her first of six European championships. On the horizon was Sarajevo and the 1984 Winter Olympics.

Though Katarina had yet to win a world championship, she was favored to win a medal in Sarajevo. Her closest competition would come from the United States's Rosalynn Sumners. Coming into the free skate long program, Sumners had a slight overall lead, but after dazzling the crowd and the judges by skating her routine to a medley of American show tunes, Katarina edged out Sumners and won her first Olympic gold medal by one-tenth of a point. Shortly after her gold-medal-winning performance in Sarajevo, Katarina came in first at the World Championships in Ottawa, Canada.

In 1985, Katarina continued to dominate women's figure skating, winning both the European and world championships. Though she came in first again at the Europeans in 1986, she was upset at the Worlds in Geneva, Switzerland, coming in second behind America's Debi Thomas. Thus began one of the most intense rivalries in women's figure skating. The following year at the world championships held in Cincinnati, Ohio, Katarina came from behind, skating a flawless long program to the music of *West Side Story* to recapture her title. She was unquestionably the best female figure skater in the world.

At home in East Germany, Katarina was treated like a hero. In a country where two or three families often had to live together in smaller quarters, the government gave her a spacious apartment. She drove around Karl-Marx-Stadt in a Soviet-made Lada sports car while many of her countrymen couldn't even afford to buy a car. In 1988, she would have a chance to bring yet more honor to her country at the Olympic Games in Calgary, Canada.

No figure skater had won back-to-back Olympic gold medals since Norway's Sonja Henie won the second of her three gold medals at the Lake Placid Winter Games in 1932. In what became known as the "Dueling Carmens" competition, because both women chose to skate their long program to the passionate Bizet opera, *Carmen,* Katarina would have to skate better than rival Debi Thomas to win her second consecutive Olympic gold medal.

Katarina skated first, turning in a moving, emotional performance. Her marks were good, but there was still a chance for Debi to win. The more athletic of the two, Debi knew she had to pull out all the stops—a conservative skate would not be enough to beat Katarina. Unfortunately, she missed a triple jump, landing on both feet, and her program began to unravel. Not only had Debi lost the gold medal, she dropped to third behind Canada's Elizabeth Manley, and had to settle for the bronze. Katarina then capped off a brilliant year by winning her fourth world title.

Katarina decided to turn professional after the world championships, teaming up with America's 1988 Olympic gold medalist Brian Boitano. The two made a number of television specials, including *Carmen on Ice,* which earned them an Emmy Award. Professionally things were going well for Katarina, but the political situation at home was quickly changing and Communism was crumbling all over eastern Europe. On November 9, 1989, Katarina turned on the TV set in her hotel room in Spain and was stunned as she watched many East Germans begin tearing down the Berlin Wall and heading for the freedom of West German soil.

With the collapse of the Communist government in East Germany, Katarina's life changed dramatically. For the first time in her life she was free to come and go as she pleased. She could keep all the money she earned. She got an apartment in New York City, and kept her apartment in Germany.

Katarina and Boitano were touring America in an ice show they created called "Katarina Witt and Brian Boitano—Skating II." She also worked as a commentator at the 1992 Winter Olympics for CBS-TV, and for NBC-TV at the 1993 world championships in Prague, Czechoslovakia. It was during her time off the ice that Katarina decided she would attempt to make it to the 1994 Olympics in Lillehammer, Norway, to try to win a third gold medal.

Calling on her old coach Jutta Mueller, Katarina trained at Kuchwald, the familiar rink of her youth. Though she made it to the Olympics, she finished seventh. By 1994, women's competitive skating was different. Much more emphasis was placed on athleticism. Nonetheless, Katarina skated her program, a tribute to the people of Sarajevo, depicting the emotion and pain of the civil war that raged there. It was also special because it was the first time her parents had ever seen her skate.

In the last few years, Katarina has been involved in many ventures—testing the acting waters, she got a small part in *Jerry Maguire* and more recently in *Ronin*. And in January 1999, she made a few guest appear-

Katarina continues to dazzle international audiences at ice shows.

ances on the Home Shopping Network to introduce her new line of sterling silver and gemstone jewelry called *Feelings*.

Katarina released her autobiography, but has only made it available in Germany, Japan, and France. The honors continue too—in 1995, Katarina received the Jim Thorpe Pro Sports Award and was inducted into the World Skating Hall of Fame. She still plans to skate professionally, doing so with the same artistry, emotion, and feeling that made her one of the most successful and decorated figure skaters the sport has ever known.

Silken Laumann

1965–
Rowing

"I chose to work on the premise that there was a little light at the end of the tunnel, and that I could work towards that light."
—Silken Laumann on rowing at the Barcelona Olympics, though seriously injured

The most important thing in the Olympic Games is not to win but to take part, just as the most important thing in life is not the triumph but the struggle. The essential thing is not to have conquered but to have fought well.
—The Olympic Creed

There are few athletes who personify the meaning of the Olympic Creed better than Canada's Silken Laumann. Though seriously injured just a couple of months before 1992 Olympic Games in Barcelona, Spain, Silken was determined to take part in one of the more physically demanding competitions—rowing. The injury to her right leg was so severe that her doctors weren't sure she would ever be able to row again, let alone compete in the upcoming Olympics. Everyone who witnessed her 2,000-meter single sculls performance will forever remember Silken for her gutsy determination on that bright day in August 1992.

Born in 1965, Silken Laumann was raised in the lakefront town of Mississauga, Ontario, 20 miles (32 km) from the city of Toronto. Hans Laumann and his wife Seigrid owned and operated a small window-cleaning business in Mississauga, while raising Silken and her sister Danielle. As teenagers, the two sisters began sculling in their double shell (the name of the boat used in competitive rowing) on the Credit River. They were good enough to earn a spot on the rowing team that would represent Canada at the 1984 Summer Olympic Games in Los Angeles, California. Danielle and Silken made the finals in the double sculls and won a bronze medal, finishing third behind Romania and the Netherlands. At only 19 years of age, Silken was an Olympic champion. Excited about her success at the Los Angeles Games, Silken looked forward to a promising future in competitive rowing.

Though she continued to train, Silken began to experience a lot of pain in her back about a year after the Olympics. The more she rowed, the worse the pain. Doctors discovered that Silken was suffering from lateral curvature of the spine. The condition had been present since birth, and rowing had made it worse. Intent on continuing to row, Silken tried to work through the pain. With another partner, she competed in the double sculls at the 1988 Summer Games in Seoul, South Korea. She was discouraged by a seventh-place finish.

Silken briefly thought about retiring from sculling, but still believed that by practicing harder, and with more demanding workouts, she would strengthen her back and improve her sculling abilities. Because she felt the Canadian women's rowing teams were not training well, she decided to train with the men's team. She would also have the chance to assess their new coach, Michael Spracklen.

Silken's instincts were right. Working with Mike and the men's team was hard, but she was seeing positive results. In July 1991, having compiled the most cumulative points in a series of race events, Silken was awarded the World Cup for rowing in the women's single sculls in the heavyweight division. She also defeated Elisabeta Lipa of Romania in the 2,000-meter singles to win the world championship.

At the top of her sport, in the best physical condition of her career, Silken was the odds-on favorite to win a gold medal at the 1992 Olympics in Barcelona. With two Olympics behind her, number three was sure to be the charm. In a career that had weathered so many setbacks and disappointments, she was close to realizing her dream of Olympic gold. But two months before the Olympics, her dream was shattered when Silken's shell was struck by another boat.

In preparation for Barcelona, Silken had gone to Essen, Germany, to compete in a regatta. During that race, her boat was struck by another boat. The impact forced part of her boat into her right leg, severing the muscles, tendons, and ligaments from her ankle midway up her shin. After several surgeries, including a skin graft, Silken began doing exercises in her hospital bed to keep herself in shape. Though everyone else told her Barcelona was an impossibility, Silken never gave up.

After missing 26 days of training, Silken lowered herself into her shell. She was rowing again before she was even walking. Though her rehabilitation and return to training were terribly painful, Silken was determined. Initially, she had only set a goal to make it to Barcelona. Now, she was going to give her all to try to win a medal.

On August 2, 1992, Silken made the final of the 2,000-meter singles race and turned in a performance that will never be forgotten. For most of the race, she was trailing behind Romanian Elisabeta Lipa, Annelies Bredael of Belgium, and Anne Marden of the United States. With half the race behind her, Silken knew she could not win the race, but she was determined not to come in fourth—and just miss a medal. So she focused on Anne Marden, who was still in third place just ahead of her. Little by little, lifting and slicing her 10-pound (4.5-kg) oars in and out of the water, Silken moved her 27-foot (8-m) shell ever closer. Finally, with just a few meters to go before the finish line, she passed Marden and moved into third place. Incredibly, Silken had won the bronze medal in a gutsy, inspiring athletic performance. One of the most poignant moments of the Barcelona Games came when Silken stepped up on the podium to receive her medal. In Canada, she became an instant hero.

In 1995, Silken won gold medals in both the singles and quadruple sculls at the Pan American Games. Unfortunately, the medals were taken away from her. Without realizing it, Silken had taken over-the-counter extra-strength Benadryl, which contained a banned substance, instead of the legal regular-strength decongestant.

However, still satisfied with being one of the best scullers in the world, Silken hoped to compete in an unprecedented fourth Olympic Games, to be held in 1996 in Atlanta, Georgia. At age 31, she made the finals in the singles sculling race. She had just as much chance to win the gold as did her two closest competitors, but she had to settle for the silver, finishing second with a time of 7:35.15. The gold medal went to Yekaterina Khodotovich of Belarus. Her time of 7:32.21 was just over two seconds faster.

Silken Laumann may not be the most decorated athlete to compete in four Olympics, and in fact she never won the elusive gold medal. But her place in sports history is secure because of that moment on the river in Barcelona. She never gave up, never let her trials and struggles defeat her. After all, that's what the Olympic Creed is all about.

Gail Devers

1966–

Track and Field

"The word 'quit' is not a part of my vocabulary. I love the sport, and I want to continue to excel. I think that my best is yet to come."
—Gail Devers on her extraordinary return to track and field competition

Fans who watched the women's 100-meter hurdles final during the 1992 Olympic Games in Barcelona, Spain, might not remember who won the race, but they undoubtedly remember Gail Devers's gutsy crawl-stumble to the finish line. Having exploded out of the starting blocks, Devers was well ahead of her competitors and seemed assured of victory. But on the last hurdle, her leg hit the top of the gate, and she lost her momentum and fell. On her knees, she scrambled to the finish line, ending up in fifth place.

Barcelona was not a complete disappointment, however. Earlier in the week Gail was crowned the "fastest woman in the world" when she won the gold medal in the closest women's 100-meter sprint in Olympic history. It was an especially poignant moment for Gail—only 17 months earlier, it was doubtful that she would ever walk again, let alone run.

Yolanda Gail Devers was born into what she often refers to as a "Leave It To Beaver" household on November 19, 1966, in Seattle, Washington. (The family moved to San Diego, California, when Gail was very young.) Gail's father Larry was a Baptist minister, and her mother Alabe was a classroom assistant at a nearby elementary school. The Devers already had one child, a son with a very unusual name—Parenthesis.

In 1980, when Gail was a sophomore in high school, she took up distance running and later realized that she was better suited to sprinting. Sweetwater had no track coach, so students who wanted to participate in track and field designed their own training routines. Even without a coach, Gail was so fast that she won many of her races easily. The support and guidance she would have received from a coach was provided by her father, who took her to meets and was waiting for his shy daughter when they ended. By her junior year, Gail was running the 100-meter dash in under 12 seconds. She also began running 100-meter hurdles, a more demanding event than straight sprinting.

Eventually Gail became one of the top track and field competitors in California. Her athletic and academic excellence earned her a scholarship to the University of California at Los Angeles (UCLA) in 1984. There Gail met Robert (Bob) Kersee, the well-known coach of track star Jackie Joyner. Kersee had a reputation for being demanding. He told Gail that she needed to start thinking of herself not as a high-school star but as a world-class competitor. He saw her as a record-breaking hurdler who would qualify for the 1988 U.S. Olympic team and win a gold medal in 1992. Gail just thought he was talking "future crazy."

But Bobby Kersee had a keen eye for spotting potential champions. Under his direction, sprinter Valerie Brisco had captured three gold medals at the 1984 Olympic Games in Los Angeles. After two years under Kersee's tutelage, Gail was ranked seventh in the United States in the 100-meter dash and 100-meter hurdles. By 1987, she had truly become a world-class athlete, finishing second in the 100-meter dash at the NCAA Collegiate Track and Field Championships and winning the same event at the Olympic Festival and the Pan American Games.

By 1988, Gail's senior year at UCLA, she was headed for Seoul, South Korea, to compete in the Olympics. She had just completed her best season ever, twice setting an American record in the 100-meter hurdles. When she arrived in Seoul, however, Gail felt sluggish and tired, but she could not identify exactly what the problem was. Her poor health showed in her performance; she was eliminated in the semifinal heat when she finished last with her slowest time since high school. Gail's high hopes for her first Olympic competition ended in crushing disappointment and with many unanswered questions. Had she overtrained? Had she pushed too hard to reach Olympic-level competition? Was she having trouble concentrating? Neither Gail nor her coach, Bobby Kersee, knew the answers.

After Gail returned home, she began to develop other health problems, including migraine headaches, uncontrollable shaking, weight swings, hair loss, and fatigue. For the next two years she suffered from a mysterious illness which left her so weak that she was unable to continue competing. Finally, in 1990, Gail was diagnosed with Graves' disease, a relatively rare illness affecting the thyroid gland. She was unable to take the standard medication for Graves' disease because the International Olympic Committee had banned its use for athletes competing in the Games. Instead, she tried an alternative treatment—radiation therapy—but while it helped alleviate her symptoms, it also damaged her skin, especially the skin on her feet. Her condition became so serious that doctors considered amputating her feet. Fortunately for Gail, the doctors eventually realized that it was the radiation treatment that was destroying her feet. They discontinued it and put her on a thyroid medication. For the first time since Seoul, Gail began to feel better.

As soon as Bobby Kersee heard that Gail's condition was improving, he urged her to get back out on the track. Although she could barely put shoes on her feet, Gail and Kersee began by walking the track together—Gail in stocking feet and Bobby in track shoes. By the end of 1991, Gail had regained her form, becoming the number one hurdler in the United States and number two worldwide. In one of the greatest comebacks in sports history, Gail Devers qualified for both the 100-meter dash and the 100-meter hurdles in the 1992 Olympics.

Having struggled to recover from a disease that threatened to end her athletic career, Gail was thinking not about medals but about just having the opportunity to compete again. The only goal she set for herself at the Barcelona Games was to finish both races. Though she was favored to win in the 100-meter hurdle and stumbled on the last gate, she was determined to cross the finish line, and she earned her first gold medal in the dash.

Now that she had recovered and was in good form again, Gail's next goal was to win the "double" at the 1993 world championships. In a controversial photo finish, Gail beat Jamaican track star Merlene Ottey in the 100-meter dash, and won the hurdles easily. Her achievement earned her the title of U.S. Women's Athlete of the Year. In what seemed like an instant replay of the 1993 world championship 100-meter dash, Gail once again beat Ottey by a slim margin in the 1996 Olympics in Atlanta, Georgia, tying the record set in 1968 for winning the event in two consecutive Games. Gail aims to be the first to achieve a third consecutive gold for the 100-meter dash by competing in the 2000 Olympics in Sydney, Australia.

Today, Gail Devers lives in Los Angeles with her beloved pet rottweilers, making preliminary plans for a day care center she hopes to open when she retires from competition. Of the disease she lives with, she says, "I'm stronger as a person, and it's not hard for me to concentrate on the job at hand. . . . [T]here's nothing that can come up in my life that I can't get over after going through what I did."

Steffi Graf

1969–

Tennis

*"What am I most proud of?
Just to have come through. I'm
proud that with everything I've
been through, I've managed
to do what I've done."*
—Steffi Graf reflecting on her career

At the end of the French Open singles final in June 1999, Martina Hingis may have had second thoughts about her underestimation of the woman on the other side of the net. Her opponent, Steffi Graf, had just soundly defeated Martina, and captured the 22nd Grand Slam title of her career in the process. Plagued by injuries over the last few years, Steffi had not been able to play the same kind of tennis she had played throughout her career—the kind of game that will undoubtedly earn her a place in the Tennis Hall of Fame. Though she officially announced her retirement in August 1999, she made plans for a farewell tour of exhibition matches later that year. Steffi also intends to concentrate on her marketing company and on helping young German tennis players develop their games.

Many in the tennis community think Steffi Graf is the greatest player the game has ever seen. She is one of only three female players in the history of the sport to complete the Grand Slam (Maureen Connolly, 1953, Margaret Smith Court, 1970). With her 1999 French Open victory, Steffi was only two Grand Slam titles away from tying Margaret Smith Court's record of 24, one that has stood for 29 years. But Steffi has accomplished something unique: she has won each of the Grand Slam titles at least four times (Australian 4, French 6, U.S. Open 5, and Wimbledon 7). The 1999 French Open may have been Steffi's sweetest victory because she won it after battling for two years with debilitating injuries, and fought her way all the way back to the top echelons of women's tennis.

Stefanie Maria Graf was born June 14, 1969, in Mannheim, West Germany. Her brother Michael, now a Formula 3 race car driver, was born two years later. Steffi's parents, Peter and Heidi, both played tennis. Peter made his living selling cars and insurance. When Steffi was about three years old, her father sawed down the handle of a tennis racquet and gave it to his daughter. Using the family's basement as a makeshift court, he tied some twine between two chairs, and Steffi hit a ball back and forth to her father. Steffi's reward for playing well was a plate of strawberries and ice cream.

Steffi's progress in tennis was so rapid that Peter Graf was convinced that his daughter could become a world-class competitor. He sold his business and moved the family to Brühl, West Germany, where he opened a tennis school. Steffi was his first pupil. When she was six years old, Steffi won her first junior tennis tournament, and by the time she turned 13, she had already won the European championship in her age group, and the German junior title for 18-year-olds and under. With no real challenges left in the junior ranks, Steffi decided to turn professional. In October 1982, at just 13 years and 4 months old, Steffi became the second-youngest player to receive a WTA ranking (124).

In her first pro match, in Stuttgart, Germany, Steffi was soundly beaten by America's Tracy Austin, 4-6, 0-6. By the end of 1984, however, Steffi's rise in the ranks of women's tennis was being noticed. She made it to the quarterfinals at Wimbledon, and won the Olympic gold medal at the Summer Games in Los Angeles when tennis was reintroduced as a demonstration sport. Still, by the end of 1985, Steffi had not won a tournament—yet.

In 1986, Steffi really started to come into her own as a tennis player. She won 8 of the 14 tournaments she entered, and made it to the finals three times. Steffi beat Chris Evert in the Family Circle Cup, and was putting top-ranked players on notice that she was up and coming in the sport that had been dominated for so long by the likes of Chris Evert and Martina Navratilova.

Steffi was also beginning to mature physically and mentally. Now a bonafide teenager at 5 feet 9 inches (175 cm) tall and weighing 132 pounds (60 kg), Steffi was a powerhouse. She was quick and strong, and it showed in her play. Steffi won her first Grand Slam singles title in 1987, beating Martina Navratilova at the French Open. At the time, Steffi set a record as the youngest player ever to win the women's title at Roland Garros Stadium. Steffi reached the finals at Wimbledon and the U.S. Open, but was defeated by Martina both times. The losses didn't really matter—by the end of 1987, having won 70 of 72 matches, and winning 11 tournaments out of 13 played, Steffi was named the number 1 player in the world.

If 1987 was Steffi's year of ascension, 1988 was her year for making history. If there were any doubts about Steffi's abilities at the start of the tennis season, she certainly erased them by the conclusion of the U.S. Open that fall, and she did it by beating some of the best in the game. Steffi started her charge at the Grand Slam record by beating Evert in the Australian Open. In the next major, the French Open, she defeated Natasha Zvereva in 32 minutes without losing a single game. Then she beat Martina Navratilova in the final on center court at Wimbledon, having made a dramatic comeback in the match to seal the victory. Steffi and partner Gabriela Sabatini also won the women's doubles title.

A jubilant Steffi, after defeating Gabriela Sabatini at the 1988 U.S. Open

With three Grand Slam tournament victories, only one remained—the U.S. Open. If the pressure was mounting on Steffi, she did not show it. In the final match, Steffi squared off against Sabatini. They split the first two sets by identical scores of 6-3. But Steffi was not to be denied. She came out smoking and won the third set convincingly, 6-1. Excited and relieved, Steffi threw her racket in the air and ran up in the stands to embrace her parents and her brother. She had accomplished what only two other women in tennis history had, and she was still just 19 years old. For completing the Grand Slam, Steffi was awarded a $275,000 prize check and a gold bracelet with four diamonds. In September, just days after her U.S. Open win, Steffi capped off an incredible year by winning the gold medal at the Olympics in Seoul, South Korea.

The following year, only a loss to Arantxa Sanchez Vicario at the French Open prevented Steffi from achieving back-to-back Grand Slams. Her two victories over Martina Navratilova in the finals of Wimbledon and the U.S. Open affirmed that there was clearly a changing of the guard in women's tennis. Steffi was so dominant in the game that from June 1989 to May 1990 she compiled 66 straight match victories, the second-longest winning streak in tennis history.

In women's tennis, there have always been great rivalries—Wills and

Mallory, Court and King, Evert and Navratilova. For Steffi Graf, the challenge came from a two-handed forehand hitter from Yugoslavia named Monica Seles. It was Monica, who, in 1990, beat Steffi at the German Open, ending Steffi's 66-match winning streak. Seles also beat Steffi at the French Open that year, and finally ended Steffi's record 186-week reign as the world's number one player on March 11, 1991.

What should have been the greatest women's rivalry of the 1990s was ended when a deranged fan stabbed Monica in the back on April 30, 1993, in Hamburg, Germany. The greatest damage was emotional—it would be 27 months before Monica would step on a court again. In Monica's absence, Steffi reigned as queen of the courts once more, winning three of the four Grand Slam tournaments in 1993, 1995, and 1996. In 1997, Steffi became the second woman to hit $20 million in career earnings.

In spite of her continued success in tennis, not everything was wonderful for Steffi in the 1990s. Her father was jailed for failing to pay taxes on more than $10 million, and admitted to having an affair with a young woman the same age as his daughter. Injuries and an aching back began to interfere with Steffi's ability to play. Finally in 1997, Steffi underwent surgery to repair the patellar tendon and cartilage in her left knee. Though the prognosis was good for a complete recovery, doctors could not promise Steffi that she would ever regain her championship-level form.

Returning to the game in 1998, Steffi decided to take it match by match, tournament by tournament. The 1999 French Open win over Martina Hingis was Steffi's first major tournament win since 1996. After claiming her trophy, she announced that it would be her last appearance at Roland Garros Stadium. The news of her retirement came a month later. At the time the announcement was made, Steffi was just two Grand Slam singles wins away from tying Margaret Smith Court's record, but with more than 100 career victories, her place in tennis history is secure.

Myriam Bédard

1969–
Biathlon

"I want to go to the Olympics again. Maybe I'll make the top 10 this time around, maybe not. The victory rests in just being there."
—Myriam Bédard on why she didn't retire after her illness

At the 1992 Winter Olympics in Albertville, France, the women's biathlon made its debut as a medal sport. Since the biathlon has not been a traditional sport in North America, very few people realize the extraordinary skill and endurance necessary to be successful. A biathlete must have excellent cross-country skiing abilities as well as expert marksmanship. It isn't as simple as ski, stop, and shoot, either. You must ski, stop, and shoot accurately at pre-positioned targets along the course. Missed targets result in time penalties, which can be costly to the skier's finishing time and overall standing in the race.

Most biathletes take years to develop into international-level competitors. However, at the 1992 Winter Games, a 23-year-old Canadian took home the bronze medal in the 15-kilometer race. The feat was even more exciting because it was the first time a North American had ever won an Olympic medal in the biathlon. Her name is Myriam Bédard, and her success brought the sport into prominence in Canada and the United States.

Myriam was born in Loretteville, Quebec, on December 22, 1969. As a young girl growing up in Canada, Myriam was rather quiet and pretty much of a loner. She enjoyed the solitude of ice skating, however, and had dreams of becoming a champion Olympic figure skater. Unfortunately the expense of competitions, costumes, training, and ice time was putting a terrible financial burden on her parents, Francine and Pierre Bédard. So shortly before her 14th birthday, Myriam traded in her skates for a pair of skis and a target rifle, and enrolled as an army cadet with the 2772 Corps de Cadets du Camp Valcartier. As a cadet, Myriam learned the skills she needed to become a champion biathlete.

During her years as a cadet, Myriam moved through the ranks quickly. By late 1984, she had earned her Green Star and Red Star, and was promoted to corporal. After attending the national Army Cadet Camp in Banff, Alberta, in 1986, Myriam was named the Top Female Cadet and was presented the Army Cadet League of Canada Centennial Award. A year later she was promoted to master warrant officer. She finished her cadet career in 1988, at the age of 19.

While she was a cadet, Myriam began competing in biathlon events. Because it was illegal to carry a rifle on public transportation, Myriam dismantled the gun and concealed it in a violin case. She won her first race at the tender age of 15 in a pair of ski boots that were so large she had to stuff them with tissue to make them fit. At 17, Myriam was crowned Canadian Junior Biathlon champion. In only her second year on the Canadian senior team, she came in second overall in the 1990-1991 World Cup. She had a great season winning six medals, and was in the running for the World Cup title up to the last race of the season.

After her bronze medal performance at the 1992 Winter Olympics in Albertville, Myriam continued to climb up the ranks in the sport, and was soon considered the greatest biathlete in the world. She cemented her place at the top by winning the world championship in 1993 at Borovets, Bulgaria. She finished more than sixteen seconds ahead of her closest competitor—Nadezhda Talanova of Russia.

At the 1994 Olympics in Lillehammer, Norway, the biathlon 15-kilometer race did not start well for Myriam, who was the favorite to win the gold medal. Tired after a restless night's sleep and distracted by the boisterous crowd, Myriam started the race in 67th position. However, she was soon able to tune out the crowd and focus on the race, dramatically catching up even though she missed 2 of 20 shots and was hit with a two-minute penalty. She won the race easily, almost 30 seconds ahead of everyone else, earning her first Olympic gold medal.

A few days later Myriam earned her second gold medal, winning the 7.5-kilometer race by a mere second. What is even more astonishing about her accomplishment is that after the race Myriam discovered she had been competing on a mismatched set of skis! Myriam became the first and only Canadian woman to win twice in a single Olympics.

In the spring of 1994, Myriam married her longtime companion, fellow biathlete Jean Paquet. She became pregnant shortly afterward, and gave birth to a baby girl named Maude at the end of the year. Everything seemed wonderful in Myriam's life. She was happy, successful, a champion athlete, and revered in Canada. But about six months into the new year, her performances started to drop off and she began to complain of severe fatigue. Doctors just attributed the loss of energy to her recent childbirth experience.

Her condition showed no improvement, however, and after several rounds of tests, Myriam was finally diagnosed with chronic fatigue syndrome and hypothyroidism—a condition that slows down the body's metabolism. She later discovered that she had also developed allergies to many foods, including dairy products such as milk and eggs. She was put on a strict diet, and medication was prescribed to manage the thyroid condition. It would be a long climb back to be competitive again in any biathlon event, but climb back she would.

At the World Cup competition in Ostersund, Sweden, in 1997, Myriam had her best finish in more than a year, coming in 15th in the 15-km race. The placement was good enough to earn a spot on the Canadian Olympic biathlon team going to the 18th Winter Games in Nagano, Japan. Though there were no Olympic medals to bring home this time, Myriam finished both biathlon races, coming in 32nd in the 7.5 km, and 50th in the 15 km.

In August 1997, at age 28, Myriam announced her retirement from biathlon competition, but she will not be idle. She has come full circle—well, almost—by trading in her rifle and skis for a pair of ice skates—not the figure skating type she hung up as a young teen to become an Olympic biathlete, but speed skates. Canadian national team speed skaters Patrick and Sylvain Bouchard suggested that Myriam try speed skating. She did, and she likes it. She plans to train for the next two years, and then enter competition again. In the summer of 1999, Myriam spent several weeks practicing at the Olympic Oval in Calgary, the site of the 1988 Games. She hopes to return to the Olympics in 2002, and perhaps win another medal. If she can stay healthy, there's every reason to believe that she'll be in the chase to the end.

Janet Evans

1971–
Swimming

"At this point in my career, winning another medal isn't as moving as looking into the stands and realizing that all those people have come to see me swim. They appreciate what I've accomplished, and I feel I have a lot to give them in return."
—Janet Evans at the 1996 Olympics in Atlanta, Georgia

At the end of her last strokes toward the wall in the 800-meter freestyle final, three-time Olympic gold medalist Janet Evans ducked under the lane ropes and found her way over to the event's newest gold medalist, Brooke Bennett. As the two hugged, the audience realized that Janet was also saying goodbye. This was Janet's last race in a spectacular, highly decorated swimming career. At 24, she had matured from being a teenage champion to a young woman who understood that winning wasn't the only thing in life. There was also the fun and joy of just being an Olympic competitor.

Prior to Janet's last race, she was reminded of what the Olympics were really all about. On the scoreboard overhead, she could see the Olympic Creed, written by the father of the modern games, Baron Pierre de Coubertin: "The most important thing in the Olympics is not to win but to take part, just as the most important thing in life is not the triumph but the struggle. The essential thing is not to have conquered but to have fought well." At these Summer Olympic Games in Atlanta, Janet had come not just to compete, but also to participate in the Olympic experience. She attended other events, including the opening and closing ceremonies, something she had not done in her prior two Olympic Games. She was also given the honor of handing off the Olympic torch to boxing legend Muhammad Ali, who lit the Olympic flame to open the Games. In a sense, Janet had grown up in the eight years since she first stepped into the spotlight in 1988 in Seoul, South Korea.

Janet Beth Evans took to the water almost as soon as she could walk. She was born on August 28, 1971, in Fullerton, California, the youngest child of Paul and Barbara Evans, who already had two sons. When she was barely two years old, Janet learned how to swim. By age three, she was swimming all four competitive strokes—freestyle, butterfly, breaststroke, and backstroke. Janet began swimming competitively by age four, and had broken several national records while she was still a preteen.

Janet was not your average swimmer, even as a youngster. Her stroke was very unorthodox—often described as looking similar to a windup toy in the bathtub. At 5 feet 3 inches (160 cm) tall and weighing 102 pounds (46 kg), she was smaller and lighter than most of her competition. But her love of the sport motivated her to work harder. In an interview with *USA Today* during the 1996 Atlanta Games, Janet explained: "When I was a little girl, I really, really loved swimming. I couldn't wait to work out. My motivation was really, really high."

Janet's dedication and hard work paid off. In 1986, at age 15, she won the Phillips Performance Award, which is given to the individual with the best performance in a specific event at the U.S. Open or spring or summer nationals. Janet broke Tracy Caulkins's 400-meter individual medley record at the U.S. Open. While still in high school, Janet set national records for both the 200-yard individual medley and the 500-yard freestyle swim. All the while, Janet just wanted to be "Janet," going to the mall with her friends, doing her homework, and dating. But she was setting new records at an astounding pace and becoming something of a celebrity.

In 1987, Janet was selected American Swimmer of the Year, an honor she would receive three more times in her career. The following year she became the only female swimmer to hold three world records at the same time in the 400-, 800-, and 1,500-meter freestyle. Excited at having made the U.S. Olympic team, Janet headed to Seoul, South Korea, a bubbly, enthusiastic 17-year-old. By the time her competitions were over, Janet's name would be in the record books for setting a world record in the 400-meter freestyle and winning three individual gold medals for the 400-meter individual medley, the 400-meter freestyle, and the 800-meter freestyle. Her exuberance was contagious and she soon became a crowd favorite.

Once she returned home, Janet found her instant celebrity status a bit difficult to handle. Her performance at the Olympics, though exciting, was just another swim meet. She had broken world records before and had been awarded other honors. But instead of still just being Janet, she was now "Janet the Olympic gold medalist." And the honors kept coming. In 1989, she was named

Sportswoman of the Year by the U.S. Olympic Committee, won the Sullivan Award as the top U.S. Amateur Athlete, and for the second time was selected as both American and World Swimmer of the Year.

In the fall of 1989, Janet enrolled at Stanford University, but stayed only two years because of a new rule restricting practice time for college athletes. She moved to Texas to continue her training with coach Mark Schubert. In 1991, Janet won two gold medals and a silver medal at the world championships.

By the time of the 1992 Olympics in Barcelona, Spain, Janet was no longer the petite darling she had been four years before. Now 20, Janet was 5 feet, 7 inches (170 cm) tall and she weighed 120 pounds (54 kg). Her physical maturity had an impact on her swimming. No longer as fast as she once was, world-record performances were fewer and farther between. Although she was still winning, the media began noting that she wasn't the spectacular athlete she had been in Seoul. The pressure was mounting.

In the 400-meter freestyle final, Janet was not able to repeat as champion. She came in only 0.19 second behind Germany's Dagmar Hase, and had to settle for the silver medal. It was Janet's first 400-meter loss in six years, and when the press asked her how it felt to be a loser, she broke into tears. With the support and reassurance of Coach Schubert and her parents, however, Janet went on to win a gold medal in the 800-meter freestyle a few days later. Still, Janet was upset by her performance in Barcelona, and when she returned home, she stopped swimming for four months.

The girl who had been used to winning suddenly felt like a failure. She was afraid people wouldn't care about her as much anymore. It took a while for the loving support of her family and true friends to help Janet realize life was about more than wins, world records, and medals. During her time away from the pool, Janet traveled, making appearances for sponsors and accepting product endorsements. Slowly, she made her way back to swimming, which she truly missed. She made a commitment to Coach Schubert to swim competitively through the 1994 world championships in Rome, Italy. There, though she came in fifth in the 400, Janet won the 800-meter freestyle race.

Because swimming was once again enjoyable, Janet decided to try to qualify for the 1996 U.S. Olympic team. Much more accepting of her limitations now, Janet knew her career was coming to a close, and she wanted to enjoy the whole Olympic experience she had missed out on in her two previous appearances. Janet didn't win any medals in Atlanta, but she had the time of her life. She still holds 6 American records, and has won 45 national titles in her career. She finished her degree at the University of Southern California in 1994, and divides her time between endorsements, charity work, and motivational speaking engagements, as well as hosting the Janet Evans Annual Invitational swim meet. She has also thought about pursuing a career in sports marketing or broadcasting. Perhaps we'll soon see Janet in front of a TV camera, giving color commentary at some future Olympics.

Kristi Yamaguchi

1971–
Figure Skating

"I skate because I love skating. Sometimes I ask myself, 'Why do I compete?' But I never say, 'Why do I skate?'"
—Kristi Yamaguchi commenting on her love of figure skating

Little girls' heroes are often athletes. We were awestruck as Russia's exuberant gymnast Olga Korbut did a back somersault on the balance beam, a feat never before attempted in competition. After those Munich Olympics, gymnastics schools were overflowing with new enrollments.

We didn't dare look away for a moment during the women's 100-meter sprint race, or we would have missed Florence Griffith Joyner run faster than any woman had in Olympic history. Not only was FloJo fast, she was beautiful and flashy. Her presence brought a style and glamour to track and field that no one had seen before. In 1976, 5 1/2-year-old Kristi Yamaguchi became enchanted with figure skating after watching Dorothy Hamill's elegant gold medal performance at the Olympic Winter Games in Innsbruck, Austria.

Kristi Tsuya Yamaguchi was born on July 12, 1971, in Haywood, California. Kristi and her older sister Lori (a younger brother Brett would be born in 1974) were raised by their parents Jim, a dentist, and Carole, a medical secretary. As a fourth-generation Japanese-American, Kristi was only vaguely aware of her family's heritage. Her parents had been among the 120,000 Japanese-Americans who suffered through the indignities of living in internment camps during World War II. Jim was just four years old when his family was moved off their ranch in California and sent to a camp in Arizona. Carole was born in a camp in Colorado, while her father, George Doi, was in Europe serving in the U. S. Army. Fortunately, by the time Kristi was born, the injustices endured by her parents' generation had become a sad chapter in American history.

Kristi was a very small baby, weighing a mere 5 pounds, 15 ounces (2.5 kg) at birth. Though she was tiny, her size was not the primary concern of Carole and Jim. Kristi had a far more serious and immediate problem—she was born clubfooted—both of her feet turned inward. Kristi's doctors put plaster casts on her feet that were reinforced with metal bars to keep them in the correct position. After the casts were removed, Kristi had to wear corrective shoes and a special brace at night.

In 1976, when Kristi saw Dorothy Hamill skate her long program during the televised coverage of the Winter Olympic Games, the graceful gold medalist became Kristi's idol. She got a Dorothy Hamill doll as a gift, and took it with her everywhere she went. Then Kristi began asking her mother to take her skating. Carole had been encouraging her daughter to participate in athletic activities to help strengthen her legs and feet, so she was happy to take Kristi to the rink. She had to hold onto her mom as they moved around the rink, but Kristi loved the way it felt to glide on the ice.

About two years later, when Kristi was six, she saw her first ice show at a local mall. She fell in love with all of it—the costumes, the music, and the skating. Shortly afterward, Kristi began taking group skating lessons with other kids her age. She grasped figure skating basics quickly, learning how to do spins, crossovers, and a mini jump called the bunny hop. In time, Kristi was ready for private lessons with her own coach. She signed on with Christy Kjarsgaard Ness and worked endless hours to learn the various jumps and moves necessary to become a competitive skater.

Kjarsgaard was impressed by Kristi's dedication and felt that the young skater indeed had the potential to become a top-ranked figure skater. Kristi joined the Palomares Figure Skating Club, a member of the U.S. Figure Skating Association. The USFSA regulates skating competitions and tests skaters before they can move up in competitive divisions (juvenile, intermediate, novice, junior, and senior).

Rising every day at 4 A.M. to practice for five hours at the ice rink, Kristi had little time for anything else besides her schoolwork. At age 11, she competed at the Central Pacific Championships where she met 13-year-old Rudi Galindo, who was looking for a pairs partner. Rudi's coach, Jim Hulick, thought Kristi was a perfect match for the young teen. Soon Kristi's time was divided between training in pairs and singles skating.

In 1986, at the Nationals Competition on Long Island, though Kristi and Rudi had only been skating together for three years, they won the junior pairs championship. Kristi's singles skating was improving too. At the 1989 Nationals, Kristi and Rudi won the pairs title. Kristi took the silver medal in the women's singles competition and earned the right to compete at the world championships in Paris, France. She also made history by becoming the first woman to win medals in two events at nationals since 1954.

The year 1989 brought many changes. Coach Hulick died of cancer at the end of the year. Kristi's beloved grandfather George Doi also passed away from lung cancer. Coach Kjarsgaard married and moved to Edmonton, Canada. Eventually Kristi moved in with her coach, so Rudi had to fly back and forth to Canada to work on their pairs' training. Though they won the gold medal again and Kristi won her second silver medal at the nationals in 1990, the worlds were a major disappointment. In pairs, Kristi and Rudi finished fifth. In the singles competition, Kristi finished in fourth place. With the Olympics only two years away, Kristi decided it was time to concentrate exclusively on her individual skating. It turned out to be the best decision for her.

By devoting all her time and energy to singles training, Kristi hoped to make it all the way to the 1992 Olympic Games in Albertville, France. In preparation, she competed in many events. Though she came in second at the 1991 Nationals, Kristi won the world championship title after skating a technically proficient and artistically beautiful program. She was even awarded her first perfect 6.0 mark.

Kristi's dreams were realized in 1992. First, she finally won the championship title at the nationals. *Sports Illustrated* described Kristi's skating as "one of the most complete performances ever seen on American ice." Just prior to taking to the ice for her long program at the Olympics, Kristi had a surprise visitor—Dorothy Hamill. The former Olympic champion came backstage to hug Kristi and wish her good luck. Kristi went out and skated the program of her career. Of her performance, newspapers wrote that Kristi "interpreted her music, *Malagueña,* as if the melodies were written on her skates." Kristi won the gold medal, the first American to do so since her idol, Dorothy Hamill, had won in 1976. Kristi followed in Dorothy's steps again by completing the "triple crown" of skating—the national, Olympic, and world titles—when she defended her title at the world championships in front of a hometown crowd in Oakland, California. Kristi also became the first American woman since Peggy Fleming to win back-to-back world championships.

Because of her success, Kristi was in demand for interviews, appearances, and product endorsements. She hired a management firm to handle her schedule and business opportunities. She signed contracts with Evian bottled water, Ray-Ban sunglasses, and Kraft Philadelphia cream cheese. She turned professional in 1993 and joined the "Stars on Ice" show. Still, Kristi found time to do volunteer work. She became the official spokesperson for the American Lung Association, and started the

Kristi performs at the 1997 Equal World Professional Figure Skating Championship in Washington, D.C.

Always Dream Foundation, which assists organizations in their efforts to provide a positive influence on countless childrens' lives. Part of the funding is contributed by Kristi from her own endorsements and career income.

Kristi Yamaguchi feels blessed by her success. Her hard work, determination, and belief in her abilities should inspire others to strive to reach their own dreams and be the best they can be.

Manon Rheaume

1972–

Ice Hockey

"I didn't try to be the first woman to do this, I just want to play. . . . I love hockey and want to go higher. It's a passion for me."
—Manon Rheaume on playing in the National Hockey League

On September 23, 1992, an NHL exhibition hockey game between the Tampa Bay Lightning and the St. Louis Blues had a slightly unusual twist—the all-male teams had a woman among them for the first time in the league's history. In the first period, Manon Rheaume—20 years old, 5 feet 6 inches (168 cm) tall, and a 125-pound (58-kg) leftie—was in goal for the newly franchised Tampa Bay Lightning.

Manon played well in her debut game, stopping seven of nine shots in her only period of play. Only Blues defenseman Jeff Brown's 35-foot (11-m) rocket and left-winger Brendan Shanahan's slap shot made it past Manon into the net. Her performance on the ice captured the attention of players and coaches from both teams. Her appearance that day was yet another breakthrough for women in professional sports.

Manon Rheaume knew she wanted to be an ice hockey goaltender from the time she was five years old. Born on February 24, 1972, in Lac Beauport, a suburb of Quebec City, Quebec, Manon was the second child and only daughter of Pierre and Nicole Rheaume. Her father was a carpenter and her mother worked as secretary in the local school. In his spare time, Pierre also ran Lac Beauport's outdoor ice rink and coached his son Martin's hockey team.

Shortly after Manon learned to walk, she was learning how to lace up her ice skates. Pierre flooded part of the family's backyard so that Martin, Manon, and her younger brother, Pascal, could skate. Manon often went with her father and brothers to the rink, where she watched endlessly as they practiced ice hockey. When they used the backyard "rink," Manon joined in.

At about five or six, Manon got a chance to play in her first real game when her father Pierre needed a goalie during one of his son's team practices. Manon eagerly volunteered to fill in. Pierre was hesitant at first, but then he realized that his daughter had already practiced with her brothers and agreed to let her play. As she grew older, Manon continued to play hockey, fitting it in between schoolwork and a few other extracurricular activities such as ballet and skiing. The more she played hockey, however, the more she realized that it was her real passion. And because of her skills, she was permitted to play on some of the boys' teams in school. At times she even participated in competition games in the boys' youth league.

After high school, Manon played for a time in Canada's Junior B league, and briefly made it to Junior A, just below the coveted National Hockey League level—a remarkable accomplishment. It was in the Quebec Major Junior Hockey League in November 1991 that Manon showed her toughness. She had replaced Jocelyn Thibault (now with the Montreal Canadians) as goal-tender for the Trois Rivieres Draveurs against the Granby Bisons in a tie game. A shot hit her face mask and shattered it, creating a 3-inch (8-cm) gash above her left eye that would later require three stitches. Yet she continued to play without leaving the ice.

When the city of Tampa Bay, Florida, was awarded a hockey franchise in 1992, Manon was invited to try out. After her now-historic appearance in an exhibition game against the Blues that September, Tampa Bay Lightning's general manager Phil Esposito signed her to a three-year contract with the Atlanta Knights, the Lightning's farm team. In March 1992, Manon was also goal-tender for the Canadian national team in the World Women's Hockey Championship. She was instrumental in winning the gold medal for Canada by recording two shutouts in three games, and she went unbeaten, 3-0-0. For her performance, Manon earned the tournament MVP trophy. (She repeated her achievement two years later in Lake Placid, New York, by going unbeaten 3-0-0 and winning a second gold medal.)

Also in 1992, Manon wrote her autobiography, *Manon: Alone in Front of the Net,* which was released the following year. In it, she discusses her childhood love of hockey and the hurdles she had to overcome to be successful in the male-dominated sport. That December, she made professional hockey history once more when she played in a regular-season game for the Knights against the Salt Lake Golden Eagles. She allowed the Eagles only one goal when opposing player Todd Gillingham fired one past her on a breakaway.

From 1993 to 1994, Manon played for four teams: After being traded from Atlanta to the Knoxville Cherokees, she was sent to Nashville; in 1994, she was traded from Nashville to the Las Vegas Thunder and then to the Tallahassee Tiger Sharks. Manon continued to play through the 1996-1997 season with the Reno Renegades. Unfortunately, at the end of the 1997 season she was cut from Canada's women's national team. But Manon would not be denied: The members of the women's team would be participating in the 1998 Winter Olympics in Nagano, Japan, and she planned to go with them.

Manon embarked on a rigorous training schedule and came back quicker and stronger than ever, making the team in time to travel to Nagano. The Canadian hockey team made it all the way to the gold medal round against the United States. With Manon in the net, team Canada was in the final game until the end, trailing by only one goal. In an attempt to tie the game and send it into overtime, Manon was pulled in order to get an extra player on the ice. But team USA shot a goal into the empty net, winning the game 3-1. Manon and her teammates shared the 1998 Olympic women's hockey silver medal.

In June 1998, Manon Rheaume married professional hockey player Gerry St. Cyr. She and her husband have traveled throughout Canada teaching hockey and goaltending for Volcanix Pure Hockey schools. While playing in an NHL exhibition game and being signed to a minor league has won Manon a considerable amount of attention, many other female hockey players are virtually unknown. For example, in 1990, a U.S. women's national team participated in the first-ever women's world tournament—and won a silver medal. As of the 1994-1995 season, more than 300 girls' ice hockey teams, excluding high school and college teams, were registered in the United States.

Mia Hamm

1972–
Soccer

"I was given a tremendous gift in terms of athleticism, and I believe I was given it for a reason. Maybe it was because I wasn't so confident in other areas."
—Mia Hamm on how playing soccer affected her life

In Athens, Georgia, on August 1, 1996, 76,000 spectators filed into Sanford Stadium. They came to see the competition for the first gold medal in women's soccer in the history of the Olympic Games. The two women's teams vying for the honor were the United States and China. Down on the field, American soccer sensation Mia Hamm glanced around the stadium, reflecting on what was about to take place. When she played in the U.S. Soccer Federation tournament as a teenager in 1987, Mia had dreamed about playing in the Olympics. Now, the dream was about to come true.

Mariel Margaret Hamm was born on March 17, 1972, in Selma, Alabama. Her father Bill was a colonel in the United States Air Force, so the family moved a lot throughout Mia's childhood. Her mother Stephanie had been a ballerina before she married. With four children—Mia, her older brother, and two older sisters—Stephanie now devoted all her time to her family.

A year after Mia was born, her father was transferred to Florence, Italy. Though his first love was flying planes, his favorite pastime was watching sports. Before long, Bill became an avid fan of soccer, one of the most popular sports in Europe. He took the family to games and bought his kids a soccer ball to play with.

A few years later, Bill was transferred back to the United States, and the Hamms settled in Wichita Falls, Texas, in 1977. Thrilled to discover that the town was part of a soccer league, Bill became a coach and referee and Mia's older siblings joined the league. On Saturdays, Mia watched them play and chased after the ball when it rolled off the playing field toward her. Meanwhile, Stephanie enrolled her youngest child in dance school. But Mia took only one class. Ballet was too slow and methodical for the energetic child. Mia wanted to run, chase after her brother and sisters, and kick around a soccer ball.

When Mia was five, Bill and Stephanie adopted an eight-year-old Thai-American boy named Garrett. The boy played soccer very well, and soon Mia and Garrett were inseparable. They often played soccer with other neighborhood kids. Mia also played basketball, baseball, and even football with the boys, but she soon realized that she loved soccer more than any other sport.

At Notre Dame High School, Mia was not only one of the best soccer players on the school team, but she was also among the best in Wichita Falls. It was a good time for American women soccer players; the sport was rapidly becoming popular across the country. John Cossaboon, a coach of the newly created U.S. women's soccer Olympic development team, saw Mia play in a state tournament, and was impressed by her speed and natural athleticism. Without hesitation, he asked Mia to join the Olympic development team.

After working with Mia for a while, John Cossaboon contacted Anson Dorrance, the most influential coach in women's soccer, and asked him to watch Mia play. Dorrance's Tar Heels at the University of North Carolina had already won three NCAA soccer championships, but he had never seen this kind of speed or this uncanny ability to discard defenders on her way to the goal. Not long after, Dorrance put Mia in his summer training camp, and then named her to the national team—the youngest player ever to join.

Mia emerged from training with two goals—to play soccer under Coach Dorrance at the University of North Carolina (UNC), and to win a world championship. The Hamms moved to Burke, Virginia, in 1988, and Mia finished high school there by completing her last two years simultaneously while playing with the high school soccer team. In the fall of 1989, Mia entered UNC at Chapel Hill on a soccer scholarship. During that year, the Tar Heels won their fourth consecutive NCAA soccer championship, and Mia was named MVP of the Atlantic Coast Conference (ACC) tournament. In her second season, Mia led the NCAA in scoring, with 24 goals and 19 assists, as the Tar Heels won their fifth straight title.

But for Mia, the event was bittersweet. The International Soccer Association (FIFA) had announced that it would hold the first women's World Cup tournament in 1991, and if Mia was going to play on the U.S. National Team, she would have to quit school. The World Cup tour required that she commit to playing full-time for a year. Mia chose to join her teammates on the national team. It was a tough decision, but it proved to be a good one—the international experience was invaluable, and the U.S. team became world champions. "When we started the team, we never thought there would be a World Cup," teammate Julie Foudy said, "And now we're holding it."

Mia returned to UNC in 1992. In her last two years there, she racked up record-breaking stats, leading the Tar Heels to two more NCAA championships, and earning Player of the Year awards in 1992, 1993, and 1994. She also received the Hermann Trophy as the nation's top athlete two years in a row. In all, over her four-year collegiate career, Mia had scored 103 goals, made 72 assists, and earned 278 points in 92 games. But what Mia remembers most about her days at UNC is the spirit of her teammates: "The goals and the championships are nice, but the emotions, the tears, and the smiles on my teammates' faces are my championships," she said.

After graduating in 1994 with a degree in political science, Mia married long-time beau Christian Corey. They didn't have much time together, however: Mia joined the national team in Florida, which was preparing to defend its World Cup title in Sweden, and Christian headed to U.S. Marine basic training in Quantico, Virginia.

In the World Cup tournament the U.S. team came in a disappointing third, but in the 1996 Summer Olympic Games, America won over Denmark and Sweden, and was poised to face the Norwegians. Mia had severely sprained her ankle in the game against Sweden, but the U.S. team won the game 2-1, and entered the gold medal match against China. With all Mia's family members cheering her on, the U.S. team pulled ahead 2-1. With time running out, Mia's ankle gave out, and she had to be carried off the field. But the U.S. team had beaten the Chinese and won the gold!

A whirlwind of activity followed. Mia was contacted for interviews and product endorsements; her face appeared on magazines all over the country. What should have been the most exciting time in her life, however, was clouded with worry and concern. Garrett had aplastic anemia, a rare bone marrow disease, and though he had been in remission for a number of years, the disease had reemerged. Despite a bone marrow transplant in February 1997, Garrett died from complications two months later. Mia was devastated. "I'd give up all of this in a heartbeat to have him back," she said, "just to give him one more day or one more week. But I know he wouldn't want that. . . .Now, no matter where I play, I feel Garrett is there."

It took a while for Mia to turn her heart back to soccer, but she returned with a vengeance in 1998. The national team beat Norway in the International Women's Tournament and turned in a gold medal performance at the Goodwill Games. In the final game against China, Mia scored the only two points, and she finished the season as the all-time leading goal-scorer in U.S. soccer history.

That year, Mia was named Female Athlete of the Year by the U.S. Soccer Association and one of the "50 Most Beautiful People in America" by *People* magazine. She also signed an endorsement contract with Nike. But Mia routinely deflects attention to her individual accomplishments and focuses on being a member of a team. Though her talents make her one of the most successful athletes in the world, Mia Hamm is much more comfortable being recognized as the consummate team player.

This is My Game, This is My Future, Watch Me Play

"We came to understand that this World Cup wasn't just about us making it to Pasadena and winning. This is a historic event far beyond any single result."
—Mia Hamm on the U.S. Women's Soccer Team's World Cup victory, 1999

Twenty-seven years after the passage of Title IX—legislation that requires equal financing and opportunities for girls' athletic programs in schools and colleges that receive federal funds—a women's sporting event took center stage around the world. On Saturday, July 10, 1999, at the Rose Bowl in Pasadena, California, the United States and China faced off in the World Cup Women's Soccer final. The sold-out crowd of more than 90,000 set a record for women's sports, and an estimated 40 million TV viewers tuned in to ABC to watch the game—the largest TV audience ever to watch a soccer match.

In a grueling match that ran 120 minutes and included two overtime periods, the two teams were locked in a scoreless tie. That left the victory to be determined by a "shoot-out"—a series of five penalty kicks by each team. Each penalty kick is delivered by one player positioned 12 yards from the opposing team's goal. Even without the incredible pressure of the World Cup championship hanging in the balance, a goalkeeper turning away just one shot can be miraculous.

China was up first. Xie Huilin fired the ball past U.S. goalie Briana Scurry into the lower left corner of the net. The U.S. team's first kicker was Carla Overbeck. Facing Hong Goa—so imposing a goalie that she is nicknamed the "Great Wall of China"—Overbeck drove the ball into the lower right corner as Goa, who guessed wrong, lunged in the opposite direction to block the kick. The score: China, 1; United States, 1.

Qiu Haiyan kicked her ball up and over Scurry's right shoulder. Joy Fawcett responded by firing her shot past Goa. Only Liu Ying was thwarted in her attempt to score on Scurry, and an amazing diving fingertip deflection turned Ying's shot aside. That miss opened the door for the U.S. team to pull ahead of the Chinese for the first time in the match. Though Goa guessed where Kristine Lilly's shot was headed and threw herself across the goal, she couldn't stop the ball from sailing into the net. China scored on their last two kicks, and Mia Hamm scored on her penalty kick, tying the game again at 4-4. Only one player and one kick remained, and it rested with the American team's Brandi Chastain.

The road to the 1999 Women's World Cup Championship had begun more than 140 matches and two years earlier. But the real journey began in the early 1990s when Dr. João Havelange, then president of the Fédération Internationale de Football Association (FIFA), the governing body of soccer, brought Women's World Cup Soccer to life.

The first Women's World Cup ran from November 16 to 30, 1991, and was hosted by the People's Republic of China. The U.S. team's forward line, dubbed the "Triple-Edged Sword" by the Chinese media, was made up of team captain April Heinrichs, Michelle Akers, and Carin Jennings. They blazed through the first round of the tournament, defeating Sweden 3-2, Brazil 5-0, and Japan 3-0. In the "knockout" round, the U.S. routed China 7-0 in the quarterfinals on the strength of five goals by Akers. The second round is called the "knockout" round because the losing team is eliminated from the tournament. Three goals by Carin Jennings helped eliminate Germany from the semifinals. In the first Women's World Cup Championship final, pitting the United States against Norway, 65,000 fans crowded into Guangzhou's Tianhe Stadium. The game was tied 1-1 with just minutes to go when Akers scored her second goal and sealed a victory for the United States.

While professional soccer is a popular sport around the world, it has been overshadowed by football, basketball, and baseball in the United States. And women's soccer, like most women's sports, was further overshadowed by men's soccer. As a result, the victorious U.S. women's soccer team returned home in 1991 to a lukewarm reception. However, the seeds of women's soccer in America had been planted.

The second FIFA Women's World Cup tournament took place in Sweden in 1995. The defending champion U.S. team suffered a major setback in its first match when Michelle Akers was injured seven minutes into a game against China. The game ended in a 3-3 draw. The U.S. team bounced back, defeating Denmark and then Australia to clinch a spot in the quarterfinals. Against Japan, the U.S. women had their way for most of the match, earning a 4-0 victory, but in the semifinals they lost to Norway. That team became the newest World Cup champion after defeating Germany in a match played in torrential rain. As the U.S. team headed home, they vowed to regain the top spot.

Under the direction of coach Tony DiCicco, the U.S. team regrouped. DiCicco's coaching style was based on positive reinforcement—a tactic he calls "catching them at being good." During postgame analysis, instead of running video footage of player's mistakes, he showed clips of the players at their best, displaying their strong defensive skills and making the moves that signaled a championship team. DiCicco also fostered team unity and individual self-confidence with physical and psychological exercises aimed at strengthening the players' camaraderie and trust in one another.

The first challenge for the newly cohesive team was to reclaim number one status. At the 1996 Summer Olympic Games in Atlanta, Georgia, women's soccer made its debut as a medal event. The international recognition boosted fan support in the United States to an all-time high and Team USA did not disappoint. The players advanced through the first round of competition with two wins, no losses, and a scoreless tie with China. Against their nemesis, Norway, the U.S. players were tied 1-1 until Julie Foudy passed the ball to Shannon MacMillan, who tucked it into the left corner in the 100th minute of the game. That win set up the final match: the United States versus China for the gold medal.

Star forward Mia Hamm was nursing a sore ankle and an injured groin muscle going into the final on August 1. At halftime, the teams were deadlocked at 1–1, and Mia considered taking herself out of the game to avoid hindering play. Her teammates would have none of it, however, and 68 minutes into the game, Mia spotted teammate Joy Fawcett running down the right wing and passed the ball to her. Joy then centered a pass to the streaking Tiffeny Milbrett, who kicked the ball past two defenders and goalkeeper Hong Gao. With only a minute remaining and the U.S. team leading 2-1, Mia Hamm was taken off the field on a stretcher—but she was carried back after the clock ran out to celebrate the U.S. Olympic gold medal victory. The team turned its attention to Pasadena in 1999.

The third Women's World Cup tournament was jump-started in June 1996 when the Women's World Cup Organizing Committee was incorporated. The nonprofit organization was established to forge "a breakthrough event for

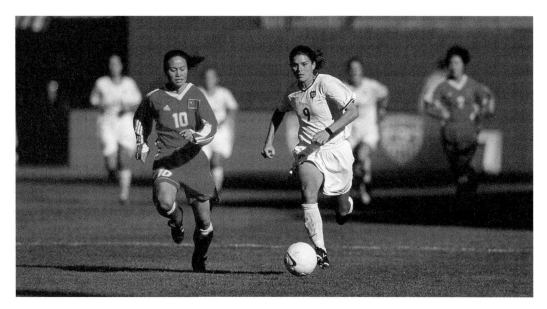

In April 1999, Mia Hamm (number 9, in white) and Team USA faced China at Giants Stadium, New Jersey.

women's sports and inspire the next generation of female athletes." Their aggressive marketing campaign attracted 19 corporate sponsors for Team USA including Adidas, Gatorade, and Allstate, and funneled $6 million into the tournament. The team members also made promotional appearances that included TV spots, autograph sessions, and interviews. The committee hoped to sell 350,000 tickets for the 32-game tournament. They were more than successful: the actual number sold—650,000—translated into nearly $23 million.

On August 21, 1997, in Hjørring, Denmark, the 1999 Women's World Cup Soccer tournament opened its qualifying rounds to 63 countries. By June 19, 1999, that number had been pared to 16 including the United States, which earned an automatic berth as the host nation. The teams were divided into four groups; the United States was placed in Group A with Korea, Nigeria, and Denmark. The U.S. women defeated Denmark and Nigeria in their first two matches, then moved into the knockout round after winning against Korea.

They next defeated Germany 3-2 in the first knockout match, and as an estimated 2.9 million TV viewers watched, they went on to beat Brazil 2-0, earning a return trip to the World Cup finals against their old rival, China.

It all came down to that last penalty kick, perhaps the most dramatic way to end a game. Brandi Chastain stepped up to the ball for her shot and refused to look at China's goalkeeper, Hong Goa. Chastain knew that the veteran Goa liked to psych out her opponents by smiling and distracting them, and she would have none of it. She lowered her head and fired the ball past the diving goalie and into the net for the World Cup victory. Overcome by the moment, Chastain ripped off her jersey and waved it at the deliriously ecstatic crowd. Within seconds, she was mobbed by her teammates. Coach DiCicco saluted the Chinese team and declared, "There are two champions here. There is only one taking the World Cup home."

The 1999 World Cup tournament was clearly a rousing success, both financially and athletically. Can the U.S. women's soccer team ride this wave of enthusiasm even further and form a professional women's soccer league in America? On the heels of the Cup tournament's popularity comes the 2000 Summer Olympics in Sydney, Australia—the same country bidding for host rights to the next Women's Soccer World Cup in 2003.

Clearly, women's sports in general and women's soccer in particular are enjoying tremendous growth and recognition in the United States. Over the last nine years, more than 100,000 girls have begun playing soccer. But regardless of the future of women's soccer, there is no doubt that Team USA's 1999 victory was more than a single win. It also marked a new era in the recognition of professional women's athletics in the United States.

"This is My Game, This is My Future, Watch Me Play," was the theme of FIFA's 1999 World Cup competition. That motto should serve as an inspiration to today's young girls who hope to enjoy equality in whatever sport they choose.

Marion Jones

1975–

Basketball, Track and Field

"Before my career is over, I will attempt to run faster than any woman has ever run and jump farther than any woman has ever jumped."
—Marion Jones on her own expectations as an athlete

She has a goal—a goal she has dreamed about every day. For the last few years, sprinter and basketball star Marion Jones has closed her eyes and imagined a future moment. Every detail is etched in her mind—the gritty

feel of the track, the slight breeze blowing across her face, the clear blue sky bathed in warm sunlight, the sounds in the stadium, what she is wearing, and how the morning of this momentous day begins for her.

In this future time, the image is now in full motion, and she sees herself crossing the finish line of the 100-meter dash, a new world record time flashing on the board as she slows up her stride and jogs past it. She knows it is *her* new world record. In that instant, she is proclaimed the fastest woman in the world. But that is only one-third of the dream. She moves on to the 200-meter sprint, and again she runs in world record time. Finally, she makes her way to the long jump pit. Her takeoff down the runway is flawless. Suspended in the air for what seems like forever, she lands in the sand pit, completing the longest jump ever recorded. The fixed expression of concentration on her face is now replaced by sheer elation. She has reason to be excited—she has completed a triple crown in track and field, and can celebrate her place among the elite women athletes in history. It may still be a dream, but Marion Jones is determined to make it a reality.

Born in the southern California city of Los Angeles on October 12, 1975, Marion Jones, according to her mother Marion and stepfather Ira Toler had always been on the move. Happy to hang out with her older brother Albert on the neighborhood playgrounds, Marion explored anything and everything. Recognizing their daughter's high energy level, the Tolers steered Marion into sports, where she had a positive outlet for all that energy. She left virtually no sport unexplored—softball, basketball, gymnastics, track and field. Marion even ventured into dance for a while, taking ballet and tap lessons. She loved the freedom she felt from all the various activities she was involved with.

When Marion was 12 years old, Ira suffered a stroke and died. Marion was close to her stepfather, and the loss was devastating. Her mother often had to work more than one job to support the family, and she inspired Marion to work just as hard in her academics and sports. By the time Marion reached high school, she was one of the best sprinters in the state. As a sophomore at Rio Mesa High School, Marion clocked the season's fastest sprint times in the 100-, 200-, and 400-meter races. In 1991, she was named National Player of the Year for girls' track. She would earn the honor again the following two years.

In 1992, Marion transferred to Thousand Oaks High School for her junior year. She continued to excel in track, and became an outstanding basketball player. When the Olympic trials were held that spring, Marion missed qualifying for the 200-meter event by just 7/100 second. Still, she had earned a place on the relay team, but as an alternate. It was quite an accomplishment for the 16-year-old. However, Marion decided to pass on the trip to the Barcelona Olympics. She did not want to chance winning a medal in an event in which she probably would not compete. Marion remembered that at age seven, she wrote on her chalkboard that someday she wanted to be an Olympic champion. When and if Marion won her first Olympic medal, she wanted it to be awarded to her because she earned it.

That fall, Marion returned to Thousand Oaks for her senior year. She had a record-setting season with the school basketball team, averaging more than 22 points, and 14 rebounds a game. In the two seasons that she played for Thousand Oaks, the team compiled a record of 60 wins and only 4 losses. For her outstanding play, Marion was named California High School Player of the Year.

Moving on to track after the basketball season ended, Marion was running better than ever. At this time, Marion decided to try her skills in the long jump. Her combined speed and athleticism made her a perfect contender in the sport. Marion quickly picked up the long jump technique, and in her first competition she jumped more than 19 feet (5.8 m). When she reached the California High School Championships, her jump of 22 feet (6.7 m) was good enough to earn her the win.

Many colleges were interested in Marion and she was deluged with athletic scholarship offers. Ultimately she decided to attend the University of North Carolina (UNC). Once her athletic career was over, Marion wanted to become a writer, and UNC had a good journalism program. It also had a great athletics program, and Marion's mom thought the university structure would be good for her daughter. Besides, UNC was willing to let Marion run track *and* play basketball, which particularly appealed to her. This way, Marion didn't have to choose between the two sports she loved.

In her first season playing basketball, Marion helped the Tar Heels upset Louisiana Tech 62-57 to win the national championship. She went from basketball to track and was named All-American. In the second basketball season, the Tar Heels had a good year, winning the Atlantic Coast Conference (ACC) title, but did not make it back to the national championship. Marion was beginning to feel torn between her two sports, and moved away from serious track for a while. The upcoming 1996 Olympic Games in Atlanta pushed Marion to start thinking about whether she should try out for the U.S. women's basketball team or the track team. Ultimately, it didn't matter. Just a few months before the Olympic trials, Marion broke her ankle. Though fitted with two metal screws, her ankle gave way while she was trying to rehabilitate the injury. The closest Marion would get to the Atlanta stadium track was seeing it on television.

The year 1997 was Marion's last year at UNC. The Tar Heels won the ACC championship again, but did not make the finals. With her studies completed, Marion felt it was time to move on with her athletic career. Most people assumed Marion would opt to join one of the two new women's professional basketball leagues, the ABL or the WNBA. However, Marion's first love had always been track, so she chose not to enter either league. Instead she began working with Trevor Graham, the coach of her boyfriend C.J. Hunter, a shot putter. The two met at UNC, became fast friends, and their relationship blossomed into a romance.

Graham was impressed with Marion's skills, but not just her running ability. Graham noted that what separated Marion from other runners was that she thought out her moves, which made her very easy to coach. Soon, with little nuance changes in her physical racing technique, Marion was sprinting incredible times. At the 1997 U.S. Track and Field Championships, Marion ran a 10.92 in the 100-meter semifinal heat. She won the final easily, clocking a 10.97 run.

Just as the crowd was trying to find out who this new sprinter phenomenon was, Marion had moved on to the long jump competition. Jackie Joyner-Kersee had been the reigning long jump champ, but it

Another great day at the track for Marion

mattered little to Marion. Jackie was leading the competition as Marion made her final jump in the event. She landed an inch farther than Jackie, and with a jump of 22 feet 9 inches (6.9 m), Marion Jones became the new national champion.

Marion had a spectacular 1998 season. At the U.S. Championships, she accomplished what no other athlete had in the last 50 years—she won the 100-meter and 200-meter sprints and the long jump. In all, Marion won 36 of the 37 events she entered in 1998. When the track season was over, Marion and C.J. were married.

Now Marion is focusing on the 2000 Summer Games in Sydney, Australia. She believes she can become the first athlete to win five gold medals in one Olympics. Many think Marion has the best chance to break Florence Griffith Joyner's world record in the 100-meters, which she set in 1988. No one has come closer to breaking it than Marion. Coach Graham is only interested in keeping his track star focused on being faster than anyone else. If world records are achieved, all the better, but the primary goal is to win. Whatever the outcome, spectators are sure to witness an athletic performance by the next century's heir apparent superstar of track and field.

Shannon Miller

1977–

Gymnastics

"My family brought the spirit of the people of Oklahoma with them to Barcelona. And a vibrant spirit it is—people willing to give of themselves so that our family could be there to share in my dreams. I'm so proud to be part of such a generous, thoughtful, and loving community."

—Shannon Miller acknowledging the citizens of Oklahoma who raised $35,000 so she could compete in the 1992 Olympics in Barcelona, Spain

Two months before the 1992 U.S. Gymnastics Championships in Columbus, Ohio, Shannon Miller's dream of going to the Summer Olympic Games in Barcelona, Spain was almost shattered. During a practice in the gym, Shannon missed a move, fell, and severely injured her elbow. The doctors gave her a choice—wear a cast for six weeks and let the elbow heal naturally, or have surgery to correct the problem. If she opted for the cast, she would miss the Olympics, but the surgery still wouldn't guarantee that she'd be healed enough to compete. Shannon wanted a fighting chance to make the Olympics, so she had the surgery.

Amazing even her coach Steve Nunno, Shannon competed at the nationals a month later, winning the balance beam competition and placing third in the vault. At the Olympic trials, Shannon stunned everyone by finishing first overall, securing a place on the U.S. gymnastics team going to Barcelona. The dream was alive and well.

Shannon Miller, 4 feet 11 inches (150 cm) tall, weighing 90 pounds (41 kg) and the pride of Edmond, Oklahoma, at the height of her fame, was born on March 10, 1977, in Rollo, Missouri. Unlike many gymnastic hopefuls who train far from their families, Shannon lived at home with her parents. Her father Ron is a physics professor and her mom Claudia is a bank vice president. When Shannon was five, she and her sister got a trampoline for Christmas. Naturally the girls tested the limits of their new apparatus, bouncing about, doing flips and spins. Ron and Claudia, concerned for their daughters' safety, enrolled the girls in the local gymnastics school.

When Shannon was nine, she went with her club to Moscow to participate in a two-week training camp. There, Shannon caught the attention of Steve Nunno, a U.S. gymnastics coach who had worked as an assistant to the legendary Bela Karolyi. By chance, Nunno was from Oklahoma, and ran a gym called Dynamo about half an hour away from Shannon's home. Nunno was impressed as he watched Shannon. Though she was frustrated because she was having difficulty with some of the maneuvers, Nunno felt that he could help Shannon become a better gymnast if he could teach her to channel her energy in a more positive way.

The matchup worked well. In a very short period of time, Shannon was performing on a par with her contemporaries, and soon she was a world-class competitor. In 1990, when she was just 13, Shannon made the senior U.S. national gymnastics team. At the world championships in Indianapolis, Indiana, in 1991, Shannon caught everyone's attention when she qualified for all four events in the finals, becoming the first American female to do so. She won a silver medal in the uneven bars. As the top scorer on the U.S. squad, Shannon helped her team capture second place in the team competition, thus assuring the U.S. women their first medal ever in a world gymnastics championship.

All the pressure of competition reached a crescendo in 1992, an Olympics year. Shannon survived the early challenge of coming back from her elbow surgery to make the Olympic team, and upset favored Kim Zmeskal at the Olympic trials by winning the all-around competition. In Barcelona, Shannon's performance did not disappoint. She won five medals, earning three of them in one night. Her silver medal in the all-around marked the highest finish by an American gymnast, and she was the only member on her team to win an individual medal.

After Barcelona, Shannon continued to perform brilliantly, remaining the top female gymnast in the world. She won the all-around gold medal at the world championships in 1993, successfully defending her title in 1994. In all, by the end of 1994, Shannon had won seven world championship gold medals, more than any of her countrymen had in the history of gymnastics.

A truly dedicated athlete who practiced more than 45 hours a week while attending school full-time, Shannon's grades were as bright as her medals. In 1994, she graduated from Edmond North High School with a 4.0 average, and

Shannon displays her extraordinary talent at the 1996 Atlanta Olympics.

was a member of the Oklahoma Honor Society as well as the National Honor Society.

Though injuries plagued Shannon off and on during the 1995 season, she wore the true heart of a champion by bouncing back whenever she faltered or had a poor showing. She won the all-around at the Pan American Games, and after falling on the balance beam at the nationals, Shannon climbed back on, finished her routine and nailed a difficult twisting double-back dismount. She failed to win the all-around by just two-tenths of a point. Undaunted, Shannon went on to win the individual gold medal in the vault.

Nursing a tender ankle and sore wrist, Shannon could only manage a 12th-place finish at the 1995 world championships in Sabae, Japan. However, she never lost her self-confidence. Continuing to be plagued by nagging injuries, Shannon decided to take some time off to rest and heal. Recharged and determined, she came back to competition better than ever. She won the balance beam event, even though she fell, and had incorporated new moves in several routines. Though Shannon's wrist problem actually worsened by the time of the 1996 Olympic trials, her national championship scores were good enough to earn her a spot on the Olympic team.

At 19, Shannon was considered old for a gymnast, but she dazzled the crowds in Atlanta, quieting the whispers of doubt about her abilities. Shannon led her teammates, known as the Magnificent Seven or "Mag 7"—Dominique Moceanu, Dominique Dawes, Kerri Strug, Amanda Borden, Amy Chow, and Jaycee Phelps—to the first gold medal ever won by a U.S. women's gymnastics team. Shannon had finally captured the elusive Olympic gold medal. She topped off her marvelous 1996 Olympic Games by winning an individual gold medal on the balance beam.

With her seven Olympic medals, and nine world championship medals, Shannon Miller is the most decorated gymnast, male or female, in U.S. history. In her amazing career, Shannon has won more than 100 national and international competition medals. After the 1996 Atlanta Games, Shannon competed in some fun events, and enrolled at the University of Oklahoma to work on a degree in business. In 1997, Shannon released a book called *Winning Every Day* in which she shares her thoughts about how she was able to realize her dreams through strong commitment, self-confidence, and setting definable goals. Shannon's volunteer work includes acting as the national spokesperson for Drug Free Youth USA and the Children's Miracle Network.

On September 27, 1998, Shannon announced her engagement to fourth-year medical student Chris B. Phillips. They were married in the summer of 1999. Though Shannon will be 23 years old by the opening of the Summer Games in Sydney, Australia, she is leaving all of her options open. She's considering a tryout for the U.S. team, but hasn't firmly committed yet. However, judging by her past achievements, there is no doubt Shannon will devote the same dedication and discipline that carried her to the top of her sport, and earned her the title *champion*.

Martina Hingis

1980–
Tennis

"My game came so naturally. I won everything I wanted to win. No one could beat me. I had no motivation to work harder because I didn't think I needed to. I guess I was wrong."
—Martina Hingis on why she lost her number one ranking

Though unseeded, 19-year-old Amelie Mauresmo of France made it to the women's final of the 1999 Australian Open. Waiting to meet her on the court was Martina Hingis, the 18-year-old former number one ranked women's tennis player in the world. Martina's reign at number one ended in October 1998, when she lost to Dominique Van Roost in the quarterfinal match at Filderstadt, Germany. Since 1975, only eight players have held the number one ranking including tennis greats Chris Evert, Martina Navratilova, Tracy Austin, and Steffi Graf. Martina felt she was the best in the world and wanted to reclaim her place on top.

Amelie's appearance in the final against Martina was not a fluke. She stunned the crowd with an upset victory in her semifinal match against number one ranked Lindsay Davenport of the United States. Though Amelie gave Martina a good battle, fighting off six match points, she finally succumbed to the three-time Australian Open singles champion. With Davenport's loss and this tournament in the win column for herself, Martina could only wait for the new rankings to be announced. Few felt that it would be anybody else.

To understand Martina's drive, you need look no further than her coach, who also happens to be her mother. Melanie Molitar is the powerful force behind her daughter. Once a top-ranked tennis player in her own right, Melanie's athletic career was severely restricted because she lived under the oppressive veil of Communism in Roznov, Czechoslovakia. Another young woman was also making her presence felt in tennis circles—Martina Navratilova. She became Melanie's idol. Navratilova eventually defected to the United States, but Melanie was not good enough to attempt a defection too. Instead she married Karol Hingis, also a tennis player and sometimes a coach. They moved to Koùsice, Slovakia, and Melanie became pregnant.

Martina Hingis, who was named after Martina Navratilova, was born on September 30, 1980. Martina is sure her career was already decided while she was still in her mother's womb. When her daughter was only two years old, Melanie sawed down the handle of a tennis racket, placed it in Martina's tiny hands, and hit balls to her every day. At first it was just 10 minutes of practice. By age three, Martina was hitting the ball back and forth to Melanie. When

Martina turned four, her mother doubled her practice time to 20 minutes. Martina played her first match at the tender age of five.

At six years old, the young protégé was so athletically gifted that she was able to serve the ball after tossing it over her head. She won her first tennis match that same year. Still, being so young, Martina got bored easily and it challenged Melanie to come up with a practice routine to keep her daughter training and interested in the sport. Instead of forcing Martina to stay on the court hitting balls for hours, Melanie mixed in other athletic activities. Martina enjoyed skiing and soccer, and later developed a passion for horseback riding.

On the home front, Martina's parents became estranged, and filed for divorce. Martina was rocked by the split. Melanie took her daughter back to Roznov, a five-hour journey away from Karl, so Martina didn't get to see her father very often. In 1988, Melanie married a Swiss computer salesman named Andreas Zogg, and the family moved to Grabs, Switzerland. The adjustment was very hard on Martina, then eight. The language was difficult to grasp, and she felt out of place in school. Eventually, Martina learned Swiss-German and her youthful resiliency helped her adjust to the new surroundings.

Outside the classroom, tennis continued to dominate Martina's life. At age nine, she became Swiss champion for girls under 12. At 10, she finally beat Melanie in a match. Martina moved through the junior ranks, winning tournament after tournament, and in 1993 Melanie felt her daughter was ready for a "major" challenge. Martina entered the French Open, becoming the youngest player ever to win the junior singles title at Roland Garros Stadium. Martina repeated the feat the following year, and also collected the youngest champ title at Wimbledon. With her number one female world ranking, it was time to move ahead.

On October 4, 1994, just one week after she turned 14, Martina joined the professional tennis circuit. Playing older, more seasoned players was an important step for Martina. Though she didn't win any major tournaments over the next two years, she made her mark on the game and an indelible impression on the other players. Wins over a host of top-notch opponents such as Jana Novotna, Anke Huber, and Arantxa Sanchez Vicario earned Martina the WTA's Most Impressive Newcomer of 1995 honors.

Martina had personal growing pains in 1996, too, as a maturing teenager. Martina and Melanie often clashed about many things, including practice time, commitment to the game, and laziness. Finally, after Martina was upset in the first round of the Lipton Championships in Florida, Melanie gave her young daughter an ultimatum: "Work harder, train my way, or quit tennis." Martina chose tennis, and began a more rigorous training program that included aerobics and shadowboxing. Building up her endurance and strength paid great dividends. In July, with her doubles partner Helena Sukova, Martina became the youngest woman ever to win at Wimbledon. In two important matches at the end of the year, Martina beat idol Monica Seles to win the Bank of the West Classic, and lost to number one tennis star Steffi Graf in a hard-fought match in the finals at the Chase Championship.

Martina made a vow to herself to come out blazing in 1997, and she made good on her pledge. It was a highly successful and history-making year for the determined 17 year old. At the Australian Open, Martina and partner Natasha Zvereva won the doubles title. She also captured her first Grand Slam singles title, beating Mary Pierce in the final. By winning both titles at Melbourne, Martina became the youngest ever champion of the Australian Open, and the youngest singles player in 110 years to win a Grand Slam event! Shortly after the tournament, Martina again entered the record books by being named the world's number one ranked female player.

A knee injury was perhaps the only thing that kept Martina from becoming the fourth woman in tennis history to complete the Grand Slam. Six weeks before the French Open, Martina ripped some ligaments in her knee after a fall while horseback riding. Surgery corrected the injury, and Martina played

Martina celebrates her win at the 1999 Australian Open.

well, but lost in the final to her best friend Iva Majoli. After some much-needed rest, Martina headed off to play at Wimbledon. Another championship win put Martina in the record books. Just shy of 17, Martina was the youngest player to win at Wimbledon since 1887!

The last of the Grand Slam tournaments that year also belonged to Martina. She won the U.S. Open, beating America's Venus Williams 6-0, 6-4. With that win, Martina completed an incredible 63-1 season, and became the first female player to earn more than $3 million in one year. She was also named Associated Press Female Athlete of the Year.

Martina was certainly on top of the tennis world during the 1998 season, but it was a year of ups and downs for her. She successfully defended her Australian Open title, and by early summer enjoyed a number one ranking in both singles and doubles simultaneously. Martina also completed the Grand Slam in doubles, with victories at the Australian, French, and U.S. Opens, and Wimbledon. However, she slacked off on practice and in workouts. The lack of intensity or interest in maintaining the hard work that got her to number one showed in Martina's singles play.

After the Australian Open, Martina went the rest of the year without another major tournament victory. She lost three times to Davenport, twice to Seles and Venus Williams, and once to a younger player, Anna Kournikova. After an 80-week reign as the number one player in the world, Martina dropped to number two on October 11, 1998, after her quarterfinal loss at Filderstadt.

Some lessons are hard to learn. Martina realized she could no longer win on talent alone. After getting back to serious training, she did well in the 1999 season. At the Australian Open, Martina won her third consecutive singles title. She also won in doubles, her fifth straight Grand Slam doubles championship. But that was only the first step on the road back to her goal of reclaiming her number one ranking. Two weeks after the Australian Open win, Martina reached her goal, defeating Amanda Coetzer at the Pan Pacific Open, 6-2, 6-1.

Martina did not like losing her number one ranking, but she was only away from the top for 17 weeks. She has been on a winning streak, beating almost all comers—including former number one Lindsay Davenport, Monica Seles, Steffi Graf, Jana Novotna, and Mary Pierce. How long will she stay on top? Many tennis watchers feel that is really up to Martina herself. Unquestionably the talent is there, but will the grit and determination last? Martina says "I've gotten my game back, and I am very professional about tennis now. But I know I still act like a teenager off the court. I have a lot to learn about life and being an adult. I'm not there yet. But hopefully, I have learned to separate that from tennis. I guess we will see this year."

Play By Play: Women In Sportscasting

"Progress of women in sports is slow for the same reason that it's so slow in the business world. It's a male-dominated society that we live in, and on top of that, most people in the sports world are chauvinists."
—male sports executive who asked to remain anonymous

Women make up 52 percent of the adult population, and as of 1997, comprise about 46 percent of the workforce in the United States. For much of the twentieth century, they have been fighting an uphill battle for gender equality, working for a stronger voice in government, better educations, job positions and salaries equal to those of their male counterparts, and entry into every area of sports. Though some gains have been made, only a small percentage of women hold government positions or executive positions in the private sector.

The world of sports for women hasn't fared much better. Until 1920, American women could not take part in the Olympics, and it wasn't until the 1972 Munich Games that women were permitted to run distances longer than 1,500 meters. Ironically, 1972 was also the first year women were officially permitted to enter the Boston Marathon. Just a little over 25 years ago, no college athletic scholarships were available to women, and the only professional sports open to women were golf and bowling.

The good news is that more girls and women are participating in sports today than ever before. In 1976, the male-to-female ratio of Olympic competitors in Montreal was 6:1; in 1996 in Atlanta the ratio was narrowed considerably to 3:1. However, in many circles sports is still viewed as a "male" domain, so it should come as no surprise that the number of women in professional sportscasting is negligible despite the endless hours devoted to broadcasting sporting events such as basketball, baseball, ice hockey, football, auto racing, golf, and tennis. A major reason for this is that sports audiences are dominated by men who do not want to hear a woman describing a quarterback sack, a double play, or a slam dunk. That job has traditionally been left to lifetime sportscasters such as Jack Whitaker, Dick Stockton, and Pat Summerall, or former players such as Terry Bradshaw and Bill Walton and former pro coaches like John Madden.

Finally, in the late 1970s two women did appear in front of the camera. During NFL pregame shows, Phyllis George, a pretty, personable southern gal, and Jayne Kennedy, a young, beautiful black actress-in-training, were both facing the camera. However, they were given fluff piece roles—asking players and coaches about how they met their wives and girlfriends, for example. The hard-core sports reporting, analysis, and play-by-play responsibilities were still handled by men.

A few women, former athletes who had excelled in their chosen sports, were hired to provide some color commentary on their sports during special events like the Olympics or a women's NCAA basketball championship. Donna de Varona, the teenage Olympic gold medal swimmer, had retired from amateur competition at age 17, and wanted to get into television broadcasting. She landed a job with ABC and was the first woman to appear on network television as a sportscaster. Her early assignments were to cover AAU swimming championship meets in New Haven, Connecticut. Eventually de Varona also became an assistant to ABC Sports president Roone Arledge.

Hannah Storm arrives at the 1994 Women's Tennis Association Benefit.

Mary Carillo accidentally fell into her broadcasting career. As a tennis pro, Mary was not really a standout. During broadcast coverage of the Avon Championships in 1980, a couple of announcers who were working the tournament for a cable network interviewed Mary to fill some time between matches. She was so interesting to talk to, and discussed tennis so naturally that she stayed through the evening's telecast, providing commentary on the matches taking place. Mary was courted by USA network, and later CBS, primarily to cover professional tennis.

Today, fewer than 50 women work as sportscasters for the more than 600 network affiliate stations nationwide. A few women appear on network television covering sports, but it is not due to any groundbreaking efforts by the three big networks—ABC, CBS, and NBC. Any such praises should go to the cable television industry, particularly ESPN. The all-sports network, based in Bristol, Connecticut, hired its first female talent in 1983—Gayle Gardner. Today she is one of the most successful and highest-paid women in the business.

Gardner, described as a tiny, intense dynamo, grew up in Brooklyn, New York, watching sports as a closet fan. She particularly enjoyed football, especially the New York Giants. She started her career in television as a talk show producer in Boston, and has worked in almost every capacity in broadcasting, both in front of and behind the camera. Gardner had worked in quite a few broadcast city markets—from New York to Detroit and Baltimore—when she got the call from ESPN in 1983. Then, in 1988, she was hired by NBC as a sports anchor and chief features reporter. Gardner was the first woman seen on a weekly basis in the studio sports anchor role.

CNN, the all-news cable network brainchild of owner Ted Turner, followed

ESPN's example by hiring sports anchor Hannah Storm in the late 1980s. Hannah knows sports; while she was growing up, her father served as commissioner of the American Basketball Association and president of the NBA Atlanta Hawks organization. Storm got her first broadcasting experience while attending the University of Notre Dame. She worked at the college's television station, WNDU, covering a vast array of sporting events.

Leslie Visser's on-air polish took years of dedicated practice to perfect.

With a degree in communications and political science, Storm sent out almost 200 résumés for sportscasting jobs, but came up empty. Instead, she wound up on radio as a disk jockey and eventually parlayed her on-air experience into radio sports work. Storm finally got her break in 1989, when she was hired by CNN. Though she often worked 12-hour days, the experience prepared her for the network level.

In 1992, Storm was hired by NBC where she covered a variety of sports, including tennis and college football. Gradually she worked her way into sideline reporting for the NFL, and as a reporter for the NBA. She broke through in 1995, becoming the first woman to host a weekly network pregame show in a major league sport—"Baseball Night In America." Since then Storm has coanchored two Olympics, and in 1997 she replaced Bob Costas as host of "NBA Showtime." When NBC assigned Storm to do the play-by-play for the WNBA, the new women's basketball league, she was thrilled. After all, she was raised on basketball.

Perhaps one of the most experienced and knowledgeable women working in sportscasting today is Lesley Visser. Her résumé is long and extensive. Visser has covered 10 NCAA Final Four tournaments, 12 Wimbledons, 5 NFL Super Bowl games, 5 NBA Finals championships, 2 NLB World Series, and 1

Olympic Games. She has often been quoted as saying "I wasn't at the dawn of women covering sports. But I made the breakfast."

As a child, Visser was an avid sports fan. She loved watching the Green Bay Packers and the Boston Celtics. Her sports idols, however, were female sports pioneers Wilma Rudolph and Billie Jean King. When she was a teenager, Visser decided she wanted to work as a sportswriter, a job that didn't exist for women at the time. After earning a degree in English at Boston College in 1975, Visser began her career as a sportswriter for the *Boston Globe*. When she was 21, she became the first woman to cover the NFL beat for the paper. Football can be particularly shaky territory for a woman, and Visser quickly found that she was not welcome in the locker room after games to interview players, as the male writers and broadcasters were.

In 1980, CBS took a chance with Visser. At the network level, most people are hired first for their television experience, and then learn their assigned area. In Visser's case it was the opposite—CBS wanted somebody who was very knowledgeable about sports, someone they would teach how to appear on camera. For Visser it was a slow, and sometimes embarrassing process, but eventually she got the hang of listening to the technical staff talking in her earpiece on-air, while she continued to speak in her microphone. When CBS lost the NFL television rights in 1993, Visser moved on to ABC and ESPN. In 1998, after covering the NFL for almost 25 years, Visser earned a spot as a sideline reporter for ABC's "Monday Night Football." As the first female on the Monday Night broadcast team, Visser said: "Credibility doesn't come from gender. It comes from the work you've done. . . ."

Before 1972, Robin Roberts couldn't find an organized little league baseball or basketball team to join. Girls were not allowed. But Robin wanted to play sports, so she learned bowling and wound up the junior state champion. But the new law known as Title IX gave girls the same sports opportunities as boys, and Robin jumped into basketball. She later took her skills to college on an athletic scholarship, where she was a standout on the Southeastern Louisiana Lions. When she graduated in 1983, Robin's stats placed her as the third highest leading scorer and rebounder at the school with 1,446 points and 1,034 rebounds.

Since the only pro-basketball options for women were in Europe, Robin decided to combine her love of basketball with her strong interest in journalism, and stayed stateside. She gave little thought to the barriers facing women who wanted to work in sports. Nor was she deterred because she is not only a woman, she is also African-American. Perhaps it was because of her upbringing. Roberts's father Laurence wanted to fly airplanes from the time he was a child, though he was told that black men did not fly planes. Today, retired Air Force Colonel Roberts can tell you stories about his flying days as a member of the first black squadron known as the Tuskegee Airmen.

Like her colleague Hannah Storm, Roberts got her first job as a sports reporter for a radio station in Louisiana. She worked her way around the South, doing stints on radio and TV stations in places like Hattiesburg, Biloxi, and Nashville, before landing a spot in 1988 as a sports anchor for WAGA-TV in Atlanta, Georgia. Roberts got the call from ESPN just two years later.

Roberts has shown her versatility as a sports reporter, commentator, and desk anchor, having covered the men's NCAA Final Four, women's LPGA tournaments, tennis, including Wimbledon, the Summer Olympics, hosting ESPN's "Sunday SportsDay" and ABC's "Wide World of Sports," and anchoring "SportsCenter." In 1998 she also did the play-by-play for ESPN's Monday night WNBA telecasts. For Roberts, setting her goals and achieving them has been very rewarding: "I don't see many women of color doing this. I'm a trailblazer doing things on my own terms and enjoying it."

The sportscasting profession may not yet display total gender blindness. However, with the experience and talent already established by the women working in the field, it should only be a matter of time before sports fans don't notice whether they are listening to a man or a woman in the broadcast booth.

66 Other Extraordinary Women Athletes

Michelle Akers (1966–   )   *Soccer*

The all-time leading scorer on the women's U.S. national soccer team, Akers helped lead Team USA to its first World Cup championship in 1991. It was a big year in her soccer career, as she also set the record for most goals in a match (5), most goals in a season (39), and most points in a season (47). With women's soccer making its debut at the 1996 Olympics in Atlanta, Akers won the first gold medal awarded as a member of the U.S. winning team.

Yael Arad (1967–   )   *Judo*

A native-born Israeli, she became a national hero when she won a silver medal in judo at the 1992 Summer Games in Barcelona, Spain—the first Olympic medal ever awarded to an Israeli athlete. Arad dedicated the medal to the Israeli athletes who were slain at the Munich Olympics twenty years earlier.

Evelyn Ashford (1957–   )   *Track and Field*

One of the greatest sprint stars ever to compete in track and field, Ashford appeared in four Olympic Games. At the 1984 Summer Games in Los Angeles, she ran the 100-meter race in world record time (10.97), a record that stood until Flo Joyner broke it four years later. The winner of four Olympic gold medals and one silver, Ashford amazed the crowds at the 1992 Summer Games in Barcelona, when, at age 35, she won a gold medal as a member of the 4 x100-meter relay team.

Tracy Austin (1962–   )   *Tennis*

A superstar at 16, and essentially retired before she turned 20, Austin is the youngest player ever to win the U.S. Open (in 1979 at age 16). Tracy and her brother John made tennis history at Wimbledon the following year becoming the first brother-sister team to win the mixed doubles title. Unfortunately, a back problem began to plague Austin in late 1980, and though she took some time off over the next few years, the pain continued to recur. She won the U.S. Open once more in 1981, but was not much of a factor in top-ten tennis after that. Recognizing her achievements, however brief her time in the sport, Austin was inducted into the International Tennis Hall of Fame in 1992.

Oksana Baiul (1977–   )   *Figure Skating*

The petite orphan from the Ukraine captured the hearts of the audience as they watched her passionate gold medal winning long program performance at the 1994 Winter Games in Lillehammer, Norway. What few people knew was that Baiul's brilliant skating performance came just hours after receiving stitches for an injury.

Ann Bancroft (1955–   )   *Journeyer, Dogsledder*

She thrives on life's challenges, and has met them head-on. Bancroft is the first woman to complete expeditions to the North and South Poles. In 1985, Bancroft traveled by dogsled to the North Pole with the seven member all-male Steger International North Pole Expedition. Bancroft and five of the men completed the 55-day trek on May 1, 1986. In 1993, Bancroft, Sunniva Sorby, Anne Dal Vera, and Sue Giller skied the 660 miles (1,062 km) to reach the South Pole.

Fanny Blankers-Koen (1918–   )   *Track and Field*

Though two Olympic Games were canceled because of World War II (1940, 1944), the 30-year-old mother of two held six world records, including the 100-meter dash, 80-meter hurdles, long jump, and high jump. Many thought she was too old to be a medal contender at the London Games in 1948, but Blankers-Koen surprised everyone by turning in an individual triple gold medal performance, and winning another gold as a member of the 4 x 100-meter relay. Her outstanding showing at the Games earned Fanny the 1948 AP Athlete of the Year honors. She was inducted into the International Women's Sports Hall of Fame in 1982.

Ila Borders (1975–   )   *Baseball*

As the only girl member of her Little League team, Borders was making sports history while still just a youngster. She played through high school, amassing a record of 16-7, and an earned run average of 2.37, and was named the Most Valuable Player on the all boys' team. In 1994, pitching for Southern California College, Borders became the first woman to pitch in a men's college baseball game. When the Cooperstown Hall of Fame opened its "Women's Baseball" exhibit, among the things on display were Borders's jersey, hat, and glove.

Hassiba Boulmerka (1968–   )   *Middle Distance Runner*

Algerian runner Boulmerka, a devout Muslim, was celebrated and condemned by her countrymen when she returned home after winning the 1,500-meter event at the 1991 World Championships. Running in track attire, with much of her body uncovered in public, Boulmerka's "nakedness" outraged many in the Muslim community. Undaunted, Boulmerka continued to compete. Crossing the finish line first at the 1992 Olympics, she celebrated her gold medal victory by chanting "Algérie! Algérie!"

Valerie Brisco (1960–   )   *Track and Field*

Though a naturally gifted runner, Brisco didn't really become a world-class sprinter until she committed to a grueling training program with famed track coach Bob Kersee. All the work paid off. At the 1984 Olympics in Los Angeles, Brisco won individual gold medals in the 200-meter and 400-meter races, becoming the first athlete ever to win both events at a single Olympics. She earned her third gold of the Games as a member of the U.S. women's 4 x 100-meter relay.

Susan Butcher (1954–   )   *Dogsledder*

She was the second woman, after Libby Riddles, to win the more than 1,000-mile (1,609-km) dogsled race through the rough Alaskan weather and terrain. However, Butcher is the only musher, male or female, to win the Iditarod three consecutive years (1986-1988). In her fourth win in 1990, Butcher set a course record with a time of 11 days, 1 hour, and 53 minutes.

Vera Caslavska (1942–   )   *Gymnastics*

The Russian great Larissa Latynina dominated women's gymnastics until the graceful, expressive performances of the younger Caslavska of Czechoslovakia emerged. In her 10-year career, Caslavska won 10 Olympic medals, including seven gold and one silver for individual competitions. A well-rounded gymnast, she captured titles on every apparatus, and is one of her country's most decorated athletes. After the Soviet Union invaded her country in 1968, Caslavska gave all of her medals to the Czech Nationalist leaders. She retired from the sport a short time later.

Mary Ellen Clark (1962–   )   *Diving*
Though suffering from severe bouts of vertigo (dizziness) throughout her career, Clark won the bronze medal in platform diving at the 1992 Olympics in Barcelona. She won her second bronze four years later in Atlanta. At age 29 in 1992, Clark was the oldest American woman to win an Olympic diving medal. She broke that record with her bronze medal performance in Atlanta in 1996, at age 33.

Alice Coachman (1923–   )   *High Jump*
Undoubtedly one of the most dominant high jumpers in history, Coachman held the AAU outdoor championship title throughout the 1940s. Winning the high jump event at the 1948 Olympics, Coachman made history by becoming the first African-American woman to win an Olympic gold medal.

Maureen Connolly (1934–1969)   *Tennis*
Affectionately known as "Little Mo," Connolly became the first woman to complete the Grand Slam of tennis, winning the Australian, French, and U.S. Opens, and Wimbledon, in 1953. The following year, a riding accident ended a brief but splendid career in which she won nine major titles. Sadly, at the age of 34, Connolly died of cancer.

Christl Cranz (1914–   )   *Skiing*
With 12 world championship skiing titles, German-born Cranz is the winningest skier, male or female, in the history of the sport. She dominated the downhill and slalom events from 1935 to 1939. At the 1936 Winter Games in Garmisch-Partenkirchen, Germany, Crantz won the first Olympic gold medal awarded in the Alpine combined event. Only the cancellation of the Winter Games in 1940 and 1944 due to World War II prevented Cristl from competing for more Olympic gold.

Ann Curtis (1926–)   *Swimming*

Curtis was the first woman in the history of amateur athletics to receive the prestigious Sullivan Award as the top athlete of the year (1944). In both national indoor and outdoor meets between 1943 and 1948, Curtis won at almost every distance. Though World War II prevented the Olympics from being held in 1944, Curtis was not to be denied Olympic success. At the 1948 Summer Games in London, she won a silver in the 100-meter freestyle and a gold medal in the 400-meter freestyle.

Donna de Varona (1947–)   *Swimming*

Though she won no medals in the 1960 Olympic Games in Rome, 13-year-old Donna was the youngest member to make the U.S. Olympic swim team. More mature at 17, Donna was one of the fastest sprint swimmers the sport had ever seen. She broke 18 world records, and won two gold medals at the 1964 Summer Games in Tokyo. She retired from competition after the Olympics and landed a job with ABC's *Wide World of Sports,* becoming the first woman sportscaster on network television. A tireless advocate for women's athletics, Donna helped found the Women's Sports Foundation with Billie Jean King, Wyomia Tyus, Micki King, and Sheila Young.

Charlotte (Lottie) Dod (1871–1960)   *Tennis*

A true all-around female athlete, Dod was definitely ahead of her time. In 1887, she was the youngest player, at 15, to win the singles title at Wimbledon, a tournament she won a total of five times in her tennis career. Versatile in many sports, Dod was also the Amateur British Golf champion in 1904, and a silver medalist in archery at the 1908 Olympics in London.

Teresa Edwards (1964–)   *Basketball*

It was a fitting moment when Edwards took the Olympic oath on behalf of the thousands of athletes who came to compete at the 1996 Summer Games in Atlanta. She grew up not far from the Athens, Georgia, stadium playing basketball—first on the blacktop courts in her neighborhood, then on the hardwood floors of her alma mater, the University of Georgia, where she was a two-time All-American. To date, she is the only American, male or female, to play on four Olympic teams (1984, 1988, 1992, 1996), winning a medal at each appearance. Edwards was the youngest member on the 1984 gold-medal squad, and the oldest on the 1996 team, which also won the coveted gold.

Krisztina Egerszegi (1974–) *Swimming*

At just 14 years old, the Budapest native won her first Olympic medal at the 1988 Olympics in the 100-meter backstroke. She was just one second slower than East Germany's gold-medal winner Kristin Otto. Egerszegi went on to win the gold medal in the 200-meter backstroke, the first of five individual Olympic golds (four in backstroke events) she would earn in her career. No other swimmer in history had ever won that many individual golds.

Lyubov Egorova (1967–) *Cross-country Skiing*

Born in Siberia, Russia, cross-country skier Egorova is one of the greatest athletes to compete in the Winter Olympics. She was the most decorated athlete at the Games in Albertville, France, in 1992, winning five medals (three golds, two silvers). In 1994, at the Winter Olympics in Lillehammer, Norway, Egorova captured three more golds and another silver, bringing her medal total to nine, one shy of the all-time record set by Raisa Smetanina who made five Olympic appearances (1976-1992).

Nawal El Moutawakel (1962–) *Track and Field*

It is fitting that in the first appearance of the 400-meter hurdles in the Olympics (1984), the first gold medal awarded in the event went to El Moutawakel. She became the first woman from an Islamic country to win an Olympic medal, and she won the first medal ever awarded to Morocco.

Kornelia Ender (1958–) *Swimming*

A powerhouse East German swimmer, Ender was the first woman to swim the 200-meter in under two minutes. At the age of 13, Ender won three team silver medals at the 1972 Munich Olympics. Over the next three years, 15 world records fell to Ender. At the 1976 Summer Games in Montreal, she made history by becoming the first woman to win four gold medals in a single Olympics.

Mae Faggs (1932–) *Track and Field*

One of Ed Temple's Tennessee Tigerbelle track and field stars, Faggs led the U.S. Women's Olympic teams of 1952 and 1956 to gold medals in the 4 x 100-meter relay race. At the end of her competitive sprint career, Faggs had broken every American track record.

Dawn Fraser (1937–   )   *Swimming*

A fabulous sprint swimmer, Fraser was the first woman to swim the 100-meter freestyle in under one minute. She is also the only swimmer to win the same event (100-meter) in three consecutive Olympic Games (1956, 1960, 1964).

Diana Golden (1963–   )   *Skiing*

An avid skier from the age of five, Golden was diagnosed with bone cancer as a preteen and had to have her right leg amputated. As soon as she was able, she was skiing downhill once more, at times clocked at over 65 miles (105 km) per hour. In her career, she won more than 29 gold medals in world and national competitions, including the gold medal in the downhill at the Winter Para-Olympics in Calgary, Canada. Golden was honored by the U.S. Olympic Committee in 1988, when she was named its Female Skier of the Year.

Dorothy Hamill (1956–   )   *Figure Skating*

The last female figure skater to win an Olympic gold medal without performing a triple jump, Hamill introduced her own special move called the "Hamill Camel," a standing spin into a sit spin. She competed only in the 1976 Olympics in Montreal, but in her short career she captured three U.S. national titles, and the gold medal in the world championships shortly after the 1976 Winter Games. Hamill purchased the Ice Capades in 1993, saving the show from bankruptcy. She revamped the show, turning it into a Broadway production on ice.

Lis Hartel (1921–   )   *Equestrian*

Striken with polio at age 23, Hartel suffered paralysis in her arms and legs. Though she never regained the use of her legs below the knee, Hartel displayed her incredible courage when she won a silver medal in the Olympic equestrian competition in Helsinki, Finland, in 1952. Making the team again in 1956, Hartel won her second silver at the Melbourne Games in Australia.

Nancy Hogshead (1962–   )   *Swimming*

In the 100-meter freestyle at the 1984 Olympics, Hogshead and teammate Carrie Steinseifer finished in a tie, the only time that has ever happened in the history of Olympic swimming. Though Hogshead suffered from severe asthma, which wasn't diagnosed until she had been competing for several years, she also won two golds as a member of the 4 x 100-meter freestyle relay and 4 x 100-meter medley relay teams.

Flora (Flo) Hyman (1954–1986) *Volleyball*

Without question Hyman was the greatest American woman in volleyball. At 6 feet 5 inches (195 cm), she was a towering presence on the court, and the first American woman named to the All-World Cup team. In 1984, with Flo's guidance, the U.S. women's volleyball team had its best showing ever, winning the silver medal at the Olympic Games in Los Angeles. Only two years later, as she sat on the bench during a game in Japan, Hyman collapsed and died from a congenital defect of the aorta.

Nell Jackson (1929–1988) *Track and Field*

A successful sprinter who held the American record in the 200-meters from 1949 through 1954, Jackson went on to make history off the track when she was appointed the first African-American head coach of a U.S. Olympic team (1956, 1972). A lifelong advocate for women's sports, Jackson was inducted into the Track and Field Hall of Fame in 1989.

Nancy Kerrigan (1969–   ) *Figure Skating*

Overcoming a knee injury that resulted from an attack masterminded by the husband of skating rival Tonya Harding just weeks before the 1994 Lillehammer Olympics, Kerrigan skated brilliantly, mesmerizing the audience with her grace and beauty on the ice. Only Oksana Baiul, who skated slightly better, prevented Kerrigan from winning the gold medal. Kerrigan does, however, have two medals from two Olympic appearances—a bronze (1992) and a silver (1994).

Micki King (1944–   ) *Diving*

Though she didn't really start diving seriously until her sophomore year in college, Micki entered the 1968 Mexico City Olympics as the favorite to win the gold medal in the springboard competition. However, she hit her arm on the board and broke it during a dive, finishing in fourth place. King returned to the Olympics in 1972, and though almost twice as old as her competition, she swept through the event and won the gold medal. In 1973, then a captain in the U.S. Air Force, King broke new barriers for women in the military by becoming the first female to hold a faculty position at the U.S. Military Academy where she coached diving. Now a lieutenant colonel, King is one of the founding members of the Women's Sports Foundation, and has served as president of the U.S. Diving Association.

Marion Ladewig (1918–   )   *Bowling*

Named the "Greatest Woman Bowler of All Time" in 1973 by the BPAA, Ladewig dominated the sport throughout the 1950s. As the first woman bowler to be named International Bowler of the Year (1957), Ladewig also has the distinction of being the only bowler inducted into the International Women's Sports Hall of Fame (1984).

Suzanne Lenglen (1899–1938)   *Tennis*

Truly the French "Grand Dame" of tennis, Lenglen was one of the first stars in women's sports. As a child she suffered from asthma, and was encouraged to play tennis by her doting father. Her flamboyant style was matched by her stunning play. Among her many accomplishments, Lenglen won five consecutive singles titles and six doubles championships at the prestigious All-England Croquet & Lawn Tennis Club, better known as Wimbledon. Her career ended early, and she died of acute anemia at the age of 39.

Tara Lipinski (1982–   )   *Figure Skating*

At just age 12, Tara became the youngest figure skating competitor to win a gold medal at the Olympic Festival in 1994. She continued to make history when she won the U.S. Nationals after landing a triple loop/triple loop combination in her program. Tara was the first athlete to successfully complete the maneuver, and the youngest U.S. champion in the history of figure skating. In 1998, at the Winter Games in Nagano, Japan, 16-year-old Tara made history again when she became the youngest skater to win an Olympic gold medal in the sport.

Donna Lopiano (1946–   )   *Softball*

Her contributions to women's sports have had an impact both on the field and off. In the nine seasons Lopiano played softball with Raybestos Brakettes, she was named series MVP three of the six times they won the national championship. Lopiano has also worked tirelessly for women's sports rights, and today serves as the director of the Women's Sports Foundation, a nonprofit organization founded by Billie Jean King and dedicated to expanding opportunities in every area of athletics for girls and women throughout the United States.

Deborah Meyer (1952–   )   *Swimming*

By winning the 200-, 400-, and 800-meter freestyle races at the 1968 Summer
Games in Mexico City, Meyer became the first swimmer to win three gold medals
in one Olympiad. She holds another "first"—breaking four records in her five years
of competition, including swimming the 1,500-meters in less than 18 minutes, and
the 400-meters in less than 4.5 minutes.

Ann Meyers (1955–   )   *Basketball*

A true pioneer in helping to forge respectability for women's basketball, Meyers was
the first woman to receive a full athletic scholarship at the University of California at
Los Angeles, where she led her team to a national championship in 1978. After graduation, she was offered a one-year contract to play with the all-male NBA Indiana
Pacers, another first for women. A Basketball Hall of Famer, Meyers went on to
become one of the first female sports commentators, and was married to Don
Drysdale, a member of the Baseball Hall of Fame.

Fu Mingxia (1979–   )   *Diving*

At age 11, China-born Mingxia won the platform diving competition at both the
Goodwill Games and the FINA/USA Diving Grand Prix. Often practicing 10 hours
a day, her hard work paid off. At the 1996 Summer Games in Atlanta, Mingxia
became the first female diver since American Patricia McCormick to win gold
medals in two consecutive Olympic Games. She also won the gold in the 3-meter
springboard event. Mingxia was the first to capture golds in both events since
Germany's Ingrid Kramer (1980).

Rosi Mittermeirer (1950–   )   *Skiing*

A darling of the ski slopes at the 1976 Winter Games in Innsbruck, Austria,
Mittermeier just missed triple gold when she mistimed a gate in the giant slalom.
She came in second behind the eventual winner, Kathy Kreiner of Canada. However,
that takes nothing away from her gold medal performances in the downhill and
slalom. Prior to her 1976 Olympic appearance, Mittermeier had never won a downhill race. Considered old at 25, she had also captured the overall World Cup title.
Undoubtedly, 1976 was the year of her career.

Ann Moore (1912–1990)   *Golf*

Just as Althea Gibson broke the racial barrier in tennis, Moore broke the racial barrier in her chosen sport—golf. In 1956, while much of America remained segregated, Moore became the first African-American woman to play in a United States Golf Association-sponsored national tournament. Moore never did win a major nonsegregated tournament, but her presence in the sport was just as important as any title—opening the door for all black female golfers who want to play the game.

Rosa Mota (1960–   )   *Marathon*

The pride of her country, Mota won a bronze medal in the debut marathon at the 1984 Olympics. She was the first-ever Portuguese woman to win an Olympic medal. Four years later in Seoul, South Korea, Mota took home the gold, another first in her country, finishing 75 meters ahead of her nearest competition.

Margaret Murdock (1942–   )   *Shooting*

A pioneer in the sport of shooting, Murdock set a world record in the small-bore rifle competition with a final score of 391 at the Pan-American Games in 1967. It was a historic achievement—the first time a female athlete had surpassed a man's record in any sport. In coed competition at the 1976 Montreal Olympics, Murdock won the silver medal.

Angelika (1971–   ) and Doris Neuner (1973–   )   *Luge*

The sisters from Innsbruck, Austria, made Olympic history at the 1992 Winter Games in Albertville, France, when they finished one-two in the luge to capture the gold and silver medals. It was the first time in Olympic history that siblings came in first and second in the same event. Younger sister Doris took the gold with a time of 3:06.696; Angelika won the silver with a time of 3:06.769, just 7/100 second slower than Doris.

Diana Nyad (1949–   )   *Marathon Swimmer*

One of the greatest endurance swimmers ever, Nyad never made it to the Olympics or won a national championship. As a young teen, she contracted viral endocarditis, an infection of the heart, and was not able to swim the short, fast races of sprint swimmers. Instead she began training for longer distances, and achieved many "firsts" in her marathon swimming career. She was the first woman to swim around Manhattan Island; the first person to swim Lake Ontario from south to north; and the first to complete a world-record 102.5-mile (164.5-km) swim from the island of Bimini, in the Bahamas, to Jupiter, Florida.

Margo Oberg (1953–) *Surfing*

A true pioneer for women in the sport of surfing, Oberg won the Western Regional Surfing Championship at the tender age of 11. Over the next two decades she would become the most decorated woman in surfing history, capturing the Women's World Surfing title twice in each decade during the 1960s, 1970s, and 1980s.

Kristin Otto (1966–) *Swimming*

One of the world's greatest female swimmers, Otto was a product of the athletic system from East Germany. She smashed the previous record for most gold medals won in one Olympiad (4, set by another East German, Kornelia Ender) when she won six gold medals at the 1988 Summer Games in Seoul, South Korea. In recent years, Otto's brilliant performance has been questioned due to allegations of anabolic steroid use.

Uta Pippig (1965–) *Marathon*

When the Berlin Wall was dismantled in 1990, East German marathoner Uta was free to compete and travel wherever she pleased. In 1993, she won the New York City Marathon in 2:26:24. She won the Boston Marathon in 1994, with a record time of 2:21:45. She won again in 1995 and 1996, becoming the first woman to win the race in three consecutive years. The 1996 marathon victory was hard-won. After the race, Uta spent two days in the hospital being treated for severe dehydration.

Mary Lou Retton (1968–) *Gymnastics*

Inspired by Nadia Comaneci's performance at the 1976 Olympics, Retton moved to Houston to train with legendary gymnastics coach Bela Karolyi. At the 1984 Olympic Games in Los Angeles, Retton exploded through her routines, winning 2 bronze, 2 silver, and the coveted gold medal in the all-around competition. By doing so, Retton became the first American woman to win an Olympic gold medal in gymnastics.

Aileen Riggin (1906–)   *Swimming and Diving*

Though only 4 feet 8 inches (142 cm) tall and weighing 70 pounds (32 kg), Riggin made a big mark in the sports of swimming and diving. She won her first Olympic medal at age 14 by winning the springboard competition at the 1920 Games in Antwerp, Belgium. Four years later, she won a silver medal in diving and a bronze in the 100-meter backstroke in swimming. The double medal win was the first time anyone had won medals in both swimming and diving.

Betty Robinson (1911–1999)   *Track and Field*

In the 1928 Amsterdam Games, the first Olympics in which women were permitted to compete in track and field, Robinson, just 16 years old, edged out Canada's Fanny Rosenfeld to win the 100-meter sprint race. Because the 100-meter was the first of five women's track and field events, Robinson became the recipient of the first gold medal awarded in her sport. Though critically injured in an accident in 1931, Robinson fought her way back into competition in time to make the 1936 Olympic Games in Berlin. Running the third leg of the 4 x 100-meter relay, Robinson helped the American women's team win the gold medal.

Christa Rothenburger-Luding (1960–)   *Speed Skating, Cycling*

With her two Olympic medals in speed skating (a gold and a silver) at the 1988 Winter Games in Calgary, Canada, and a silver medal in the 1,000-meter match sprint in cycling at the 1988 Summer Games in Seoul, South Korea, Rothenburger is the only athlete to win medals in both Winter and Summer Olympics. Since the Winter and Summer Olympic Games are now staggered instead of being held the same year, no one will ever match Rothenburger's record.

Ildikó Rejtö Ujlaki Sagine (1937–)   *Fencing*

One of the most decorated fencers in Olympic history, Hungarian-born Sagine was born deaf. She did not let her handicap prevent her from learning her sport. From 1960 to 1976, she won two individual and three team Olympic medals in her five appearances.

Summer Sanders (1972–)   *Swimming*

Awarded an athletic scholarship to Stanford University, Sanders was named NCAA Swimmer of the Year in 1991 and 1992. An Olympian star at the 1992 Summer Games in Barcelona, Spain, Sanders won four individual medals. She was also the first American female swimmer to compete in four events since the 1976 Summer Games in Montreal, and the first to win four medals since the Los Angeles Summer Games in 1984.

Monica Seles (1973–   )   *Tennis*

It was the mental trauma more than the injury from an attack by a deranged fan during a match in 1993 that forced Seles into seclusion for two years. Prior to that, the Yugoslav-born tennis star had taken over the number one ranking from Steffi Graf, who had held the position for a record-setting 186 weeks. Among Seles's accomplishments are her wins at the French Open in 1990 and the Australian Open in 1991. She was the youngest woman at that time to win both tournaments. Seles returned to the game in 1995, and won her third Australian Open singles title in 1996.

Marilyn Smith (1929–   )   *Golf*

A charter member of the Ladies Professional Golf Association (LPGA), Smith was one of the sport's greatest ambassadors. As an amateur attending the University of Kansas, she won three consecutive state championships. She traveled extensively in the United States and several foreign countries after the founding of the LPGA to promote women's golf, and served as the organization's president from 1958-1960. Smith made television broadcast history when she worked as the first female commentator during a men's golf tournament.

Junko Tabei (1939–   )   *Mountaineering*

One of the most rigorous, demanding, and dangerous sports, mountain climbing was once considered much too difficult for participation by women. Junko was still in grade school when she climbed her first mountain. In May 1975, as part of a 15-member Japanese women's expedition, Junko became the first woman to reach the 29,028-foot (8,848-m) summit of Mount Everest.

Debi Thomas (1967–   )   *Figure Skating*

The first African-American female to win a gold medal in figure skating in world competition, Thomas did so by beating 1984 Olympic gold medalist Katarina Witt of East Germany. Two years later, Thomas won the bronze medal at the 1988 Winter Games in Calgary, finishing behind Canada's Elizabeth Manley and Witt, who captured her second consecutive gold.

Lyudmila Tourischeva (1952–   )   *Gymnastics*

It is unfortunate that Lyudmila entered gymnastics competition at the same time as Russian teammate Olga Korbut. She never received the same "star" attention as the charismatic Korbut, but Lyudmila was a more successful gymnast. With 15 individual medals from world and Olympic championship competitions, and three Olympic Games appearances, Lyudmila retired after the 1976 Summer Games in Montreal, married, and went back to school to earn her postgraduate degree in education.

Wyomia Tyus (1945–   )   *Track and Field*

Tyus was the first athlete, male or female, to win consecutive Olympic gold medals in the 100-meter sprint race. A Tennessee Tigerbelle, Tyus achieved the back-to-back record, which has yet to be equaled, with wins in the 1964 (Tokyo) and 1968 (Mexico City) Summer Games.

Amy Van Dyken (1973–   )   *Swimming*

Afflicted with asthma as a child, Van Dyken began therapeutic swimming to help strengthen her lungs. The true testament of her courage and determination came at the 1996 Summer Games in Atlanta when Van Dyken became the first female swimmer in U.S. history to win four gold medals in a single Olympics.

Margaret Wade (1912–1995)   *Basketball Coach*

For her lifetime contribution to women's basketball, a trophy bearing her name is awarded each year to the outstanding women's college basketball player. Wade played at a time when basketball was considered too strenuous for women. With few playing options available after she graduated from Delta State College, Wade became a high school basketball coach. In 1959, she was named the chairperson of the physical education department at her alma mater, where she resurrected women's basketball. At age 60 she went back to the bench, where she stayed until retiring from the game in 1979. Wade's overall collegiate record as a coach: 157 wins and 23 losses.

Greta Waitz (1953–   )   *Marathon*

One of Norway's most popular sports heroes, Waitz's athleticism shone brightest as a long-distance runner. With the encouragement of her coach and husband Jack Waitz, Greta competed in her first New York City Marathon in 1978. She ran the race nine times in nine years, and won each of them, setting a remarkable record in the sport. When the marathon was finally introduced as an Olympic event in 1984, Waitz won the silver medal behind America's Joan Benoit-Samuelson.

Lynette Woodard (1959–   ) *Basketball*

A four-time basketball All-American at the University of Kansas, Woodard led in scoring, rebounds, or steals at one time or another from 1977 to 1980. Woodard won an Olympic silver medal at the 1984 Summer Games and in 1985 she became the first woman to play for the famed Harlem Globetrotters. With the founding of the WNBA, Woodard signed with the Detroit Shock and is coached by colleague and Hall of Famer Nancy Lieberman-Cline.

Organizations and On-Line Sites

Althea Gibson
http://www.altheagibson.com/

Canadian Association for the Advancement of Women and Sport and Physical Activity
1600 James Naismith Drive
Gloucester, ON
K1B 5N4
http://www.caaws.ca/Milestones/milestones.htm

ESPN's Top North American Athletes of the Century
List countdown, individual biographies of each athlete represented
http://espnsportszone.com/sportscentury/athletes.html

Fédération International de Football Association (FIFA)
Box 85
8030 Zurich, Switzerland

Full Court Press: The Women's Basketball Journal
http://www.fullcourt.com/

Hickok Sports.Com
Comprehensive sports web site including Sullivan and Associated Press Award winners, biographies, history of sports, quotes, links, etc.
http://www.hickoksports.com/

International Amateur Athletic Association
http://www.iaaf.org/

International Gymnastics Hall of Fame
120 North Robinson
East Concourse
Oklahoma City, OK 73102
http://www.int-gym-hof.org/

International Olympic Committee
http://www.olympic.org/home.html

International Tennis Federation
http://www.itftennis.com/fl_index.html

Ladies Professional Golf Association
100 International Golf Drive
Daytona Beach, FL 32124
http://www.lpga.com/

The National Women's Hall of Fame
76 Fall Street
Post Office Box 335
Seneca Falls, New York 13148
http://www.greatwomen.org/

Olympic History Timeline
http://www.timeblazers.com/olym_timeline.html

Tennis Canada
3111 Steeles Avenue West
Ontario M3J 3H2 Canada
http://www.tenniscanada.com/

United States Olympic Committee
http://www.olympic-usa.org/

United States Swimming
One Olympic Plaza
Colorado Springs, CO 80909-5707
http://www.usswim.org

United States Tennis Association (USTA)
70 West Red Oak Lane
White Plains, NY 10604
http://www.usta.com/

U.S. Biathlon Association
421 Old Military Road
Lake Placid, NY 12946

U.S. Cycling Federation
One Olympic Plaza
Colorado Springs, CO 80909

U.S. Diving
Pan American Plaza, Suite 430
201 South Capitol Avuene
Indianapolis, IN 46225

U.S. Figure Skating Association
(USFSA)
20 First Street
Colorado Springs, CO 80909

U.S. International Speedskating Association (USISA)
Box 16157
Rocky River, OH 44116

U.S. Rowing Association
Pan American Plaza, Suite 400
201 South Capitol Avuene
Indianapolis, IN 46225

U.S. Soccer
Communications Department
1801-1811 South Prairie Avenue
Chicago, IL 60616

USA Basketball
5465 Mark Dabling Boulevard
Colorado Springs, CO 80918

USA Gymnastics
Pan American Plaza, Suite 300
201 South Capitol Avuene
Indianapolis, IN 46225
http://www.usa-gymnastics.org/

USA Track and Field
Box 120
Indianapolis, IN 46206
http://wwwusatf.org/

Wilma Rudolph
http://www.lkwdpl.org/wihohio/rudo-wil.htm

The WNBA
http://www.wnba.com

Women's Professional Volleyball Association
840 Apollo, Suite 205
El Segundo, CA 90245-4701
http://www.volleyball.org

Women's Sports Foundation
Eisenhower Park
East Meadow, NY 11554
http://www.lifetimetv.com/WoSport/index.html

For Further Reading

Anderson, Dave. *The Story of the Olympics.* (New York: Beech Tree, 1996).

Biracree, Tom. *Althea Gibson.* (New York: Chelsea House Publishers, 1989).

—————— . *Wilma Rudolph.* (New York: Chelsea House Publishers, 1988).

Benoit, Joan, with Sally Baker. *Running Tide.* (New York: Alfred A. Knopf, 1987).

Brooks, Philip. *Steffi Graf: Tennis Pro.* (Danbury, Conn.: Children's Press, 1996).

Browne, Lois. *Girls of Summer.* (Toronto: HarperCollins Publishers Ltd., 1992).

Christopher, Matt. *On The Field with… Mia Hamm.* (New York: Little, Brown & Company, 1998).

Chronicle of the Olympics. (New York: DK Publishing, Inc., 1996).

Coffey, Wayne. *Katarina Witt (Olympic Gold!).* (Woodbridge, Conn.: Blackbirch Press, 1992).

Deford, Frank. "Truly Amazing Trudy." (Lands' End catalog, May 1998).

Donohue, Shiobhan. *Kristi Yamaguchi: Artist on Ice.* (Minneapolis: Lerner Publications Company, 1994).

Golden, Kristen and Barbara Findlen. *Remarkable Women of the Twentieth Century.* (New York: Friedman/Fairfax Publishers, 1998).

Goldstein, Margaret J., and Jennifer Larson. *Jackie Joyner-Kersee: Superwoman.* (Minneapolis: Lerner Publications Company, 1994).

Gregorich, Barbara. *Women at Play: The Story of Women in Baseball.* (Orlando: Harcourt Brace & Company, 1993).

Gutman, Bill. *Gail Devers.* (Austin: Raintree Steck-Vaughn Publishers, 1996).

——————. *Shooting Stars: The Women of Pro Basketball.* (New York: Random House, Inc., 1998).

Hamm, Mia. *Go for the Goal: A Champion's Guide to Winning in Soccer and Life.* (New York: HarperCollins Publishers, 1999).

Harrington, Geri. *Jackie Joyner-Kersee.* (New York: Chelsea House Publishers, 1995).

Jackel, Molly and Joe Layden. *WNBA Superstars.* (New York: Scholastic, Inc., 1998).

Jennings, Jay. *Moments of Courage: Bravery Under Pressure.* (Englewood Cliffs: Silver Burdett Press, 1991).

Johnson, Anne Janette. *Great Women in Sports.* (Detroit: Visible Ink Press, 1996).

Joyner-Kersee, Jackie, with Sonja Steptoe: *A Kind of Grace: The Autobiography of the World's Greatest Female Athlete.* (New York: Warner Books, 1997).

Kerrigan, Nancy, with Steve Woodward. *Nancy Kerrigan: In My Own Words.* (New York: Hyperion Paperbacks for Children, 1996).

King, Billie Jean, with Cynthia Starr. *We Have Come a Long Way: The Story of Women's Tennis.* (New York: McGraw Hill, 1988).

King, Billie Jean, with Frank Deford. *Billie Jean.* (New York: Viking Press, 1982).

Layden, Joe. *Women in Sports.* (Los Angeles: General Publishing Group, 1997).

Leder, Jane. *Grace & Glory: A Century of Women in the Olympics.* (Chicago: Triumph Books, 1996).

Littlefield, Bill. *Champions: Stories of Ten Remarkable Athletes.* (Boston: Little, Brown & Company, 1993).

Lobo, Rebecca and RuthAnn Lobo. *The Home Team: Of Mothers, Daughters, and American Champions.* (New York: Kodansha International, 1996).

Lynn, Elizabeth A. *Babe Didrikson Zaharias.* (New York: Chelsea House Publishers, 1989).

Macy, Sue. *Winning Ways: A Photohistory of American Women in Sports.* (New York: Henry Holt & Company, Inc., 1996).

Markel, Robert, Susan Waggoner, and Marcella Smith, eds. *The Women's Sports Encyclopedia.* (New York: Henry Holt & Company, Inc., 1998).

Marvis, Barbara J. and Theresa Scott Swanson. *Famous People of Hispanic Heritage.* (Elkton, MD: Mitchell Lane Publishers, 1997).

Navratilova, Martina, with George Vecsey. *Martina: An Autobiography.* (New York: Alfred A. Knopf, 1985).

Nelson, Mariah Burton. *Are We Winning Yet? How Women Are Changing Sports and Sports Are Changing Women.* (New York: Random House, 1991).

Ponti, James. *WNBA: Stars of Women's Basketball.* (New York: Pocket Books, 1999).

Quiner, Krista. *Shannon Miller: America's Most Decorated Gymnast: A Biography.* (New York: Bradford Book Company, 1997).

Rheaume, Manon, with Chantal Gilbert. *Manon: Alone in Front of the Net.* (Canada: HarperCollins, 1998).

Rutledge, Rachel. *Women of Sports Series.* (Brookfield, Conn.: The Millbrook Press, Inc., 1998).

Stewart, Mark. *Florence Griffith-Joyner.* (Danbury, Conn.: Children's Press, 1996).

——————— . *Lisa Leslie: Queen of the Court.* (Danbury, Conn.: Children's Press, 1998).

——————— . *Marion Jones: Sprinting Sensation.* (Danbury, Conn.: Children's Press, 1999).

——————— . *Mia Hamm: Good as Gold.* (Danbury, Conn.: Children's Press, 1999).

——————— . *Monica Seles: The Comeback Kid.* (Danbury, Conn.: Children's Press, 1997).

Teitelbaum, Michael. *Grand Slam Stars: Martina Hingis and Venus Williams.* (New York: HarperCollins Publishers, 1998).

Woolum, Janet. *Outstanding Women Athletes: Who They Are and How They Influenced Sports in America.* (Phoenix, AZ.: Oryx Press, 1992).

Index

Numbers in *italics* represent illustrations.

Photo Credits

Photographs ©: AllSport USA: back cover bottom center, 7, 233 (Al Bello), 7, 250 (Clive Brunskill), back cover bottom right, 235 (Stephen Dunn), 5, 73, 104, 149 (Hulton Deutsch), 6, 215 (Bob Martin), 7, 239 (Jamie McDonald), 3, 15 (Ralph Merlino), 6, 161 (Gary Newkirk), 176 (Doug Pensinger), 179 (Mike Powell), 7, 255 (Todd Rosenberg), 6, 206 (Howard Roylan), 7, 224 (Ezra O. Shaw), 191 (Richard Martin/Vandystadt), cover bottom center, 129; AP/Wide World Photos: 3, 31, 35, 39; Archive Photos: 159 (Mike Blake), back cover left center, 6, 181 (Gary Cameron/Reuters), 153 (Frank Capri/SAGA), 123 (Express Newspapers), 89 right (Louis Goldman/Fotos), cover bottom right, 6, 196 (Gary Hershorn/Reuters), cover bottom left, 4, 5, 70, 120, 144 (Popperfoto), cover top left, 1, 246 (Ray Stubblebine/Reuters), 6, 192 (Jeff Vinnick/Reuters), 5, 94, 125; Art Resource, NY: 3, 10 (SEF); Corbis-Bettmann: 4, 45 (Minnesota Historical Society), back cover top left, 6, 147, 186, 210, (Reuters), back cover center right, back cover bottom right, 3, 4, 5, 6, 14, 17, 40, 54, 58, 62, 66, 80, 90, 99, 100, 101, 106, 110, 115, 130, 132, 134, 139, 154, 164, 166, 175, 204 (UPI), 3, 4, 24, 86; Courtesy of the International Tennis Hall of Fame, Newport, RI: 3, 21; Liaison Agency, Inc.: 7, 241 (Bourg), 219 (Karin Cooper), cover top center, 1 center, 6, 170 (Pam Francis), 3, 4, 28, 33, 49 (Hulton Getty), cover top right, 1 left, 7, 220 (Jeff Scheid), 201 (Art Seitz), back cover top right, 244, 254; North Wind Picture Archives: 9; Sygma: 89 left; University of Texas: 4, 75.

About the Author

Judy L. Hasday, a native of Philadelphia, Pennsylvania, received her B.A. in communications and her Ed. M. in instructional technologies from Temple University. A multimedia professional, she has had her photographs published in many magazines and books. As a successful freelance author, Ms. Hasday has written several books, including an award-winning biography of James Earl Jones and biographies of Madeleine Albright and Tina Turner. She has also coauthored *Marijuana,* a book for adolescents that presents the facts and dangers of using the drug.